Gorgeously
Green

Gorgeously Green

8 Simple Steps to an
Earth-Friendly Life

Sophie Uliano

Collins
An Imprint of HarperCollinsPublishers

HarperCollins books may be purchased for educational, business, or sales promotional use. For information, please write: Special Markets Department, HarperCollins Publishers, 10 East 53rd Street, New York, NY 10022.

FIRST EDITION

Designed by Paula Russell Szafranski

Library of Congress Cataloging-in-Publication Data

Uliano, Sophie.
  Gorgeously green:every girl's guide to an earth-friendly life/Sophie Uliano.—1st ed.
    p. cm.
  ISBN 978-0-06-157556-3
  1. Sustainable living. 2. Women environmentalists. I. Title.

  GF78.U45 2008
  333.72082—dc22   2007043677

08 09 10 11 12 ID2/RRD 10 9 8 7 6 5 4

To Joe and Lola

CONTENTS

Chapter Five

STEP 5: *Your Palace: Creating the Home You Deserve*

Week 5 moves into your home. You deserve to have a beautiful toxic-free home, and this chapter will show you exactly how. Find out which chemicals must be avoided and the fabulous alternatives that you can start using right now. Turn your bedroom into a romantic and eco-friendly haven. See how simple it is to create a small, lovely organic garden and how glamorous composting can actually be!   132

Chapter Six

STEP 6: *Every Last Bite*

The sixth step is all about food. We'll look at some nonorganic foods that must be avoided at all costs! There's advice on how to eat organic without going broke. Get healthier and happier by getting into your kitchen and trying out some of my fabulous recipes.   189

Chapter Seven

STEP 7: *Out and About Having Fun*

The seventh step deals with transportation, travel and entertainment, and gifts. A fun, information-packed step with loads of tips and tools covering how to throw a Gorgeously Green dinner party, how to create fabulous green gifts, how to vacation with a difference, and more.   242

Chapter Eight

STEP 8: *Go Supergreen*

The last step will take you out into the world to discover what your passion is. We'll talk about how you can really make a difference and how fabulous it feels to become an activist! There will be a final checklist/quiz for you to see how much your life has changed. I conclude with my Gorgeously Green simple maintenance program designed to help you stay Gorgeously Green forever more.   274

FOREWORD

BIBLE (*noun*): any book, reference work, periodical, etc., accepted as authoritative, informative, or reliable.

Where to start?

It is a question I ask myself every day.

I am a wife and mother of three.

My days are busy and fun and full of questions that need answers.

What to wear?

What to cook for breakfast?

Is your blanket my responsibility?

Do I have time to work out?

Paper or plastic?

Has anyone seen my keys?

Why is your sister crying?

What time will you be home?

Where to start?

I absolutely believe I am in the majority of people who are concerned about the environment and the state of our planet.

Mother Earth has seen better days.

I also believe I am in the majority of people who want to do something, anything to help, and simply do not know *where to start?*

Well, good people, wonder no more.

This is what I have been waiting for . . . someone to tell me what to do!

Someone to help me understand there is good plastic and bad plastic.

How can cotton be bad?

Where does my garbage go? And how can I make less of it?

I quite simply cannot list all the amazing aspects of this book you are about to read, but I can tell you this:

I love to shop, I love to cook, I love to feel I have done one thing a day to educate myself and my children in making the world a better, stronger place to live in.

Easier said than done, right?

We would all do the right thing/things if only we had the resources, the answers, the advice we need.

What can I tell you, but *here it is!*

Sophie is one of those rare people that to be with her is to be so caught up in the thrill of the potential of good!

Good works, good food, good ideas, good cupcakes (who knew vegan anything could be so yummy?).

Good choices for you and your family that have a light and gentle impact on our planet.

As soon as she leaves my house, I want her to come right back!

Tell me more!!!!!!

Well, here is the *more*.

Here is Sophie and all her vibrant knowledge for everyone to access and apply little by little to every single thing we do in the day.

Her guidance casts a wide and understanding net.

I am absolutely altered.

This *Gorgeously Green* book has provided my household with a bible of hope and help (not to mention a good cleansing mask and a source for eco-cashmere).

So where to start?

Congratulations—you are already there.

Mahatma Gandhi said, "Be the change you want to see in the world."

Nothing stopping you now!

—*Julia Roberts*

ACKNOWLEDGMENTS

I want to thank the many people who helped make this book possible:

My husband, Joe, who fanned the flame with a pair of bellows when *Gorgeously Green* was just a flicker of an idea, and for his continued support, strength, and love.

My daughter, Lola, for her frequent admonishments of "You're not being very Gorgeously Green, mommy!" And for her six-year-old passion concerning everything that *is* still gorgeous about this planet. Thank you, Lola, for being my muse.

My long-suffering mother, who has spent many a late, late night listening and laughing, and my father, for his infectious optimism, humor, and boundless energy.

Genevive Lyons, who has inspired me for many years to keep on reaching for something greater.

In our many writing sessions at my kitchen table and at the Chado Tea Rooms, Lucinda Clare, who not only made me laugh and cry but also insisted that I write this book.

Mary Lynn Rapier for holding my hand throughout this whole process and for encouraging me every step of the way.

Jane and Marcus Buckingham, for being a tremendous inspiration and for providing me with their invaluable and expert advice whenever I needed it.

Brett Ollinger and Jerry Lee for getting my manuscript to the perfect person and Melinda Jason for her unbridled passion and intuition.

Joel Gotler, Scott Waxman, and Melissa Sarver, for sharing in my vision and doing such a great job in getting my book out there. Judith Regan for her enthusiasm and support of the Gorgeously Green message.

I thank Anne Cole, my editor, for stepping in at a crucial time and giving this book the attention and care that it deserves.

Kevin Small for leaping in and helping to take Gorgeously Green to the next level.

Sabine Dodane, for her talent and artistic expertise in the creation of Emerald.

And most importantly, Professor David Phillips, who woke me up to the plight of the planet and showed me how great it feels to be accountable and responsible for my each and every action.

Last, but not least, Julia Roberts, who has showered this project with humor and love. I thank her for her commitment and kindness and for being the quintessentially Gorgeously Green girl!

INTRODUCTION
One Change Makes a Difference

If I make one tiny positive change today, I consider myself green. It can be as simple as flicking off a light switch or buying an organic apple. My motto is *one change makes a difference,* and if you can make two, that's even better! The payoff is that in doing that one thing, I not only feel good about myself, but I also know that I'm part of the new, cool crowd of women who are turning their lives from gray to green.

You are about to embark on an eight-step program that will show you exactly how to live an earth-friendly life. Each step of the way, I will invite you to check off just one change you want to make. I don't want you to feel as overwhelmed as I once did. The great news about the one-change philosophy is that if every woman followed it every week—just one teeny thing—cumulatively we would create megachange in the world.

Women like me tend to be more interested in their compact than their compost. We never forget a hair appointment yet always forget our reusable shopping tote. Many of us think the whole green way of life will be tedious, time-consuming, and even boring. Wrong! I have found out that caring about this planet doesn't have to be granola/hippie stuff. On the contrary, it's the most exciting, colorful way in which we could possibly live. After all, green is the new black, and we're going to be wearing this shade for a long time. Going green is not a fad that is going to fade; with temperature and pollution levels on the rise, it is becoming a way of life.

A few years ago, I hadn't a clue. I thought organic food was a rip-off and that composting was for eco-nerds. Yoga and recycling were as far down the environmental food chain as I was willing to go. There was no way that I was going to stop dyeing my hair and painting my nails; and my gas-guzzling SUV was just fine, thank you very much!

I knew about the rain forests, or lack thereof, so I recycled the obvious things, but if I felt too lazy to walk down the hall to the recycling bin—well, a girl needs to conserve her energy for the really important things in life, like sitting down in front of the TV to find out who has been voted off the island. Then I started to hear about the ice caps melting, Manhattan submerged under water, and air pollution. It freaked me out, but it all still seemed too far away to really matter.

The Internet is not a safe place for women like me: I shop too much and scare myself silly by Googling symptoms such as "headache" and deducing that I must have a brain tumor! Several years ago, on a sunny Saturday morning, I needed some new yoga pants, so I began surfing the Web and ended up reading about pesticides in cotton. I clicked from link to link and read on about neurotoxins in cosmetics and pesticides in my favorite foods. I became obsessed and spent the rest of the weekend glued to the computer as horror upon horror mounted.

My neurosis quickly switched from hypochondria to eco-anxiety, and my long-suffering husband began to tire of the latest update. I'd begin with "They say . . ." and he would suddenly become very busy and have to take off. He was not amused by my half-baked attempt at wrapping our water heater with an old comforter to curb energy consumption; when I bought him a personal air ionizer to wear around his neck for a plane trip, he said, "I wouldn't be seen dead in it."

I turned to my friends in desperation, but this was way before green was cool, so I got a lot of glazed looks. I'm sure I bored all of my girl-friends silly in an attempt to get them on the same page. I even dragged a new acquaintance along to a Sustainable Living Conference in a ghastly hotel ballroom with orange carpets. I never saw her again. I felt powerless.

In an attempt to focus on something else, I took a psychology class at my local college and was surprised to find out that my professor

David Phillips was a hard-nut environmentalist who promised a higher grade to any student who completed an extracurricular class about sustainable living. Before I knew it, I was sitting in the scrubby backyard of a rather depressing eco-house on the college campus, where the fierce-looking crew leader, Hilary, opened up a whole new world. I was fascinated despite the fact that I was seriously distracted by her unshaven legs and long, unpainted toenails. We explored everything from the storm drains spewing out sludge into our lovely bay to organic farming. We became committed to turning our thermostats down, installing CFLs (compact fluorescent lightbulbs), growing our own veggies, and buying green power. We even baked brownies in a solar oven, which were totally inedible and closely resembled something the dog left behind.

As I got more and more involved with a plethora of green activists and organizations, I discovered a whole new universe of inspiring individuals who were passionate about preserving this planet. I realized that there was work to do and not a lot of time to be wasted. I rolled up my sleeves and educated myself about every environmental issue that affects women, because we are often the decision makers in the home; we are mothers, lovers, movers, fixers, and caretakers. We can create change very quickly when we want it to happen.

Yet I wondered how on earth I could make *all* of these changes at home. I didn't really fancy the idea of trekking to the end of my yard with soggy lettuce leaves to a smelly compost bin, and there was no way I was going to ruin my French manicure by gardening, *and* how on earth could I throw away my "Scarlet Vixen" nail polish? It may have been full of scary chemicals, but at twelve bucks a bottle, I broke out in a sweat.

Having committed to air-drying my laundry, my entire yard was strewn with towels, socks, and even underpants hanging from branches. That was when my husband put his foot down. The nail in the coffin, however, was when I arrived at a dinner date in a brown hemp yoga suit. I had convinced myself in the store that it was cute in a funky sort of distressed way. Imagining Kate Moss in it, I persuaded myself that the whole look was actually very chic until I saw my husband's expression. I hope somebody at Goodwill appreciated it.

I realized there had to be a better way of doing this whole eco-thing.

With my newfound awareness, I couldn't ever go back to the way I lived before, but I had to find a way to make it simple, easy, and a whole lot more fun.

I wanted to be green, but I also wanted to be gorgeous. So I designed the eight-step Gorgeously Green program for reluctant woman like myself. I want to live with sustainable style—*style* being the operative word. I can't and won't become like the eco-nerds who stomp around in beige Velcro sandals, pontificating about the virtues of their compost toilets. I appreciate where those people are coming from, but there is a different way to do it, the Gorgeously Green way.

I thought I'd try my eight-step course on my yoga clients first. While we're practicing, we girls like to chat about *everything*, so it seemed only natural to throw in a few eco-tips during our discussions. I talk way too much as a teacher: I begin a diatribe once I've got my clients in an impossible pose and make them hold it until I'm done. So, as you can imagine, I held many of them hostage in a headstand while outlining the designated green changes for that week.

I also spent many hours with their long-suffering housekeepers, persuading them to part with their toxic cleaning materials and energy-guzzling habits. I remember being horrified at the sight of a dishwasher being switched on with only one cup, one glass, and one teaspoon in it. I realized that I was going to have to get quite bossy. I also discovered that while some women became terrified upon learning about the chemicals in their homes, others couldn't have cared less as long as their sheets were white and their dishes were sparkling. Moreover, everyone moved at a different pace. The great thing about the course, however, was that it had a beginning and an end, and everyone wanted to complete it.

After taking numerous women through the eight-step program with one new change each week, I began to see huge smiles. Everyone felt better about themselves and the choices they were making. One girl, Lisa, asked me to do some research to find out if her favorite designer purses were made in a sweatshop. Upon hearing that they were indeed, she ceremoniously dumped three of them in her recycling bin. I can't say I wasn't tempted to retrieve the one that looked brand new, but I managed to take a deep breath and walk away, my faux-suede purse swinging in the breeze.

My six-year-old daughter, Lola, has been skipping along the emerald path with me and never fails to delight in our every green discovery. She is passionate about recycling, gardening, and nature even though we live in a concrete jungle. She also puts up with my newfangled attempts at a no-waste lunch box and is thrilled with her new hemp backpack.

The green lifestyle takes me back to my childhood, which was completely eco-friendly. I was raised in the English countryside by parents who had lived through World War II—an era that required frugality and inspired gratitude for the small luxuries in life. My mother grew a huge organic garden and engendered in me a passion for fresh local food, cooking every recipe from scratch. Everything was reused a gazillion times. If we were cold in the winter, we were told to put on another sweater. I now have to suffer regular "Duh, I told you so!" looks from my Gorgeously Green mom.

I love that I can bring the eco-ethic into every single area of my crazy life as a mother, gardener, cook, writer, yoga teacher, and consultant. I have found a way to care for myself and my family *and* my environment as never before; and I'm constantly learning new things. I am happier and more fulfilled than I have ever been. Even on a bad day, I can still manage to flick off a light switch, recycle a yogurt cup, and feel Gorgeously Green.

I don't know about you, but I have to be inspired to do something. I have tons of really good intentions and plans for the future, but the only way I'm going to get off my backside is when I see someone doing something that blows me away. Over the past few years, I have met a number of incredible people who have moved me by their compassion and love of the earth and all living things. I want what they have got. I want to walk around with my head high, feeling proud of all the choices I am making. I want to be a woman who takes care of myself *and* the world around me. I want to have self-respect *and* a great body! I want to live my deepest core values *and* look totally gorgeous. I want each year to get better as I grow older. I want to become kinder, wiser, and more beautiful, and I want to see this reflected in the world around me. I want my hair to shine, my skin to glow, and my heart to sing. I want it all. Our life on this planet is relatively short, so let's not treat it like a rehearsal—let's get the show on the road. Together we can do it.

Begin to inspire yourself and everyone around you. I'm telling you—it is an exciting and fabulous way to live.

The Eight-Step Program

Gorgeously Green is an upbeat and solution-oriented eight-step program that will show you how to live a sustainable life in style. From lipsticks to lightbulbs, you will learn how to feel gorgeous without polluting yourself or the planet. You will be led step by step down the green carpet to a lifestyle choice that can make you healthier and happier. The program incorporates beauty, style, fitness, home, kids, and cooking. It's a one-stop shop for the whole shebang.

The first step is an exciting exploration of your life. It's all about becoming aware. You will complete a checklist, which we will come back to at the end of the course. The second step dives straight into your beauty regime so that you can "green" it as soon as possible. Step 3 outlines a fabulous home yoga practice. You can join in the fight against global warming by using less fossil fuel and get a great body in the process. If shopping is your thing, you'll see in step 4 that you don't have to go without to be green. You can have your cake and eat it, too. I make the greening of your home supersimple, easy, and fun in step 5 by covering every room of your house and then moving into your yard. In step 6, we'll move into Gorgeously Green cuisine—delicious recipes that are superhealthy and completely sustainable. Step 7 is about your transportation, eco-vacations, eco-entertainment, and more. Step 8 will take you out of the home and into the world to discover where your passion lies. You will revisit the checklist from step 1 and see that you are already making a difference. Finally, you can create an eco-mission statement by going through the study pages at the end of the book.

How Do I Use This Book?

Start at the beginning of the book and slowly work your way through step by step. If you are like me, you may decide to skip certain areas that don't interest you or that you feel you are too busy to do. Don't worry—you'll probably want to go back many times, and I suggest you do. Have a pencil handy for the checklists.

Alternatively, you may just want to begin with a step that interests you. For instance, if you are specifically interested in organic and sustainable cuisine, you may want to begin with step 6. The important thing is to make a start.

I strongly suggest creating a Gorgeously Green group. Ask a few friends if they would be interested in forming a weekly or monthly gathering to discuss progress and obstacles and share new discoveries. I love creating a small community with a common purpose. I started a Gorgeously Green Girls' Club™ in my neighborhood. It was fantastic because each week someone would come in with a specific problem that we would all brainstorm. We would then come in the next time with ideas and solutions. At every gathering, we'd sample new products: nontoxic nail polish or a solar cell phone charger. We'd end by sharing fantastic organic food. More than anything, this group gave us an excuse to have a great party or night out. If we didn't feel like cooking, we'd try a new restaurant. If you would like to host a Gorgeously Green Girls' Club Evening for you and your friends, visit *www.gorgeouslygreen.com*.

It's also a brilliant idea to try to get your family involved, particularly your kids. They totally respond to the structure of a course. My husband loved the shopping step because I was compelled to practice what I preach!

What is so fabulous about the green movement is that it's mobilizing many of us to come together and fight for a cause that is relevant to everyone. There is an exciting shift in the collective consciousness. I see it everywhere—people wanting to get past themselves in order to reach for something greater. Our personal survival depends on global unity.

I have packed each chapter with numerous resources so you can easily find everything you need at the click of a button. As this information is constantly evolving, I want to introduce you to Emerald (left), your

official online go-to girl. She will lead you to the most up-to-date, earth-friendly products and information.

Girls' Club—Why not host a fabulous evening of eco-learning and fun? Simply visit gorgeouslygreen.com and type in the password. You will receive in-depth information about how to start a Gorgeously Green Girls' Club.™ Password: Club.

Whatever you can do, or dream
you can do, begin it. Boldness, has
genius, power and magic in it

—JOHANN VON GOETHE

Chapter One

STEP 1: Becoming Aware

Getting Started

In step 1, we'll talk about how you can become aware of the way you live and the changes you can make. It is not about judging yourself. It is about observing yourself with compassion. It's crystal clear that as a society we need to make some radical changes in order to avoid disaster; however, the slap-on-the-wrist approach doesn't work for me. I don't like being told off because I use too much electricity or drive the wrong car. I judge myself way too harshly, so I don't need anyone else doing it, thank you very much!

This step is about figuring out how to make the most positive choices for yourself and the planet. You deserve the best. We are going to discover exactly what that is.

What Is "Green"?

Living "green" is about taking everyday actions that have a positive impact on the environment. Each day, we make an impact, and most of the time it's negative without our even knowing it. Who would have thought that an innocent shopping trip to buy a pair of shoes could have a negative impact on anything other than your bank balance!

What Is Gorgeousness?

Gorgeousness is not necessarily an external thing. There were so many times when I tried to perfect my appearance, making sure that every hair was in place, every eyelash separated, every fingernail polished to perfection—and yet deep down I felt horribly inadequate. It was often because I was burned out, afraid, disconnected to anything other than the noise in my head. Gorgeousness is a quality of energy. When I'm connected to that part of me that is living according to my deepest values, I feel something inside of me light up. I can be wearing scraggy old jeans and an ill-fitting shirt, but I still feel happy, passionate, and alive. That is gorgeousness.

Have Your Cake and Eat It, Too

Going green doesn't mean you have to go without. On the contrary, you can have everything your heart desires, the caveat being that it has to be for the good of everyone and everything involved. *Gorgeously Green* will take you to a new level of understanding about the interconnectedness of everything—human beings, animals, nature; it is the same energy that is in all of us. On a quantum level, there is no separation between me and you and the earth we are standing on. We can go ahead and indulge in all the things we desire as long as they are produced with love and reverence for the earth and its inhabitants.

I don't want to be made to feel guilty about the way I live now. I can only do my best, according to the knowledge and awareness that I currently have. It's ironic that most of the things considered to be bad for the environment were considered to be awe-inspiring less than a hundred years ago: electricity and natural gas were miracles, and plastic was to be marveled at. Today, we know these wonderful commodities can devastate and pollute the planet, but it's not our fault. We thought we were doing the right thing, creating a better standard of living. We got more comfortable and then we wanted more.

Running Out

The problem lies in our lack of understanding about the sources of our everyday necessities. Oil was made deep in the earth's crust thousands of years ago and there is a finite amount. We didn't even think about that little problem. We just assumed that we would never run out. Ugh! No one told us, so we carelessly and greedily used all we could, and now we're in trouble. In much the same way, my six-year-old daughter thinks there is an infinite amount of money in the bank. She sees me pulling it out of a hole in a wall of my local bank and naturally can't understand when I tell her that the hamster palace she's been bugging me about costs too much.

The Solution

We got it the wrong way around. We thought the earth should take care of us when really we should have taken care of it. I'm so grateful that it's not too late. We can begin to think differently about ourselves in relation to this exquisite planet. I'm a strong believer in the collective conscious. When a deep awareness begins to germinate within the consciousness of a few, it spreads along invisible networks of energy. Before we know it, everyone will be aware and wanting to make the changes to create a decent environment for their children. So let's you and me become the pioneers—little centers of consciousness that will help to heal the earth.

I love that we can continue to evolve and change every day. I never want to be stagnant. I don't want my life to become routine and boring; however, our culture has become stuck in a bit of a rut in recent years. A weird kind of complacency has set in, and it doesn't feel good. Come on, girls—time to shake off the cobwebs, wake up, and go wild. There is so much to discover. We are beginning to understand what doesn't work anymore. Now we need to reach up and find out what does work.

The green scene is exploding and is going to evolve gradually over the next few years. What we know today may be obsolete soon, but the important thing is that we keep reaching for something greater. Human beings have one thing in common—we all live on the same small planet, yet we're too busy fighting over religion and oil to notice that the twirling ball we're standing on is in serious trouble.

Keep It Simple

The reason I wrote this book was because I wanted to create an easy-to-follow program that would dispel the confusion that is often associated with the concept of going green. If you follow and complete this eight-step program, you will have covered absolutely everything that you need to know. You can close the book, sign the completion certificate at the end, and be rest assured that you have sufficiently changed your life so that it complies with the eco-standards that even the most hardcore are throwing at us.

Many of us have become aware of global warming and the concept of going green, because we've seen or heard about Al Gore's movie, *An Inconvenient Truth*. On my travels, I have met so many women who started to make a few changes after seeing this movie. All of them said that they had no idea what was going on prior to seeing it. I applaud Al Gore for raising our awareness. His book and movie give us a simple and clear understanding of the whys and wherefores of global warming: He explains how the sun's energy enters the atmosphere and is then reradiated back into space as infrared waves. Normally the atmosphere traps some of this heat, which is why planet Earth is habitable to humans; however, in recent times, Gore believes that our atmospheric layer has been thickened by large quantities of "human-caused carbon dioxide and other greenhouse gases," so the heat cannot escape and our planet is thus getting too hot. Gore goes on to explain what all the greenhouse gases are and that a large percentage of them come from the burning of fossil fuels. His message encourages all of us to become responsible about our personal energy consumption. He says, "We can even make choices to bring our individual carbon emissions to zero."

When I talk about being eco-friendly or going green, many people automatically think of global warming because of the recent media coverage concerning reducing our carbon footprint. The words *global warming* frankly make a lot of people switch off. But this is only a very small part of our environmental concerns. Even if global warming isn't caused by carbon emissions (and there are many scientists who vehemently disagree with Al Gore's theory), there is still much to do and not a minute to be wasted. I refuse to be one of those people who will regret that we didn't clean up our acts when there was still time. If you too are a bit tired of it all, don't be put off as this book is about becoming a Green Goddess not a carbon offset bore.

Reluctant Environmentalist!

I know that "reluctant environmentalist" is an oxymoron, but that is honestly me! I want to be green and I've attempted to make many changes in my life; however, I have dragged my feet on many occasions because I am a princess who likes the familiar.

When I first spent a day of trying to be aware of how my every action affected the environment, I was even more shocked than I thought I would be. I was convinced that I wasn't really causing too much damage, and the shocker was how much I consumed. I love shopping and realized that a day didn't go by that there wasn't some serious spending! Typically, I'd run into a superstore for a toothbrush and some lightbulbs. An hour or two later, I would come out laden with plastic bags, a hundred and fifty bucks lighter. Moreover, that was the first shopping stop of the day! It felt good while I was actually filling the cart, but after a week, what did I have to show: a few plastic toys crammed into my daughter's overstuffed toy basket and a T-shirt for me that looked awful after one wash, not to mention the numerous toxic cleaning supplies that promised to transform my house into a gleaming palace, sitting unused under the kitchen sink.

I couldn't believe how many little trips I took: "I'm just going to nip to the garden center or the dry-cleaner," I'd say to my long-suffering husband, who was quick to point out that the car hadn't yet cooled down from the last trip. So when I started to become aware of my energy consumption for the week, I totally freaked out. The daily running of my beloved washer/dryer was just the tip of the iceberg. I began to imagine what it must have been like to live two hundred years ago with no lights or hot water. For the first time in my life, I felt somewhat grateful for these basics—this gratitude is sadly short lived!

I knew that my cosmetics were probably full of nasty chemicals, but I wasn't motivated enough to start squinting at the small print. Besides, I had just blown half a paycheck on a brand new line that claimed I would look ten years younger in a month. I could only find one packet in my kitchen cupboard with an organic label on it and decided that I wasn't yet ready to pay a premium for food that I didn't really believe was going to be that much better for me. I absolutely knew my kitchen cleaning products were chock-full of chemical horrors, but how otherwise would I get that squeaky clean shine?

Baby Steps

As I slowly became aware of green issues, it was as though I was waking up from a lifetime of being unconscious. Once I started to really learn about the products I used every day in my home, I became overwhelmed. This was just my house—what about the world around me? The most important thing was the baby steps that I took at the beginning. I had to realize that I couldn't change everything at once and that all I had to do was change one tiny thing a day. Soon enough, the days mounted up. Before I knew it, I had radically transformed my lifestyle. I began to feel better than ever. The more gorgeous I felt, the more I wanted to do.

I'm very lazy, so I've made peace with the fact that I just can't become an eco-freak overnight. The other evening, I was so tired that I couldn't face cooking. My husband ordered Chinese takeout, and I was horrified to see much of it arrive in Styrofoam containers—what's a green girl to do? My husband told me not to get my knickers in a twist, reminding me that most of the time I attempt to do the right thing— hello, I had ordered tofu, rice, and veggies for Pete's sake! I promised myself that I would call the restaurant the next morning to ask them to change to a greener alternative, but laziness won out and they still haven't been subjected to my annoying British-fake-polite tone. My husband says I sound patronizing when I'm complaining, so I'm working on it. Besides, I don't want to alienate the only takeout that doesn't use MSG within a three-mile radius.

No Need to Be Boring

I used to think it was all about wearing hemp and eating organic tofu. I thought I would have to turn into one of those zealous do-gooders with unshaven armpits. Trust me, this is not what the Gorgeously Green program is about. Far from it. We are going to be busting out in bright and wonderful colors. We're going to be painting our nails and our lips and wearing the latest, hippest fashions.

I am not part of the tree-huggers' "My way or the highway" movement, either. Gorgeously Green is not all or nothing. On the contrary, if you can learn to make just one small change a week, you will start the snowball rolling. In my experience, one action leads to another. I've always been put off in the past because I thought you were either a hemp-wearing do-gooder or a nasty consuming mess. I'm somewhere in the middle. With one foot in my Jimmy Choos and the other in the dirt, digging for weeds, I have to admit that I enjoy having my cake and eating it, too.

In Nazi Germany, it was said that "the road to hell was paved with indifference." I think it's the same way with saving the planet. The difficult thing is that it's not so easy to actually see what is going on. I rely on the media reports about global warming and carbon emissions, but I don't actually see the ice caps melting out of my bedroom window, I don't taste pesticides on carrots, and I don't feel the toxins in cosmetics seeping into my skin. It sometimes doesn't feel real or urgent.

In a perfect world we wouldn't have to worry about air and water pollution, about toxic foods and cosmetics that cause us to get sick, but they're a reality. Indifference is a dull and ugly attitude. Passion is exciting and inspiring. I know all you soon-to-be Gorgeously Green girls out there are not afflicted with indifference.

The situation is so scary that it's not only parts of Africa that are going to experience drastic water and food shortages—we are going to experience them as well. Have you noticed how much your water and sanitation bills have gone up? That's the first place that I began to feel it. I couldn't believe that it was costing me as much as an expensive pair of shoes a month to irrigate my backyard. I'm now desperate to get a gray water system installed that will utilize the otherwise wasted water from my shower and toilet—yes, to think that every flush is watering another rose would be pretty cool, and the savings could justify a cyber visit to *www.jimmychoo.com*.

A New Purpose

The other day I was driving out of the mall and found myself stuck in traffic. I turned on my radio, pressed the "seek" button, and all I could find were commercials trying to seduce me into buying more stuff. I looked at all the billboards around me and realized that I couldn't escape from advertisers trying to sell me yet more stuff. They are everywhere. I suddenly felt suffocated. I looked around at the unhappy and frustrated faces around me, thinking, What are we all doing? We are like hamsters running around on wheels, getting caught up in this lifestyle that is becoming hellish. It is moments like these that get me thinking about the deeper meaning of my life.

As soon as I got home, I escaped to my little vegetable garden at the end of our yard and started pulling weeds. It felt so good to be around plants and greenery and to feel that I was doing something worthwhile—plucking the suckers off my tiny heirloom tomatoes. I realized that modern life is a sucker sometimes, draining our energy and vitality, leaving us exhausted and depressed.

A trip to the grocery store or the mall can be equally draining. The time it takes to get there, the parking, and then the endless shopping—traipsing up and down neon-lit aisles, only to have to wait in a long checkout line, while contemplating packets of bubble gum and lurid photos of bikini-clad starlets trying to hide cellulite. Ugh! I often need to regenerate myself after such experiences by finding a new sense of purpose, which can make every day feel exciting and worthwhile.

What Are Your Deepest Values?

What do I value most about life? I have to ask myself this question. I have to have a sense of purpose; otherwise, I lack the drive to create wonderful things in my life. We all have the potential, no matter what our circumstances are, to create change and spread hope. It's about feeling good about yourself. Deciding to buy a reusable coffee mug makes me feel a hundred times more fabulous than chucking another paper cup into the trash.

I love that we can turn this global warming crisis into something positive. As Al Gore says in his wonderful book, *Earth in the Balance,* "we have a generational mission . . . a shared and unifying cause." There is nothing like a terrible disaster or crisis to bring out the best in human nature. My parents tell me what it was like living in England during World War II; it was a terrifying period where the whole nation had to come together and learn how to pool their resources and live on less. My mother waxes lyrical about how good it felt to "make do" and reminisces that there was a great sense of community—whether it was dragging a neighbor to a bomb shelter or sharing rations, it felt great. The situation we face today is no less terrifying, so we can again come together as we face this crisis. We can feel good, on a gut level, about helping each other and the planet.

Try This Exercise

Here's a great exercise that comes from an old Buddhist tradition. You basically imagine you are an old lady—say ninety years old—and you are sitting in a beautiful backyard or lying peacefully in bed, ruminating on your life. How well did you live? How well did you love? How much did you care? Did you live with a great sense of purpose?

Go on, try it! Look back on your life and think about the things that really mattered to you. Did you live with a deep sense of purpose?

The last time I did this exercise, it made me realize I want to leave this world in as good shape as I possibly can for future generations. If I have done everything within my power, I will be satisfied. I want to teach my daughter and her friends to do the same.

Grab some recycled paper, a pen, and get writing. Staples now carries 100 percent recycled legal pads, which are perfect. Write at the top of one page: How well did I love? The second page: In what ways did I help to make this planet more habitable for future generations? The third page: In what ways did my life have meaning?

Don't think too much about what to write—just get writing. Don't allow your pen to stop until you've filled the page. That way, you'll tap into your stream-of-consciousness writing, where you'll find gold. Remember, no one is going to read this except you! The whole exercise should take no more than fifteen minutes.

Sometimes when I get caught up in everyday life, I forget why it is so important for all of us to strive to be green. We all must remember the global crisis we are facing.

- The number of people living in poverty has increased by 100 million over the past decade, to 1.3 billion people (more than one-fifth of the world's population).
- According to the United Nations, poor environmental quality contributes to 25 percent of all preventable illness in the world today.
- According to the United Nations, about 1.2 billion people worldwide drink polluted water, causing hundreds of millions of water-related diseases every year and over 5 million deaths.
- In the United States, 60,000 premature deaths are caused by pollution annually (American Lung Association).
- Eighty percent of marine pollution comes from land-based sources. In developing countries, more than 90 percent of untreated sewage and 70 percent of untreated industrial wastes are dumped into surface waters. Human activity has degraded more than 50 percent of the world's costal ecosystems.
- Seventy-five percent of the world's fisheries require immediate steps to freeze or reduce fishing to ensure a future supply of fish. In forty years, it is likely that our children will not be eating fish at all (United Nations).
- Nearly 40 percent of the world's agricultural land is seriously degraded.
- In the United States, approximately 6.6 tons of greenhouse gases are emitted per person every year. About 82 percent of these emissions are from burning fossil fuels to generate electricity and power our cars. The remaining emissions are from methane derived from wastes in our landfills, raising livestock, natural gas pipelines, and coal, as well as from industrial chemicals and other sources (Environmental Protection Agency).

❀ Since 1950, over 50 percent of the world's tropical forests have been lost.

❀ If current deforestation rates continue, many of the 50 to 90 percent of the earth's species that live in forests will be lost by the middle of the twenty-first century.

❀ According to U.S. Geological Survey predictions, Glacier National Park will not have glaciers left by 2030.

❀ The United States is ranked as the number one global polluter.

These statistics are certainly scary enough to get a girl springing into action.

Empower Yourself

You are going to empower yourself through what you learn in this program. You will be in the driver's seat from now on. Instead of the advertisers telling you what will make you happy, you will decide for yourself. We are innately powerful as women.

If you are green about being green, you will find this awareness step quite shocking. If you have already started on this path, I want you to use this week to further your awareness. It's not a competition. Some of you will have already made a ton of changes with the threat of global warming looming, and some of you will be new to this way of living.

The Fun Begins!

To get you thinking, I've created a checklist. It will help you to take stock of where you are right now. It'll be really interesting, because in the last chapter you will repeat the checklist to show you how much you have changed.

Resistance

Trying something new can often feel uncomfortable and like a waste of time. What difference is it going to make if I recycle one yogurt cup, I've thought. The good news is that you can make a massive difference by doing just one thing a day. It has a cumulative effect. You inspire

GORGEOUSLY GREEN LIFESTYLE CHECKLIST
(YES/NO ANSWERS)

Your Beauty

☐ 1. Do you know what the ingredients are in your cosmetics?

☐ 2. Do you ever read the labels on your lotions and creams?

☐ 3. Do you know what is in your nail polish?

☐ 4. Do you use drugstore hair dye?

☐ 5. Do you buy your products from a department store?

☐ 6. Do you believe labels that say "natural" or "organic"?

Your Home

☐ 1. Do you know what energy-efficient appliances are?

☐ 2. Do you buy energy-efficient appliances?

☐ 3. Do you know what compact fluorescent lightbulbs (CFLs) are?

☐ 4. Do you buy CFLs?

☐ 5. Do you purchase paper items made from recycled or postconsumer material?

☐ 6. Have you ever cleaned your refrigerator coils?

☐ 7. Do you shut things off when not using them?

☐ 8. Do you unplug appliances and chargers when not using them?

☐ 9. Is your thermostat set at 68 degrees Fahrenheit or lower?

☐ 10. Is your air conditioner set at 78 degrees Fahrenheit or higher?

☐ 11. Is your water heater wrapped?

☐ 12. Do you use space heaters?

☐ 13. Do you purchase green energy?

☐ 14. Do you use your washer/dryer almost every day?

☐ 15. Do you ever air-dry your clothes?

☐ 16. Do you take your clothes to a regular dry-cleaner?

☐ 17. Do you have low-flow toilets and showers?

☐ 18. Do you use recycled trash bags?

☐ 19. Are you aware of how many bags of trash you generate weekly?

☐ 20. Do you use toxic cleaners in your home?

☐ 21. Do you chuck used batteries in the trash?

☐ 22. Do you know what volatile organic compounds (VOCs) are?

☐ 23. Are VOCs present in your home?

☐ 24. Have you ever visited a hazardous waste facility?

☐ 25. Do you have green houseplants in your home?

☐ 26. Do all members of your family try to conserve water?

Your Yard

☐ 1. Do you have a garden?

☐ 2. Do you grow herbs?

☐ 3. Do you know about native plants?

☐ 4. Do you grow native plants?

☐ 5. Do you use lawn fertilizer?

☐ 6. Do you use garden pesticides?

☐ 7. Is your garden organic?

☐ 8. Do you irrigate your lawn every day?

☐ 9. Do you hose your driveway to clean it off?

Your Ride

☐ 1. Do you drive an energy-efficient car?

☐ 2. If not, are you considering purchasing one?

☐ 3. Do you ever carpool?

☐ 4. Do you use a reusable mug?

☐ 5. Do you drive to the store every day?

☐ 6. Do you own a bicycle?

☐ 7. When you change your oil, do you recycle it?

☐ 8. Do you check your tire pressure once a week?

☐ 8a. Do you wash your car at home?

Your Shopping

☐ 1. Do you buy organic cotton clothes or bed linens?

☐ 2. Do you buy clothes not made with sweatshop labor?

☐ 3. Do you try to eat locally grown food?

☐ 4. Do you eat organic food?

☐ 5. Do you try to buy things with less packaging?

☐ 6. Do you shop at farmer's markets?

☐ 7. Do you buy from small local stores?

☐ 8. Do you avoid factory-farmed meats?

☐ 9. Do you buy organic produce?

☐ 9a. Do you Buy Fair-Trade Items?

☐ 10. Do you purchase genetically modified organism (GMO)-free food?

☐ 11. Do you purchase antibiotic- and hormone-free dairy?

Your Desires

☐ 1. Do you wish to become healthier?

☐ 2. Do you want to become more vibrant?

☐ 3. Do you want to live according to your deepest values?

☐ 4. Do you want to feel exhilarated?

☐ 5. Are you ready to become Gorgeously Green?

other people by your actions. Before you know it, thousands of women are recycling yogurt cups.

My daughter plays with a girl on the next block whose parents are eco-fanatics. They walk around in shoes that resemble loaves of bread. I made the terrible mistake of chucking an empty juice box into their trash can. The mom almost had a choking fit as she dove head first into the bin to retrieve it. "We recycle *everything*," she shrieked as she carefully folded it up like origami for the recycling bin.

I can assure you that we are not going down that alley. We are just going to tread a little more lightly and have a lot more fun. I know a bunch of supercool families who wear the whole green thing with style and a smile. That's what turns me on. But I have to admit that I fold the occasional juice box like origami and want to shriek at friends who don't recycle—but manage to refrain!

How Earth Friendly Are You?

I invite you to now go to *www.gorgeouslygreen.com* to take the **Green Evaluation Test** (GET). Learn how earth-friendly you really are by taking this short and easy online quiz at *http://gorgeouslygreen.com*. Simply type the password that you see below into the search bar to take this illuminating quiz and receive your personalized report. Password: Emerald.

Set an Intention

Through my yoga practice, I have learned how powerful it can be to set an intention. I spend a few seconds each day asking myself what my intentions might be for that day. I then mentally pick just one. It could be as simple as "I spread joy and laughter." I close my eyes and mentally repeat it two or three times to set it in my consciousness. It will miraculously pop back into my mind, which is very useful when I'm stuck in an impossibly long grocery store line!

It's important to say your intention in the present tense. If you say, "I will do such and such," it will stay in the future rather than happen now. Here are some Gorgeously Green suggestions:

"I am ready and willing to make the changes necessary to live a sustainable life."

"I give and receive only the best."

"I am living in a way that reflects my deepest values. I'm walking the walk."

"I'm moving mindfully through my day and making choices that are having a positive impact on the environment."

"I'm enjoying living with a deep sense of purpose."

"I am becoming Gorgeously Green."

Pick one of them or make up your own and try it on for size. See if you can remember to repeat it to yourself a few times during the day.

Get In Tune

Spend half an hour every couple of days connecting with nature—ugh! I know this sounds wishy-washy and new age; however, we need to make a connection to the earth in order to feel what this whole thing is about. As Al Gore so eloquently put it: "We each need to assess our own relationship to the natural world and renew, at the deepest level of personal integrity, a connection to it. And that can only happen if we renew what is authentic and true in every aspect of our lives."

If you live in the country, go for a walk and discover something new each time you go, maybe a different shade of green or a new smell. Living in a concrete sprawl, as I do, can be a little more challenging; however, I can always find a park or a tree-lined street. My favorite way to connect is to pull weeds in my garden.

Cell phones are part and parcel of our everyday life, like it or not. Go to *www.rareearthtones.org/ringtones* and download for free the most beautiful sounds of endangered species: For your ring tone, you can pick an owl hooting in a nighttime forest or a whale calling its mate. I picked out an eagle. Each time the phone rings, I can hear the ocean waves behind the eagle's haunting cry. And people always think it's a real bird call!

Savasana

Savasana (pronounced *sha-va-sana*) is the yoga "corpse" pose. As you lie down on the floor like a corpse, you let go of every tension in your body. I practice this pose every day because it helps me to become aware of my body and my thought processes. So I want you to lie down. If you have lower back issues, grab a pillow to put under your knees. Once on the floor, lie like a snow angel and begin to observe your breath. Is it deep or shallow? Are you inhaling through your nose or your mouth? Now, become aware of your body. Do any parts of it feel tight or blocked? (My right shoulder is always a good few inches higher than my left.) Now, deliberately let go. Lie still for a few moments. Feel the weight of your body being supported by the earth. Get up slowly and carefully, and enjoy seeing the rest of the day through green-colored spectacles!

How Did You Do?

❀ Did you complete the checklist?
❀ Did you write down your deepest values?

❀ Did you take the GET quiz at *www.gorgeouslygreen.com*?

❀ Did you do your "nature" date?

Pat on the Back

Congratulate yourself for making the effort to embark on a journey that is vitally important for you and future generations. You are going to inspire yourself and others in a way you never thought possible.

Chapter Two

STEP 2: Green Goddess

Women spend an average of four hundred hours a year on their beauty routine. That's a lot of time spent rubbing in lotions, potions, and the like. As a green girl, I realized that I needed to make absolutely sure that everything I used from bubble bath to blush was safe. Without knowing it, we slather ourselves with toxins morning and night. One product alone is unlikely to cause harm, but repeated exposure to these chemicals can eventually lead to health problems and environmental pollution.

I don't have a lot of time for my beauty routine anymore: work, husband, and six-year-old daughter meltdowns have seriously compromised my glorious "me" time. I comfort myself by using the most nourishing, luxurious, and safe products I can find. I need to know that I am not only saving myself but also the planet. Moreover, if I use harmful chemicals on my body, many of them wash down the drain and contaminate the groundwater and urban runoff. So it's a win/win situation to get Gorgeously Green in the beauty department.

I adore makeup. It makes me feel sexy and glamorous. It can transform me in seconds from an old hag into a goddess. Even on my worst day, a quick lick of shimmering lip gloss and a dab of mascara can change my mood immeasurably. When I first started becoming green, I worried that I would have to seriously compromise in the beauty department. I had visions of the vegan woman named Joy who lived next door to us growing up. She let her natural gray hair grow down to her waist and wore Abba-style beauty-without-cruelty makeup. Things have changed since then. There are so many wonderful companies that offer everything our hearts might desire.

It's time to get savvy about your choices right now. You are about to take the second step of the Gorgeously Green program, so let's examine exactly what you plaster all over your body on a daily basis. Is it really good for you or are you harming yourself and the planet?

Your Skin

Your skin is the largest organ of your body. It is living and breathing and absorbs everything you apply to it. Unlike food, which goes through your digestive system before being absorbed into your body, the chemicals you put on your skin are directly absorbed into your bloodstream. It's insane that the government demands regulations for food labeling but not for cosmetics. This will probably change in the future as the large cosmetic companies come under greater scrutiny and organizations lobby for them to remove dangerous chemicals, but for now we have to be detectives.

We are lucky that a fantastic nonprofit group called the Environmental Working Group has taken matters into its own hands and given us a ton of information. This group has also put pressure on companies that are not towing the line. It will not be a wasted journey for you to visit its Web site at *www.ewg.org* and give the group some support. This group covers every aspect of the environment, pushing the companies and organizations that need it, to make our world a healthier place.

We tend to focus mostly on the skin on our face. When I think of the crazy amounts of money I used to spend on miniscule pots of antiaging cream filled with useless and possibly dangerous chemicals, I'm

DID YOU KNOW?

According to the Environmental Working Group, only 11 percent of 10,500 ingredients in beauty products have been tested for safety. One in thirteen women are exposed every day to ingredients through their personal care products that are known or probable carcinogens and reproductive toxins. Aubrey Hampton, founder of the fabulous company Aubrey Organics, says that the average woman's morning routine puts her in contact with a hundred chemicals before breakfast!

more than a bit annoyed with myself. Seduced by the packaging, I'd bring the precious pot home with the sales assistant's claims ringing in my head: "erases every single one of your fine lines in just a week!" I'd carefully unwrap the cellophane, open the box, and fish around to find the paper leaflet, which would confirm what the assistant had told me. After a week, when all the fine lines were still firmly entrenched, I felt more than a bit silly but had to still keep on believing in the claims because I'd spent so much money. By the way, it's not just me! Women spend an average of $650 a year on beauty products.

Now that I'm older and wiser, I walk the other way when one of those painted beauties approaches me in the department store. I smile not because I think that beauty comes from within (we all know it does—but come on!), but because I'm savvy now about what's safe and effective.

We'll focus on our hair and body to begin, since these areas absorb more products. The Gorgeously Green program is going to make this supersimple for you. There is a ton of information available, so let's deal with the most important issues first.

What on Earth Is in the Products You Use?

I want you to get out your beauty-related products (shampoos, conditioners, body scrubs, bubble bath, face creams, body lotions and oils, and hairstyling products). Grab your partner's or roommate's stuff while you're at it. Put them on the kitchen table or the countertop. Grab a large magnifying glass as most ingredient lists are so tiny, you can barely see them with your naked eye. I invested in a compact magnifying glass, which I can keep in my purse and easily whip out at a moment's notice in the store.

There is a great media buzz right now about how some cosmetic companies are taking all the "bad" chemicals out of certain lines or how a particular nail polish brand is completely safe; however, these claims should be based on scientific evidence and often aren't. You will also read how many U.S. cosmetic companies are now pledging to make the necessary changes to make all their products "safe." Be very wary, though, because the regulations are not very tough and the loopholes are ridiculous.

Red Alert

The Environmental Working Group suggests that consumers should be on high alert for the following seven ingredients (listed in order of danger significance):

1. **COAL TAR:** *Used in dandruff shampoos and anti-itch creams, coal tar is a known carcinogen. Coal tar–based dyes such as FD&C Blue 1, which are used in toothpastes, and FD&C Green 3, which is used in mouthwash, should be avoided.*

2. **FRAGRANCE:** *This ubiquitous term is used to mask hundreds of ingredients, including phthalates, which disrupt the endocrine system and could cause reproductive and developmental harm.*

3. **HYDROQUINONE:** *Commonly found in skin lighteners and facial moisturizers, it is a neurotoxin and is allergenic.*

4. **ALUMINUM:** *Often used in eye shadow as a color additive and also used in deodorants, it is listed as carcinogenic, toxic, and mutagenic.*

5. **TRICLOSAN:** *This chemical is used in almost all antibacterial products, including soap, toothpaste, and cosmetics. Triclosan is often contaminated with dioxins, which are highly carcinogenic and can also weaken your immune system, decrease fertility, and cause birth defects.*

6. **P-PHENYLENEDIAMINE:** *This is the chemical that has given a bad name to regular hair dye. It can damage your nervous system, cause lung irritation, and cause severe allergic reactions. It's also listed as 1,4-Benzenediamine; p-Phenyldiamine and 4-Phenylenediamine.*

7. **LEAD AND MERCURY:** *Lead could appear in toothpaste as a naturally occurring contaminant of hydrated silica. It is a neurotoxin that also appears as lead acetate in men's hair dye. Mercury is found in a cosmetic preservative called thimerosol.*

Are they really *that* bad? Hello! Yes, these chemicals are terrible because they might contain impurities that are carcinogenic, and many of them are actually classified as neurotoxins and endocrine disruptors. It gets pretty complicated when you do the research and discover that certain chemicals mixed with other chemicals become carcinogenic or another chemical in a particular formulation may cause liver and kidney abnormalities. I will spare you the gruesome details, but it's sufficient to know that if there is a long list of chemicals in a product, don't buy it. (These products should really be taken to your nearest hazardous waste disposal unit!) I had some really expensive potions that I just couldn't throw away, so I used them up quickly on larger areas of my body—namely my bottom! Yes, I admit it—my buns got a good coating of some ridiculously expensive eye gel, probably full of horrors that I had been gullible enough to buy.

Reading Your Bottles

Now that you know the worst seven chemicals, let's get started. It's important to prioritize with the following five products, as they tend to get the most daily usage:

1. *Shampoo*
2. *Conditioner*
3. *Body wash*
4. *Lip products*
5. *Hand lotions and creams*

Most of us use one or all of these products every day. I use hand cream every time I wash my hands. Living in a desert here in Los Angeles, lip balm is always at the ready. I also slather my entire body with lotion twice daily, so these items were the first up for scrutiny.

Place your shampoo, conditioner, body wash, lip balm, and lotions in front of you on the table; make sure you find all your children's bottles, too. If a bottle contains *any* chemicals, move it to one side of the table. You are going to make three piles:

1. Chuck out immediately
2. Finish but don't buy again
3. Needs further investigation

The products containing any ingredients from the Red Alert list will obviously go in the "chuck out immediately" pile.

The "finish but don't buy again" pile works for all those products that are suspect on account of a gazillion unrecognizable ingredients but not dangerous. It can be pretty costly to start from scratch, so put them back in your cabinet and know that you can make better choices the next time.

Generally speaking, the more ingredients listed, the more wary you should be. It's likely that you will have thrown away the box that your face cream came in and the actual pot may not list the ingredients. If this is the case, put it in the "needs further investigation" pile until your next trip to the store.

When you next go shopping, take your Gorgeously Green Skincare Shopping Cheat Sheet that you can download from my Web site: *www. gorgeouslygreen.com/cheatsheet*. With this important information in hand, you can give the poor sales assistant a good grilling—chances are she won't know what you are on about, but it's within your rights to ask about all the dodgy chemicals.

Be Wary

Most products claim to be natural or say that they contain botanicals or plant extracts. This means absolutely nothing—they may well contain miniscule amounts of these ingredients but also a plethora of chemicals and additives. Also, watch out for "unscented" or "fragrance-free," which often means that synthetic ingredients have been added to mask the odor. Finally, watch out for "hypoallergenic." Although the most common irritants may have been left out, the product could still contain all the other ugly stuff. I know that it's exasperating not to be able to trust an ingredient list from a supposedly reputable company, but you can't and shouldn't! You also need to be discerning about the look of the label. You may see flowers, herbs, or a little cottage with roses around the front door—this doesn't mean it's safe or wholesome.

Be suspicious if you see the word *organic* in the name of the product. Some sneaky companies just put this word in the company name and trademark it so that it looks official. Sometimes these products don't contain one single organic ingredient!

Going Deeper

Having dealt with the worst offenders in our most-used products, it's now time to get out *all* your other products: face creams, eye gels, skin lighteners, shaving foam, hair dye—the lot! Repeat the task of sorting into three piles.

Hopefully, you will be pleasantly surprised and won't have to chuck too much out; however, it's now time to go deeper. Since you've already got your potions out, you may want to repeat the process, checking them for Orange Alert ingredients.

Orange Alert

Some of the following chemicals can create the formation of carcinogenic chemicals called nitrosamines, so I strongly suggest avoiding them:

- Cocamide DEH
- Lauramide DEA
- Cocamide MEA
- Triethanolamine (TEA)
- Diethanolamine (DEA)

Mineral Oils

They coat the skin like plastic, so it cannot breathe. They can slow down the skin's natural functions and cell development, resulting in premature aging. Mineral oils can also be contaminated with PAH (polycyclic aromatic hydrocarbon), which can be carcinogenic. They come in the form of petroleum distillates, which are human carcinogens that are prohibited in the European Union but are found in the United States in many products including mascara. It appears on labels as "petroleum" or "liquid paraffin."

Petroleum jelly, which, by the way, I touted as a cure-all as a younger girl, is now thought to be a carcinogen because of the way it is manu-factured. Ugh—to think of all those years of slathering it all over my face and lips.

Parabens (methyl-,ethyl-,propyl,butyl,isobutyl-)

Parabens are chemical preservatives that have been identified as estro-genic and disruptive of normal hormone function. Estrogenic chemicals mimic the function of the naturally occurring hormone estrogen, and exposure to external estrogens has been shown to increase the risk of breast cancer. Enough said—I don't touch them with a barge pole. I have also put them in the Orange Alert list because they are very common, so squint at the small print whenever you see a long list of chemicals.

Phthalates

These horrid little synthetic chemicals are known to cause a broad range of birth defects and lifelong reproductive impairment in lab ani-mals exposed during pregnancy and after birth. They are also hormone-mimicking chemicals, many of which disrupt normal hormone processes, raising concerns about implications for increased breast cancer risk. They are often hidden under the term "fragrance." Dibutyl and diethylhexyl have been banned in the European Union but not in the United States.

Sodium Lauryl Sulfate (SLS) and Sodium Lauryl Ether Sulfate (SLES)

This ingredient is a foaming agent that is derived from coconut oil. It is used in brake fluid and antifreeze and also in a huge variety of skin care products, including toothpaste, shampoo, bubble bath, and soap.

There is a great deal of controversy surrounding SLS, as many feel that it is not only a proven skin irritant but also could be carcinogenic. The Environmental Working Group considers it to be a carcinogen; oth-ers say that it is prone to contamination by a probable carcinogen called 1,4-dioxane, which is used for its foaming ability. Many other groups blame the hype on the natural skin care industry, who want to make a buck or two flogging their SLS-free products.

I'm not a great risk taker when it comes to my health, so I'm choosing to go SLS-free for now.

Polyethylene Glycol (PEG)

PEG is a potential carcinogen that is typically used as a grease-dissolving cleaner and a thickener for skin care products. These chemicals are deemed to be so toxic by the Environmental Protection Agency that workers have to wear protective clothing when handling them. They can easily penetrate your skin, causing brain, liver, and kidney malfunctions. Also look out for propylene glycol, isopropyl alcohol, and butylene glycol.

Formaldehyde-Producing Preservatives

Some preservatives can become formaldehyde donors, in that they release small amounts of formaldehyde into the skin. Many preservatives are cellular toxins. Formaldehyde can cause many health issues including joint discomfort, chest pains, and chronic fatigue. Examples are hydantoin, imidazolidinyl urea, and diazolidinyl urea.

Talc

Found in baby products, underam deodorants, and cosmetic powder products, talc contains a chemical that is similar to asbestos and can increase the risk of certain ovarian cancers.

Acrylates and Methacrylates

Found in nail products, these products can cause contact dermatitis.

Alcohol, Isopropyl (SD-40)

This additive is very common in cosmetics. It is a drying agent that strips off the outer layers of skin, exposing you to bacteria and other toxins. It can also promote brown spots and even accelerates aging —ugh!

Tocopherol Acetate

This may sound innocent, but it is a synthetic version of vitamin E, which is a suspected carcinogen and causes dermatitis.

Phenonip

This is a preservative blend that contains the aforementioned parabens: phenoxyethanol, methylparaben, ethylparaben, butylparaben, proylparaben, and isobutylparaben.

Quaternary Ammonium Compounds (Quats)

The oddly named "Quats" are used as preservatives. They are the primary cause of contact dermatitis. They will be listed on your ingredient list as benzalkonium chloride, cetrimonium bromide, quaternium-15, and quaternium 1-29.

Cationic Surfactants

These little guys can be found in your hair conditioner. They were originally used in the paper industry but, ironically, can make you hair dry and brittle after long-term use. They are also allergenic and toxic. Look out for these ingredients: stearalkonium chloride, benzalkonium chloride, cetrimonium chloride, cetalkonium chloride, and lauryl dimonium hydrolyzed collagen.

Benzyl Alcohol

Look out for this on your ingredient list, as it is a petrochemical that can be a severe irritant to your eyes and your respiratory system.

Silicone Derived Emollients

These chemicals coat your skin like plastic wrap—and even worse, can accumulate in your liver and lymph nodes, which can promote the tumor growth. These emollients include: dimethicone, dimethicone copolyol, and cyclomethicone.

Carbomer 934, 940, 941, 960, 961C

This chemical is used as a stabilizer and thickener in creams, cosmetics, toothpaste, and bath products. It is a known allergen that causes eye irritation.

Weeding Out the Bad Stuff

The really great news is that with so much media awareness, many of the really cool products will tell you on their labels that they do not contain parabens, sodium lauryl sulfate, or mineral oil. So remember my suggestion to get rid of the Red Alert products and put the Orange

Alert products in your "use up but don't buy again" pile. With your newfound knowledge, you can make better choices when you next run out.

Confused?

If you are in doubt or confused by a particular product you own or have thrown out the box, you can go to a fabulous Web site at *www. safecosmetics.org* from a company called Safe Cosmetics and actually type in the product to get the safety scoop on it. Using Skin Deep, the company's cosmetic safety database, Safe Cosmetics rates the product from 0 through 10 (0 being the safest and 10 having the most dodgy chemicals). I avoid products with a rating of 5 or higher.

Safe Cosmetics is an offshoot of the Environmental Working Group. I often refer to this nonprofit research organization that is based in Washington, D.C. If your product isn't listed and you are concerned about a particular chemical, go to *www.scorecard.org* and click on "Chemical Profiles." You can check your air, water, home, and general environment for toxic concerns. This site is quite addictive. You can type in your zip code and see exactly where all the most offensive polluters are located. You can also see how your area stacks up, toxicity-wise, against every other area in the United States. Plan to put aside some time for this one.

Don't Forget the Packaging

Remember that the packaging in which any of your goodies arrive will just sit in a landfill unless it is fully biodegradable or reusable. Try to look for packaging that is made with recycled materials. It will clearly say so if this is the case. I love a cosmetics company called Suki. Their cute yellow and black boxes are made of recycled materials and labeled with vegetable nontoxic ink. We can only hope that many will follow in their footsteps. If the plastic bottles have a number 1 or 2 on the bottom (in the chasing arrows), it means you can always put them in your recycling bin. Every city differs in which plastic numbers they accept, so contact your local bureau of sanitation to get the scoop.

Movers and Shakers

For those of us who want to live with a good conscience, there are quite a few amazing new companies that have developed perfect personal care products for the Gorgeously Green girl. Along the road, I have met some incredibly inspiring women, many of whom have completely turned their lives around due to something awful that happened to them or to someone they know. I have met many survivors of breast cancer who have taken matters into their own hands by starting their own nontoxic skin care companies.

> It's true: "a substantial and growing body of evidence indicates that exposures to certain toxic chemicals and hormone-mimicking compounds contribute to the development of breast cancer."—THE BREAST CANCER FUND

I am always fascinated with how the companies I love got started. I want to know who the owners are, how and why they started the company, how they create their products from plant to shelf—everything. I encourage you to do the same. You can go online and read how the company was started and by whom. If you have further questions about the purity of a product's ingredients, call the company or send them an e-mail.

Many of the companies that I recommend to you are cottage industries or started off that way. Thanks to the Internet, we can all, no matter where we live, have access to these beautiful products. Don't waste another penny on a cream or lotion that wasn't produced with your health in mind. I also love that I am putting money back into supporting these small industries, rather than filling the coffers of huge pharmaceutical corporations, many of whom own the big-name brand products that appear in every magazine we open. Here are some very cool companies, all of whose ingredients you can trust:

✿ **Suki** (*www.sukisnaturals.com*) has developed one of my favorite skin care lines. The products are every bit as wonderful as other high-end products, but they are free of synthetics, GMO (genetically modified organism) ingredients, petrochemicals, fragrances and dyes, and animal ingredients. Suki Kramer developed the line because she had very sensitive skin and couldn't use regular products. I especially love this company because it is ethical and responsible—packaging and otherwise. Suki Kramer's slogan is "Know your beauty." Suki manufactures a full skin care, hair care, and body care line. I love her Oscar Nominee Deluxe Gift Set. It was given on every 2006 nominee and includes a sample of all of her best products.

❀ **Pangea Organics** (*www.pangeaorganics.com*) has fabulous packaging. Each bottle comes in a fully biodegradable box, the paper of which is infused with wildflower seeds that you soak in water, plant, and wait for your flowers to grow. All its ingredients are plant based, and the company says it has been proven that natural ingredients are more effective than synthetics. The products contain no parabens and no petroleum-based preservatives. A portion of their profits go to the Pangea Institute, which has been set up to help teach people about sustainability. Pangea manufactures facial, hair, bath, and body products.

❀ **Dr. Hauschka** products (*www.drhauschka.com*) began in the 1930s when Dr. Rudolf Hauschka created a holistic pharmaceutical company. He was inspired by the work of Rudolf Steiner, whose teachings included biodynamic farming. This kind of farming embraces the rhythms and cycles of nature and is how all the herbs are farmed in Dr. Hauschka's beautiful products. The company was voted one of the "Top Brands with a Conscience" for 2006. If you become a dedicated Dr. Hauschka follower, as many do, you can be rest assured that there is a huge selection of products to suit every skin type. The only thing you won't find is night cream, as they believe that at the end of day, all you need is a moisturizing cleanse, and then you should let your skin breathe through the night.

❀ **Kuumba Made** (*www.kuumbamade.com*) is a beautiful company that makes every single product in the spirit of their love and reverence for botanical plants and herbs. All its perfumes and creams are handmade and hand-labeled. They specialize in bath and body products. You really feel that you are getting a little pot that was created with great care. I adore their tiny roll-on perfumes. Everyone always comments on how gorgeous I smell, which is never a bad thing!

❀ **Juice Beauty**   (*www.juicebeauty.com*) is a very cool company that was started by two Californian women who felt that an organic lifestyle should include skin care. The full line of skin care products products contain up to 95 percent certified organic ingredients—a high percentage because they have a patent-pending juice base. They are also totally yummy.

❀ **Gorgeously Green**   (*www.gorgeouslygreen.com*) is my own skin care line that I developed because I wanted to create products that were gorgeous and totally safe.

Your Face

We are persuaded that unless we use a gazillion serums and neck creams, we'll likely turn into an old crone in a matter of weeks. I like to keep my routine supersimple because I don't have time to dab on too many serums, eye gels, and the like. If you use good-quality organic products, you really only need a cleanser, a toner, a moisturizer and an exfoliator. All the rest is fun fluff, and I agree that it's fabulous if you have the time and money. But remember that buying only what you need saves packaging and waste.

Most commercial cleansers contain harsh chemicals that strip away the skin's natural oils and alter its pH balance. We are led to believe that the taut, dry feeling after cleansing means that our skin is squeaky clean. This is not the case—our skin should still feel a little moist, even after a major cleanse. Most commercial toners are mostly alcohol, water, witch hazel, and synthetic chemicals.

The key to great skin is proper exfoliation, because we need to get rid of the dead skin cells. The skin sheds cells at the rate of a million per hour, so it is essential to do a mild exfoliation daily. If you miss this step of your routine, you will be simply gluing dead skin cells back to your face with moisturizer!

If you go to the spa and get a glycolic peel, it can be way too drastic for your tender skin, making it parched and oversensitive to the sun.

It's easy to make your own fruit acid peel that is a lot gentler. See "DIY Beauty" at the end of this chapter (page 58).

Green Cleansing

Do away with tissues or cotton (unless they're organic) for cleansing or toning. By far the most effective method is to use face cloths. Twice yearly, I buy a stack of organic cotton ones and toss them in the washer when I'm doing a load. They help to exfoliate, and you're helping the planet by not using paper or pesticides.

Beauty—For the latest beauty updates and products with the Gorgeously Green stamp of approval, visit *www.gorgeouslygreen.com*. Simply type the following password that you see below into the search bar for more earth-friendly beauty secrets. Password: Goddess.

I want to recommend some great beauty products to you. All of the following have the Gorgeously Green stamp of approval:

❀ **Dr. Hauschka** (*www.drhauschka.com*) gets a green star. I have been using these products for over ten years. Many of Hollywood's top makeup artists swear by this line.

❀ **Jurlique** (*www.jurlique.com.au*) is an Australian company. All its products are organic, and they have some great cleansers. I love OPC Make-Up Remover, which works really well for removing thick makeup.

🌸 **Aubrey Organics** (*www.aubrey-organics.com*) are completely natural and made with essential oils and vitamins. The company's Rosa Mosqueta line for dry skin is brilliant. I love Seaware with Rosa Mosqueta Facial Cleansing Cream because it moisturizes as it does the job.

🌸 **Suki** (*www.sukisnaturals.com*) has an excellent exfoliating lemongrass cleanser that you sort of want to eat off your face as it drips down—yum!

🌸 **Juice Beauty's** (*www.juicebeauty.com*) mild cleanser made with white grape juice is really effective and smells wonderful.

Moisturizers

Many moisturizing creams are made up of oil and water held together with chemical emulsifiers and chock-full of preservatives to give them a superlong shelf life. Here is an example of the chemicals that are listed on a moisturizer that I recently picked up at a drugstore. It was almost twenty dollars and was labeled "natural" in the green-and-cream-colored box. I wanted to see what was in it because it appeared to be the most natural-looking product on the shelf:

> Glycerin, Nylon.66, cyclohexasiloxane, dimethicone/vinyl dimethicone crosspolymer, hydronated polysobutene, ammonium polyacryloyidimethyl taurate, solanumlycopersicum/tomato extract, ascorbyl glucoside, magnesium pca, actindia chinensis, capryloyl, salicylic acid, manganese PCA, zinc PCA, sodium PCA, tocopheryl acetate, octydodecanol, carbomer, ceteth-10, glyceryl state, laureth-4, lauroyl lysine, mica, myristyl alcohol, PEG-100 stearate, dimethyl isosorbide, polycaprolactone, sodium citrate, disodium EDTA, imdazolidinyl urea, sodium hydroxide, stearyl alcohol, T-butyl alcohol, methylparaben, propylparaben, phenoxyethanol, parfum/fragrance, linalool, benzyl salicylate

Okay, can you actually pronounce any of these words? Please be my guest. So in buying this natural-looking product, you are plastering a bucket load of chemicals all over your face that are not necessarily safe or effective, and you are paying almost twenty bucks for the privilege. Check out how much alcohol (drying or what!) there is in this cream. I also noted fourteen ingredients from our Red Alert and Orange Alert lists. The solution is to either make your own moisturizer (see "DIY Beauty" at the end of this chapter, page 58) or purchase one from one of these fabulous companies.

❀ **Max Green Naked Rescue Cream** (*www.maxgreenalchemy. com*) is a wonderful thick moisturizer for really dry skin (unscented).

❀ **Terra Nova Miracle Cream** (*www.commonscents.com*) is a gorgeous, silky cream for normal skin.

❀ **Blooming Lotus Luminous Lotion** (*www.bloominglotus.com*) is a great daytime moisturizer that smells of tangerines.

❀ **Lavera Hydrosensitive Energy Cream** (*www.lavera-usa.com*) is for sensitive skin.

❀ **Suki's Moisture Serum** (*www.sukisnaturals.com*) is for mature dry skin.

❀ **Pangea Organics Argentinean Tangerine and Thyme Cream** (*www.pangeaorganics.com*) is for oily, demanding skin.

❀ **Simply Divine Botanicals** (*www.simplydivinebotanicals.com*) makes creams that are absolutely delicious. I can't resist using the company's Amazing Face Cream every now and again. It is packed with essential oils and smells fabulous. The eye gel is called Pack Your Bags and is truly miraculous. The products are made with the highest-quality essential oils, and the first ingredient on their list is "unconditional love and gratitude."

❀ **Ikove by Florestas** (*www.ikove.com*) is a certified organic skin care company with a wonderful Rose Night Cream.

❀ **Savage Beauty** (*www.savagebeauty.net*) (love the name) carries a great Nutrient Packed Hydrating Serum. Although I'm not a serum girl, this one feels irresistibly silky.

❁ **Grateful Body**   (*www.gratefulbody.com*) has a beautiful moisturizer called Environmental Impact Facial Therapy. This company also does a great thirty-plus line, which is packed with all the nutrients that an old girl needs!

❁ **Suki Facial Cream**   (*www.sukisnaturals.com*) has vitamin liposomes and antioxidants.

❁ **Dr. Hauschka Rose Day Cream**   (*www.drhauschka.com*) will help if your skin is superdry. This is a thick emollient cream that will do the trick. If you are going skiing or flying, or anywhere where your skin becomes lizard-like, take along a tube.

❁ **Inky Loves Nature**   (*www.inkylovesnature.com*) is the first vegan-certified, all-organic body care company "with women of color in mind." The company's products can be used by everyone and are fantastic. I love the Gleaming Sheen Anti-Ash Machine Moisturizer.

❁ **Organicapoteke**   (*www.organicapoteke.com*) is a higher-end line that boasts some beautiful products. The company attempts to be sustainable across the board. I particularly like their Rejuvenating Face Cream because it has a lovely creamy texture.

Vitamin C

Many swear by topical vitamin C. It can stimulate collagen production and can minimize fine lines. Be really careful that you find a brand that only contains the good stuff. I like **Jason**'s vitamin C line, particularly their Hyper-C Serum (*www.jason-natural.com*). Be wary that vitamin C, as a cosmetic, has a really short shelf life, so buy a small bottle and use it up quickly.

You could also go the sticky route and rub a slice of an organic orange over your face three times per week.

Your Body

Regular exfoliation is the way to go. I sometimes visit a Korean spa near my home where the women indulge in some serious salt scrubbing on an almost daily basis. I once, and only once, had the salt scrub there as part of a package. Like a slab of meat, I was scraped and scrubbed within an inch of my life—layers of my skin were removed before I was forced into a hot tub, which was like a boiling cauldron, with an enormous herbal tea bag floating in it. As alarming as the experience was, my skin felt like a baby's bottom, and it has not escaped my attention that all the Korean girls I know have extremely shiny, smooth skin.

You can gently exfoliate every day, getting rid of dirt, grease, and grime, and then do a full-on scrub once a week.

✿ **Chocolate Rose Body Polish**   (*www.bloominglotus.com*) has an almost cult-like following and makes a great gift.

✿ **"I Love Organic" Sugar Scrub**   (*www.nature-girl.com*) is an incredible scrub from Nature Girl. I love this line because of its cute packaging and super-cool body products. This scrub left my skin feeling unusually soft and smelling like a freshly sliced lemon!

Lotions

Body lotion is a big part of my day. I have a love/hate relationship with the whole process depending on my mood: Being in a rush is hugely annoying, not having time to let the cream/oil absorb. Then I'm typically having to squeeze my legs into yoga leggings. By the time I get them up to my waist, they're decorated with awful grease marks (which never come off), and I have to start all over again. Conversely, after a hot evening shower, I love to sit on a towel and spend far too long massaging myself in a dreamy haze. The time-consuming element only serves to remind me that my skin is by far the largest organ of my body, so what I put on it has to be the best. Cream queen that I am, here are my Gorgeously Green picks:

✿ **Betsey Body Lotion**   (citrus and lavender) (*www.store-greenfeet.*

com) is a tribute to Betsey Medina, who is a breast cancer survivor. The proceeds all go to cancer research.

❀ **Alaffia** (*www.alaffia.com*) makes products that are simple, sustainable, and effective. I love that the company supports fair trade for African women and donates 10 percent of its sales to community enhancement programs in the United States and West Africa. The African Wild Honey Nourishing Lotion is extremely emollient and smells dreamy.

❀ **Aubrey Organics** (*www.aubry-organics.com*) is reliable. The company was one of the first to be 100 percent organic, and it makes everything from soaps, to body lotions, to shampoos. I'm very fond of its Sea Buckthorn with Ester-C Nourishing Hand and Body Cream.

❀ **Terressentials** (*www.terressentials.com*) is a fine company that handcrafts 100 hundred percent organic products. The company has an extraordinary line of Anointing Body Oils, which is a cross between a lotion and an oil. My husband is partial to the Seductive Spice blend!

❀ **Kuumba Made** (*www.kuumbamade.com*) makes my favorite coconut oil, which is a natural wonder for the skin. Its body oil comes in calendula, lavender, rose, or pure coconut.

Essential Oils

Essential oils are the most concentrated and refined form of a plant, and therefore they are most effectively absorbed by the skin through its hair follicles and glands. Many of them have antibacterial, antiseptic, antifungal, and preservative properties to boot. These wonder oils are very expensive to produce—for example, one ounce of pure rose oil requires 200 pounds of rose petals. Most of these pure essences are diluted in a base of a vegetable oil (the carrier oil). You will absolutely get what you pay for. If the essential oil is cheap, it has probably been heavily diluted. Do your research, making sure that the essences are organic if possible. Also smell oils when buying them (most have testers); they should smell really strong. Once you get the hang of the essential oils that work for you, you will never look back. They work for every aspect of your personal care.

Your Hair

When I first started to go organic with hair products, I found a line that contained only natural ingredients, so I ordered the very expensive shampoo and conditioner. The labels stated that these products could take a bit of getting used to. After the first wash, my already dry hair was like wire wool that I literally couldn't get a comb through. The conditioner was like brown water and made things worse, so I gave the whole lot to my six-year-old daughter, who was equally disgusted: "Mommy, it's like horrid mud!" she wailed. I then tried to palm the stuff off on my husband, thinking he wouldn't notice! He couldn't believe I would purchase a shampoo that had the consistency of "chocolate milk."

Watch out for that old chestnut, sodium lauryl sulfate, because it is in most shampoos and can seriously dry out your hair and irritate your scalp. Since I've stopped using it, I never get a dry scalp anymore and I don't need to use so much conditioner. I wash my hair every day (every hairdresser tells me off). If I don't, it ends up looking like a sort of fluffed-up fifties beehive.

As organic or health food store shampoos can be a bit hit and miss as far as the dry haystack look is concerned, I've done my work to find you the best.

❀ **Eco Bella** (*www.ecobella.com*) has created a line of products that smell like candy. I love the Vanilla Moisturizing Shampoo for every day.

❀ **Surya** (*www.bodyofgrace.com*) hair products are beautiful. The company's Preciosa Conditioner is a real treat and is packed with unusual essential oils and butters.

❀ **John Master's Citrus and Neroli Detangler** (*www.johnmasters. com*) is at the forefront of the organic hair care movement and all of his products are fabulous.

❀ **Desert Essences** (*www.desertessence.com*) has a line of shampoos and conditioners that are not only very effective for dry scalp conditions, but they smell lemony fresh.

Hairstyling

I am a product princess in this area—always on the hunt for something to work miracles with my unruly mop.

Be aware that some mousses can contain diethanolamine (DEA), which is a potential carcinogen, and triethanolamine, which is used to make chemical weapons. I really like the following products:

❀ **Max Green Alchemy** (*www.maxgreenalchemy.com*) is vegan and cruelty-free. The company supports the Campaign for Safe Cosmetics. My husband and I really love its Scalp Rescue Gel and Scalp Rescue Pomade.

❀ **Modern Organic Products** (*www.moporganics.com*), commonly known as **MOP,** has a huge selection of really good styling products. From straightening balm to curly lotions, this company does the whole shebang.

❀ **Miessence** (*www.miessence.com*) has a wonderful hair styling gel called Misessence Organics Shape Styling Gel.

❀ **John Master's Organics** (*www.johnmastersorganics.com*) has a Bourbon Vanilla Tangerine Hair Texturizer, which is brilliant for all hair styling and smells totally yummy.

Hair Spray

I never use hair spray because I haven't yet found a brand that satisfies my green criteria. Most commercial brands of hair spray and styling mousse contain alcohol, polyvinylpyrrolidone plastic (a carcinogen), formaldehyde, and fragrance—not a very attractive cocktail!

Hair Drying

I know it's an energy-guzzler, but I can't let go of my trusty hair dryer on account of the frizz factor if I air-dry. A great green investment is a iTech tourmaline hair dryer (*www.sprig.com*). It contains tourmaline, which helps dry your hair faster than a regular hair dryer, so it consumes less energy. Negative is really positive as far as ions are concerned. Many electrical appliances emit either positive or negative ions. If they are negative, they charge the air with great energy. It therefore makes sense to get an ionic hair dryer that not only dries your hair in half the time, but also puts you in a better mood. Check out the **Tourmaline Ionic Dryer** (*www.folica.com*).

Scalp Massage

My hair has gotten thicker since doing a daily scalp massage, which takes all of two minutes. I like to do it at night because my hair doesn't always look its best after a particularly vigorous massage. If time is an issue, you can do a quick one in the shower before you shampoo. Scalp massage not only increases the oxygen supply to the brain, but it improves circulation of cerebrospinal fluid, which stimulates brain development and relaxes nerves and muscles. If my scalp is dry, I add a few drops of lavender to my fingers before massaging. If my hair feels greasy, I add a few drops of rosemary essential oil.

Scalp massage is also a wonderful gift for the one you love. I do it to my husband while he's watching TV. He says it's the next best thing to a foot massage.

Hair Dye

Many of the worst chemicals are in regular hair dye, so it's really important to avoid it. I beg you to change to something natural or that you absolutely know doesn't contain any harmful chemicals. Generally speaking, don't buy any regular hair dye from the drugstore, and grill your colorist about what he or she uses. Regulators have recently announced the ban of twenty-two substances from hair dyes in the European Union, as they are known to increase the risk of bladder cancer and bone marrow cancer. These same regulations have not been enforced in the United States at the time of this printing.

The following dyes contain no harmful chemicals:

❀ **Tints of Nature**   (*www.tintsofnatureusa.com*) is a wonderful line that has a massive color palette.

❀ The **Henna Company** (*www.bytheplanet.com*) has a huge selection of safe dyes.

❀ **Eco Colors** (*www.ecocolors.net*) is a great company that is well worth checking out for color.

One of the chemicals that has been linked to allergic reactions and cancer is p-phenylenediamine (PPD). The following products have been specially formulated to have a low amount or none of this chemical:

❀ **Hebatint** (*www.ihealthtree.com*)

❀ **Vegetal Color** (*www.hairboutique.com*)

❀ **Naturtint** (*www.ihealthtree.com*)

❀ **Light Mountain Natural Hair Color** (*www.ibeauty.com*)

Hair Salons

I take comfort in the fact that the bleach highlights that my lovely colorist Debbie puts in don't actually touch my scalp. If, however, I had the full dye job or tint left on my head, I would need to know the scoop. Please be bold and discuss this at length with your colorist. Many of them don't offer a solution because they don't think there is anything that works as well as their tried-and-tested dyes. You could offer to bring in your own dye, which you can purchase online. Some cities boast organic hair salons; however, they are rare, so do your homework and ask around. I sometimes feel really silly bugging my colorist. I'm sure she goes to the back room with eyes rolling, telling her work mates about the ridiculously neurotic woman in her chair. That said, I would rather be neurotic, paranoid, and crazy than sick.

Showering and Bathing

In Europe, most women I know do something very strange called skin brushing. I have done it for years and have very little cellulite as a result. It is believed to stimulate the lymphatic system and thereby remove toxins. You must do it when your skin is *dry,* so before the shower or bath is the best time. You can then wash off all the dry skin that has come up through brushing. You need a sisal body brush with a long handle, and you start from your feet, brushing in long, upward strokes. Don't miss any part of your body, except of course your face. I do extra strokes on my thighs and buns for obvious reasons. This exercise will take off a few layers of dead skin to prepare it for all the goodies. The whole process should take no more than three minutes.

You can find the brush at *www.thehairdoccompany.com*. This company also carries the best hairbrushes.

Soap

Remember when you are soaping yourself up that all the suds will run off your body, down the drain, and straight into our precious water-ways. The contamination of our water supply with chemicals is becoming a huge problem, so we need to really think about what is in our suds (more of this in step 5). So take care of your body and the watershed by picking out eco-friendly soap. Also, many of us use soap or body wash twice a day, all over our bodies, so make sure it's safe. It's also more eco-friendly to buy bar soap rather than liquid soap in a plastic pomp bottle. Three companies have a great selection of chemical-free and gorgeous soaps:

- ❁ *www.bloominglotus.com*
- ❁ *www.kissmyface.com*
- ❁ *www.pangeaorganics.com*

Epsom Salts

Epsom salts are fantastic for bathing. They are inexpensive, they can be purchased at any drugstore or supermarket, and they stimulate serotonin (the hormone that makes you feel really good). Epsom salts are made up of two pure minerals: magnesium and sulfate. It is hugely beneficial for these important minerals to enter the bloodstream through your skin while soaking in a hot tub. Elevated magnesium levels can lower your blood pressure and sulfates can alleviate headaches and flush toxins from your body.

When I am feeling run-down or really stressed out, I need a little extra help to relax in the evening. Although running a full tub of hot water is not the most green thing to do (a tub uses twenty gallons of water, whereas a shower uses three), I do have a bath as a treat.

I add two cups of Epsom salts to my bath water and then about ten to fifteen drops of lavender pure essential oil and soak for about fifteen minutes. If you are having your period, add ten drops of clary sage essential oil. After drying, I slather myself in my Gorgeously Green Homemade Body Oil.

Sesame Oil

Buy a bottle of cold-pressed sesame oil from the beauty section of your health food store. Add a few drops of your two favorite essential oils and put the plastic bottle in a cup of hot water to warm for five minutes. The heat makes the oil thinner and easier to apply. After slathering yourself from top to bottom, get a face cloth and pat off the excess oil. Wrap yourself in a terry robe, as you'll still be a bit greasy. I used to slather myself without adding the essential oil until my husband said I smelled like a stir-fry.

This simple product really has magical properties. Its unique chemical structure allows it to penetrate the skin easily, providing you with health benefits including stress reduction, increased immunity, and pain relief. Best of all, it has many natural antioxidants, which explains its reputation for slowing the aging process. I can't get enough of it!

The best place to get your sesame oil and all carrier oils is *www. mountainroseherbs.com* (best quality you can find and 100 percent organic). When you purchase any plant-based oils your skin, try to make sure they are 100 percent organic and unrefined. Also, store your oils in a cool, dark place. It's important to realize that the shelf life of all unrefined oil is only six months.

Cellulite

It is impossible to get rid of cellulite completely. Sorry, but despite all the cosmetic company claims, it simply can't and won't vanish. But you could help matters a little by using products that contain algae extracts, which detoxify and increase metabolism. Green tea does the same.

❀ **Lavera Body Control Anti-cellulite Lotion**   (*www.lavera-usa.com*) is great.

❀ **Susan Ciminelli Marine Lotion**   (*www.susanciminelli.com*) is also pretty cool.

- -

From Within

Many say that taking evening primrose flax and fish oils are not only essential for women's health but also for their skin. I believe this to be true. Virtually all the Green Goddesses I know take all three oils daily.

Internationally acclaimed Julia Tatum-Hunter, M.D., founder of Skin Fitness Plus in Beverly Hills and dermatologist to the stars, takes a "holistic" attitude toward skin care. She believes that supplementation and nutrition are essential to create and maintain beautiful skin. Dr. Hunter prescribes fish oils, flaxseed oil, greens (all those awful-tasting things like wheatgrass and chlorella), and antioxidants every day and tells her patients that youthful skin begins with becoming healthy from the inside out. She clearly practices what she preaches, as her skin has an enviable glow!

So there you have it, girls. I use a blend of marine fish oil and evening primrose capsules. Go for the best quality you can find, because you get what you pay for and some cheaper brands can be rancid. I love CODmega by Garden of Life (*www.gardenoflife.com*). Independent laboratories test all their oils for heavy metals and other impurities.

One yummy way to get your omega-3 oils is to buy omega chocolate truffles. They are simply out of this world and are called **Bija Omega Truffles** (*www.florahealth.com*).

Another scrumptious treat comes in the form of the **Woman's Wonder Bar** (*www.healthbychocolate.com*), which is basically a bar of chocolate that "takes sweet revenge on the symptoms of PMS and menopause." It's filled with omega oils, rose oil, and chaste tree berry.

You can purchase a great antioxidant blend called Fruit Matrix, as well as a wonderful blend of greens called Perfect Food, both at Garden of Life. Make sure you get the capsules, as it takes some getting used to the powder.

Flaxseed oil can be purchased from some grocery stores and most health food stores. The recommended dosage is 1 tablespoon daily. You need to keep it in the fridge all the time to avoid oxidation. I actually love its nutty taste, so I often make salad dressings with it; however, most women I know can't bear it, so they favor the capsules.

● ●

Your Smile

You are going to be smiling a lot more now that you are Gorgeously Green. Is your oral hygiene green?

The most obvious way to be environmentally kind is to turn off the faucet while you are brushing. I know we were taught that on *Sesame Street*, but I still don't do it every time, so I need it emblazoned on my skull.

What about your toothbrush? Dentists recommend that you change your brush four times per year. I do it more because I love a new toothbrush. Think, however, about mountains of old toothbrushes sitting in a landfill. There is a wonderful company that has come up with a brilliant solution: it's called the **Preserve Toothbrush** (*www.recycline.com*)—you get to send this toothbrush back to them and they will recycle it into really cool-looking picnic tables and other furniture. The company also makes picnicware, toothpicks, and razors.

An eco-friendly toothbrush for kids is called the **Fun Brush** (*www.eco-dent.com*). It has a replaceable rainbow-colored head.

Toothpaste is a controversial issue because of two ingredients that some say are harmful: sodium laurel sulfate (SLS) and fluoride. SLS is also linked to canker sores. There is a huge selection of toothpastes that don't contain either of these ingredients at virtually every health food store.

❀ **Tom's of Maine**   (*www.tomsofmaine.com*) has a fabulous selection of natural toothpastes to suit everyone.

❀ **White Glo**   (*www.greatwhitetrading.com*) is a homeopathic whitening toothpaste that claims to "control your appetite throughout the day." The jury's out on that, but it's an interesting claim.

❀ **Coral White**   (*www.coralcalcium.com*) is my favorite toothpaste. It is full of good ingredients and actually helps to build up your tooth enamel.

Feminine Stuff

The Gorgeously Green girl needs to pick her tampons wisely, especially for her health. Most conventional tampons are made of two substances that can pose serious health risks. The first is dioxin, which is a by-product from the chlorine bleaching process and is a potential carcinogen. The second and most alarming is asbestos, which some claim is put into tampons to encourage heavier bleeding so that you would be forced to buy more tampons! In addition, when any products are made with chlorine bleach, harmful chemicals pollute our environment.

Natracare (*www.natracare.com*) tampons and menstrual pads are made from organic, chlorine-free cotton and bleached with hydrogen peroxide. **Seventh Generation** (*www.seventhgeneration.com*) also carries chlorine-free tampons and pads.

These are two companies' products can be found at most large health food stores or at *www.OrganicPharmacy.org*.

You should also avoid a plastic tampon applicator as it goes straight to the landfill. For more information, visit *www.whyorganictampons.com*.

Luna Pads International (*www.lunapads.com*) is a Canadian company that sells washable pads and something called a Diva Cup, which is a very strange device that you use instead of a tampon!

Deodorants

I have tried every conceivable alternative to the normal drugstore deodorants. Many brands contain aluminum, which has been linked to

Alzheimer's. I'm taking no risks and have become an expert in finding alternatives. I don't like wet patches under my arms, but I refuse to put anything containing aluminum or paraben on my delicate armpits. There are thousands of alternatives, and many of them have pretty packaging but don't do the job. I tried one of those crystals that you wet with water and then rub under your arms, but it wasn't effective enough to cope with the sweaty yoga girl that I am.

❁ **Dr. Hauschka's** (*www.drhauschka.com*) roll-on is one of the most effective I have found, and the floral scent is beautiful.

❁ **Erbaviva** (*www.erbaviva.com*) is a wonderful company with organic spray deodorants that come in amber glass bottles. The deodorant feels really cool as it goes on and smells of fresh citrus.

❁ **Herbal Magic** (*www.vitamincountry.com*) has a roll-on deodorant with a lovely jasmine scent that reduces wetness considerably.

❁ **Aubrey Organics** (*www.aubreyorganics.com*) E Plus roll-on is very safe, smells good, but shouldn't be relied on for occasions when you have to be dry.

❁ **Tom's of Maine** (*www.tomsofmaine.com*) unscented deodorant is my husband's favorite.

If you still feel that you need something stronger, which will actually stop you from perspiring altogether (unhealthy but sometimes necessary), go to *www.skindeep.com* and click on "Deodorants." You will find some commercial brands there and can see which ones carry the lowest risk factor.

Lip Balm

Make sure that your lip balm is free of mineral oils and all of the previously discussed chemicals. Here are my favorites:

❀ **Dr. Hauschka**   (*www.drhauschka.com*) is the hands-down winner in this category. I have been using its Lip Care Stick for years, and it has the best texture of the lot.

❀ **Blooming Lotus**   (*www.bloominglotus.com*) makes an exquisite Mandarin and Rose Lip Balm, which smells and tastes of freshly picked tangerines.

❀ **Burt's Bees**   (*www.burtsbees.com*) also carries a large selection of lip products that you can now buy at most large drugstores.

Your Hands and Feet

I always need to have some thick emollient hand cream in my purse and on my kitchen counter. I always forget to wear rubber gloves to do the dishes, and with all the handwashing that we're supposed to be doing after pushing supermarket trolleys and the like, my palms are constantly shriveled. Fortunately, I have found a wonderful company called Ikove (*www.ikove.com*) that makes fabulous hand and foot lotion with ingredients from the Brazilian rain forest. They are certified organic and conduct sustainable practices. You could also give someone you are close to a bit of a hint, as the foot cream says it is for "smelly and swollen feet"!

Sunscreens and Fake Tans

This is a big deal for me because I have really pale skin and I live in California, where it looks awful to have white/purple mottled legs in the summer. I have tried every conceivable fake tan, and none of them smell that great or end up standing up to the claims on the bottle, namely "streak-free tan." I, too, have been subjected to the spray gun while standing naked in a custom tanning booth. I thought I looked fabulous, but my husband thought I looked totally orange. Thinking it was the funniest thing ever, he and my daughter teased me relentlessly until it faded into blotches resembling a nasty disease. To add insult to injury, the whole lot came off on my lovely white organic sheets. Given the fact that I don't use chlorine bleach anymore, this presented me with a bit of a problem. Turns out it's probably better for me not to do the fake tan thing anyway, since most of the products contain dihydroxy acetone chemicals, which can pose a risk for cancer.

I have, however, found one self-tanner that contains only the good stuff, smells fantastic, and is as streak-free as any I've found: **Lavera Sunless Tan** (*www.lavera.com*).

We need a bit of sunshine anyway. It's really important for vitamin D production. Doctors have found low levels of this vitamin in many patients recently, and it's thought to be because of sunscreen use. Most doctors recommend allowing your bare skin (face and arms will do) to get ten to fifteen minutes of full sun a day (no sunscreen and not through glass). I always feel so much better having a bit of sun, and vitamin D is thought to protect against many cancers.

If you plan to do a bit more than your daily sun requirement and insist on tanning, there is a huge current debate about the safety of regular sunscreens. Some say they contain harmful ingredients that increase free radicals and therefore damage your skin, making it more susceptible to skin cancer. What an awful thought! I have to admit that when I was a teenager, I was so desperate to get a tan that I would lie in the sun with a sheet of aluminum foil under my head to attract the rays. Not anymore, with every women's magazine banging on about sun damage!.

❀ **Jason** (*www.jasonnatural.com*) has a sunscreen that is pure, natural, and organic and has a fabulous smell. It spreads on easily. My daughter, who is like a wild animal when I try to slick her up, stays still for Jason because she says she wants to eat it!

❀ **Aubrey Organics** (*www.aubrey-organics.com*) is completely organic and good for you. It may be a little too thick for some of you, but it smells good.

❀ **UV Natural**   (*www.uvnaturalusa.com*) is a fabulous sunscreen that contains no chemicals, and I love that a little goes a long way. It's extremely thick, so you squeeze out a dime-size amount into your palm, rub your hands together, and then apply (the heat of the hand rubbing helps to soften it).

Icing on the Cake

We all have our can't-live-without item; mine changes from year to year. It used to be mascara, and now it is tinted moisturizer and lip gloss. Either way, we all need to go totally nontoxic. There is no point doing all the skin/body care and then slapping chemical horrors on top of it.

Just know that most commercial brands of makeup contain toxic chemicals, parabens, synthetic dyes, and harmful fillers. Seventy-two percent of cosmetics contain phthalates, which are hormone disruptors. Don't fret, though, because there are a few wonderful brands that don't.

❀ **Jane Iredale**   (*www.janeiredale.com*) was the Beauty Award Winner for Best Makeup Range, and I agree with the judges. Many of her products contain sunscreen, they are anti-inflammatory, and they do not contain talc or parabens. I always spend way too much money on this line because I want everything. I adore her liquid foundations for nighttime coverage, and her lipsticks and eye shadows are divine. The Web site will locate your nearest store. Unfortunately, mine is less than a mile away—I can walk there to do my damage!

❀ **Susan Posnick**   (*www.susanposnick.com*) is a celebrity makeup artist who, after developing skin cancer, created an incredible mineral foundation called "ColorFlo." Instead of slathering sunscreen on top of her base, she developed a two-in-one product that is quite brilliant. It has an SPF factor of 26 and comes in a variety of shades to suit every skin tone. It's a great find for me, as I haven't got time to apply foundation and blush every morning, so I simply swirl the brush over my face and I'm ready to face just about anybody!

❀ **Emani Minerals** (*www.emani.com*) are simply made from mineral color dusts, crushed mineral foundations, crushed mineral cheek colors, titanium dioxide, mica, and iron oxides. They also use phenoxyethanol (one of the less irritating preservatives). If you compare that list of ingredients with a major commercial brand, you will be amazed. I love many of the products in this line but mostly their glittery eye colors that resemble fairy dust.

❀ **After Glow Cosmetics** (*www.afterglowcosmetics.com*) are made from pure crushed minerals and are really safe. I get everything from my base to my eyeliner from them.

❀ **Mineral Fusion** (*www.mineralfusioncosmetics.com*) is another great company that has a massive new collection. I particularly love its tinted moisturizers, as they leave an all-day healthy glow. The products are available in most Whole Foods stores, so if you have one near you, go and do some sampling.

❀ **Lavera** (*www.lavera.com*) is an incredible German company. The founder and owner, Thomas Haase, started the company in 1987 because he suffered from dermatitis and started to grow his own herbs in an attempt to find a formulation that would work for him. The company is now massive and sells every skin care product imaginable. I particularly love their cosmetic line. Go to this company for your lipsticks because they have a really good choice of colors and will send you samples.

❀ **PeaceKeeper Cause-Metics** (*iamapeacekeeper.com*) is the wonderful company that I mention in the nail polish section. The company also does makeup that you should check out. I love this company because it gives all its profits after tax to women's issues.
   Also try these products:

❀ **Gabriel Cosmetics** (*www.gabrielcosmetics.com*) is made from 100-percent natural ingredients. No synthetic or animal by-products are used. These environmentally safe cosmetics contain a very high percentage of active ingredients.

❀ **Ecobella**   (*www.ecobella.com*) has created a Flower Color Liquid Foundation that I really like. It's lightweight yet really smooths out the imperfections.

❀ **Aubrey Organics**   (*www.aubrey-organics.com*) lip gloss is an absolute must, as it smells fabulous and gives you a shiny smile for hours.

❀ **Nvey Eco**   (*www.econveybeauty.com*) cosmetics are from Australia, where they really have the organic thing down. Their ingredients are certified organic, and their lipsticks and glosses are a must-have.

❀ **Cargo**   (*www.sephora.com*) is a large cosmetics line that has created eco-friendly lipsticks called Plant Love Botanical Lipsticks. The bioplastic tubes are made from corn, a renewable resource. Lola, my daughter, wanted one so badly because the little tubes are all girly, with little flowers on them. Did she get it?

Heaven Scent

Now that you are pampered, polished, and made up, we need to talk about perfume. Most contemporary perfumes contain a mixture of four thousand synthetic chemicals, which have never been tested for safety. Since I have switched to greener alternatives, I have totally gone off most commercial brands. They are so strong and artificial that they take away from a woman's natural scent. I want to enhance rather than mask my natural smell. It's the same with men. It's a total turnoff when all you can smell is an overpowering aftershave—yuck!

In the daytime, I wear essential oils only. Try a blend from one of these companies:

❀ **Wyndmere**   (*www.wyndmere.com*) is a great little company that has created a bunch of blends—that is, three or four different aromatherapy oils that complement each other are blended together. Anxiety Release is my favorite. I just put five or six drops in the palm of my hand, rub my hands together, and then rub my neck and even through my hair. Everyone comments on the smell and wants to know which oils I'm wearing.

❧ **Kate's Magik** (*www.katesmagik.com*) is another company that just uses aromatherapy oils. Try its Anointing Perfumes (perfumes with a purpose). These blends will help you to "remove obstacles and reach for your goals." I'm leaning toward the "woman see bright" or "sensual lust."

❧ **Jo Anne Bassett** (*www.joannebassett.com*) is a master perfumer based in San Diego. She creates the most beautiful scents imaginable— no synthetics in sight. My favorite daytime perfume of Jo Anne's is Le Voyage.

❧ **Aubrey Organics** (*www.aubrey-organics.com*) has a line of perfumes that are very pretty and also reasonably priced.

❧ **Hood River Lavender** (*www.lavenderfarms.net*) is a certified family-run, organic farm in Oregon. Their perfumes are sublime and very reasonably priced. All their products make wonderful gifts.

❧ **Patyka Perfume** (*www.puresha.com*) is a fabulous organic perfume. My hands-down favorite is called Hesperide (fresh and very sexy).

If you want something that is a little stronger, you may want to compromise and use a brand that uses *some* synthetic ingredients. I love a company called **Le Labo** (*www.lelabofragrances.com*), which is based in New York. It uses some synthetics but also wonderful plant oils that are distilled and prepared in Grasse, which is in southern France and is known for its flower oils. One of my intentions is to go to Grasse during the lavender harvest season. I want to lie down in the middle of one of the purple fields and inhale. I may even get off my lazy behind and help with the harvesting. If you happen to be in New York, drop into Le Labo, as the company will hand-blend your perfume and write your name on the little glass test tube–like bottle.

Kuumba Made (*www.kuumbamade.com*) fragrances are strong, sexy, and last a long time. At night, I wear its Tunisian Opium.

Nail Polish

It's really important to consider your nail polish carefully, since some of the major brands contain chemicals that could cause birth defects and cancer. The main chemicals that you want to avoid are toluene, dibutylphthalate (DBP), and formaldehyde. Since becoming aware of these scary facts, I'm taking no chances. I have found a few fabulous lines that are completely safe.

❀ **Honey Bee Gardens** (*www.honeybeegardens.com*) makes a Watercolors non peel-off polish. I love these polishes, which contain no FD&C colors, toluene, dibutylphthalate, xylene, or formaldehyde. They are water-based and odor-free. Also try their peel-off polishes, which are great for kids, and their odorless polish remover.

❀ **No Miss** (*www.nomiss.com*) does gorgeous colors and its nail polish chips less than the other well-known brands. The company also has a wonderful polish remover that is completely organic, plus it's acetone-, ethyl acetate– and cruelty-free.

❀ **PeaceKeeper Cause-Metics** (*www.iamapeacekeeper.com*) gives all its distributable after-tax profits to women's health advocacy and human rights issues. The company's nail polish line includes endless shades of girly/pearly pink.

❀ **Sparitual**'s (*www.SpaRitual.com*) Vegan Lacquers come in bottles made from recycled glass. Soy ink is used for its labels.

❀ **Zoya** (*www.zoya.com*) products are sold in high-end beauty salons or you can go online. The company has a huge color selection.

❀ **Priti** (*www.abeautifullife.com*) has 100 percent soy- and corn-based nail polishes and nail polish remover—fabulous.

Make sure that all the cotton pads and swabs you buy are organic—all health food stores stock them. I have found a wonderful company that carries every conceivable nail care accessory you could wish for. It also does bath sponges and has a wonderful herbal eye pillow: *www .earththerapeutics.com*.

Acrylic Nails

Love them or hate them—they are not good news for the Gorgeously Green girl. There are numerous short- and long-term health problems from the chemicals used in fake nails. Our nails need to breathe to be healthy. Covering them in a coat of plastic resin causes them to become weak and brittle. When moisture is trapped beneath the artificial nail, fungal infections can occur—yuck. The worst bit is that removing the nails requires the use of a powerful solvent, usually acetonitrile. This toxic chemical can irritate the respiratory system and could cause an enlarged thyroid. Don't even think about fake press-on nails from the drugstore, because the glue that you need to attach them could make you dizzy and give you eczema and/or a headache.

Pregnancy

If you or anyone you know is pregnant, be very cautious about every single product you use. Some of the dangerous chemicals listed previously are especially bad for pregnant women and can affect the unborn baby.

Knowing as much as I now know about chemicals, I wouldn't set foot inside a regular nail salon while pregnant. You know that acrid smell that hits you as soon as you walk in? Not good for the little munchkin inside of you. There are so many awful chemicals flying around those salons that I feel really sorry for the people working in them.

Give every pregnant woman you know a couple of bottles of nontoxic nail polish and tell them to read this book.

As for stretch marks, they can happen anytime but especially during pregnancy. Fortunately, help is at hand with the following green products:

✤ **Pregnant Belly Oil**   (*www.motherlove.com*)
✤ **Erbaviva Stretch Mark Oil**   (*www.erbaviva.com*)

My skin got extra dry when I was pregnant. I used warm sesame oil every day. Buy a bottle of cold-pressed organic sesame oil as previously mentioned and add ten drops of clary sage essential oil, which is great for balancing hormones, and ten drops of lavender essential oil. Warm the bottle in a mug of hot water and then apply to your big, beautiful belly morning and night.

Green Baby

As a mom, I am passionate about making sure my daughter gets the good and safe stuff. When I think what was plastered over me when I was a baby, I am horrified: baby oil, which is 100 percent mineral oil, and talc, which is now linked with ovarian cancer.

The general rule with babies and children is less is more. I was disgusted to find out that many of the worst chemicals are most prevalent in baby products. It is dreadful when you consider that a small baby's body is affected much more drastically by these chemicals than an adult's.

If you have a baby or a small child, I encourage you to start label reading immediately. Your nose will also be a good guide. If the product has that clean baby smell that makes you feel all cozy, don't buy it! This smell means that it has a fragrance. It's very important to understand that "fragrance" as an ingredient is not a good thing, as you can see from our Red Alert list. You want to avoid it at all costs because of the harmful chemicals. Once you wean yourself off these ubiquitous products, you'll really go off that smell. I have a friend who insists on using the whole range of drugstore baby products. Whenever I walk into her baby's room, it smells like cheap talc. When you start exploring the alternatives by way of essential oils, you'll be intoxicated by the rich, exotic aromas.

My daughter knows the smells of lavender and lemongrass—she could probably even guess the smell of geranium or ylang-ylang. You can tell her mother is obsessed with these natural plant essences. We do want our Gorgeously Green babes to connect with nature whenever possible, and it's a great opportunity to explain how the things that they use are made and where they come from. My daughter desperately wants to visit Grasse in France, the lavender capital of the world. I've waxed lyrical about the acres of purple fields and how they harvest the flowers and boil them in massive vats to produce tiny bottles of the precious oil that we put in her bath—it's all food for thought.

We are pressured into buying so many baby products when in reality all we really need is a good diaper cream and a nontoxic hair/body wash. Babies don't need too many products on their skin—they have natural oils that do the job. It's only when we get older that we need the added moisture.

You have to become really vigilant here with label reading. Even some of the most natural-looking products are filled with bad ingredients. I keep it really simple with my daughter. My favorite routine is to put three or four drops of lavender essential oil into her tub. When she gets out, I slather her in organic sesame oil, which helps her immune system in the winter months. You can buy organic sesame oil from most health food stores or go to *www.mountainroseherbs.com.*

I don't like to use regular bubble bath because it strips a little one's skin of its natural oils. Most bubble baths from drugstores, especially the cute character bottles, are not the way to go—you're just soaking your child in a bath of chemicals. I occasionally buy the following products if my daughter feels she is missing out:

❀ **Jason**   (*www.jason.com*) makes a wonderful body wash that contains only good stuff, and you can use it to wash your kids' hair as well.

❀ **Aubrey Organics**   (*www.aubrey-organics.com*) has come out with a great line for children. The company calls it Natural Baby & Kids, and it does shampoo and soap.

❀ **Weleda**   (*www.weleda.com.au*) is a tried-and-tested company that has been around for years and carries everything you need for baby.

❀ **Target**   (*www.target.com*) has just started to carry an organic baby line called Erba Organics. It's reasonably priced and very good.

❀ **Little Twig**   (*www.littletwig.com*) is a company I love not only because it has lovely products but also because it picks a children's charity to donate annually.

If your little one has diaper rash, just put 2 teaspoons of baking soda and 2 drops of tea tree oil in his or her bath. This works like a charm, and then you can apply a nontoxic diaper rash cream.

As many of us already know, disposable diapers are not really disposable. They sit for many years, taking up an enormous amount of space in our landfills. In the United States, every year, up to 4.4 million tons of nonbiodegradable diapers are chucked away.

The Gorgeously Green mom really needs to use a biodegradable alternative or cloth diapers. I couldn't face the whole cloth diaper thing, so I found everything green that I needed at these Web sites:

❀ *www.baby'sbottomline.com*

❀ *www.organicbebe.com*

❀ *www.diaperaps.com*

❀ **G Diapers** (*www.gdiapers.com*) makes a diaper you can flush. It consists of a cute washable cotton outer pant and a plastic-free flushable refill. You can even compost the wet ones! Please note that to get the diaper cozy and comfy, you shouldn't pull it too high up the belly (like most other diapers), but you should let it sit below the belly button.

Make absolutely sure you buy baby wipes that are biodegradable. No excuse not to. **Seventh Generation** (*www.seventhgeneration.com*) carries them.

The final suggestion for kids is to always avoid conventional head-lice treatments. They contain pediculicides, which are extremely toxic. **Lice B Gone** (*www.myhealthpro.com*) is an effective and safe treatment.

DIY Beauty

The most green thing you can do for your beauty regime is to make your own face and body oil. It is so incredibly easy and fun to do and will save money, energy, and trees (for the packaging).

I want to show you how to make the best face oil in the world. All you need to do is go to (*www.mountainroseherbs.com*) and order your oils. They will arrive in a few days and you can get to work.

Remember that you will have to use only a few drops of essential oil from each bottle, so whatever you order to start with will end up making more than twenty bottles of face oil. Don't forget to also order the little brown glass bottles for your concoctions.

If you are feeling creative, make little labels and give them as girlfriend gifts or even sell them for a fortune! Last year, all my holiday gifts were Gorgeously Green face oils. My friends loved them and many have asked for more.

Make sure all the oils you buy are 100 percent organic. Aromatherapy is often a buzzword for preparations that are synthetic and full of chemicals. (All the sites I have listed are good to go.)

Gorgeously Green Luxurious Rose Face Oil

All of the ingredients are available at Mountain Rose Herbs. Also order five or six little brown bottles and a small plastic funnel. The base oil is the stuff that makes up most of your concoction.

apricot or sweet almond oil (for the base)
Essential oils:
rose, lavender, and geranium
vitamin E oil

Wash and dry your little bottles and set on the table. Then fill each one almost to the top, using your funnel, with your base oil/oils. Next add 5 drops of each of your three essential oils. Then add 1 teaspoon of vitamin E oil, and voilà!

After cleansing, work a generous amount of the oil into the skin on your face and neck with small circular movements. It smells and feels so good that you'll want to gift all of your friends.

Gorgeously Green Oil for Oily/Acne-Prone Skin

jojoba oil (for the base)
Essential oils:
Saint-John's-wort oil
black cumin seed oil
lavender and geranium

As before, fill the bottles almost up to the top with the base oil, then add 1 teaspoon of Saint-John's-wort oil and 1 teaspoon of black cumin seed oil. Finally, add 10–15 drops of lavender and geranium.

Gorgeously Green Salt Rub

2 cups fine sea salt
4 cups apricot or almond oil
20 drops of your favorite essential oil (I always like to mix lavender, geranium, and orange.)

Simply combine all of the ingredients in a glass jar and stir or shake to blend. Get in the shower, wet your skin, and then scoop out a handful of the scrub. Apply to your skin, and rub and scrub from your neck to your toes.

Gorgeously Green Alpha-Hydroxy Acid Mask

Alpha-hydroxy acids (AHAs) are derived from fruit sugars, such as glycolic acid, which comes from sugar cane. The glycolic acid sloughs off the upper layers of the skin, making way for beautiful new cell growth. You can buy commercial creams containing AHA, but be wary of the dangerous chemicals that may also be packed into the potion. Commercial brands may be way too strong and may cause your skin to become very sun sensitive, so tread lightly when going down this road, or stay on the safe side and make your own.

1/4 cup lemon juice

1/4 cup apple juice

1/4 cup grape juice

1/4 cup cane sugar

Blend all of the ingredients in a glass jar. Apply to your face with an organic cotton ball. Leave on for 10 minutes and rinse off. The mixture will keep for up to 4 days in the refrigerator.

Task

You can either visit a large health food store or one of the suggested Web sites and buy at least one new product from each of these categories: face, body, hair, makeup, and nails. Depending on what you are used to, these safe alternatives may cost a little more or a little less than you thought. Once you try them, you will never go back.

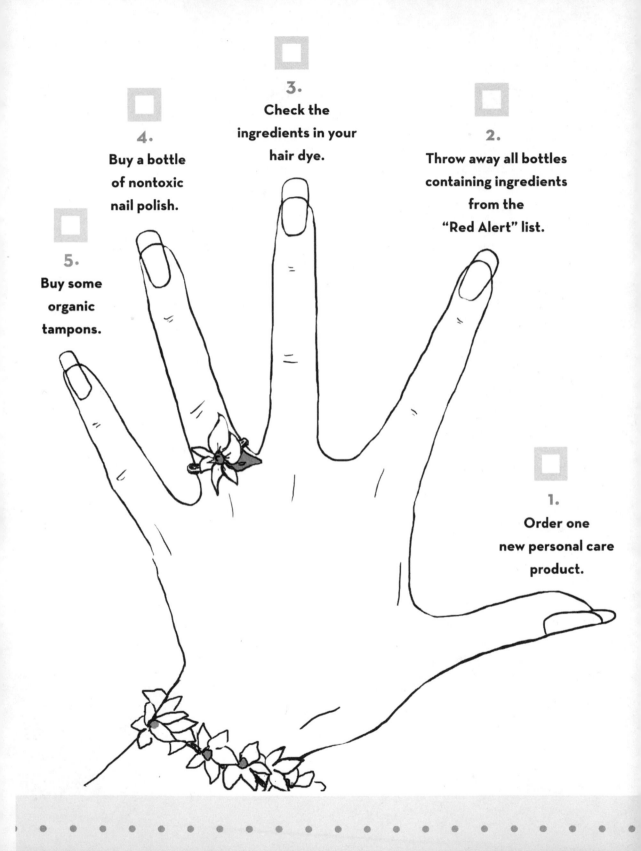

3.
Check the ingredients in your hair dye.

4.
Buy a bottle of nontoxic nail polish.

2.
Throw away all bottles containing ingredients from the "Red Alert" list.

5.
Buy some organic tampons.

1.
Order one new personal care product.

Tip

If you haven't already, create your own nail care bag to take to your next mani/pedi. Fill it with an assortment of wonderful colors from the lines in this chapter. Also pack a small bottle of tea tree oil and put five drops into the water in which your feet or hands will soak. Tea tree oil is antibacterial and smells really fresh. Don't forget the No Miss or Honey Bee Gardens nail polish remover. Your manicurist won't like it at first because it doesn't take off the polish as quickly as the usual stuff, but it doesn't fell like acid being poured on your skin, either.

Pick One

Take a look at the Gorgeously Green hand on page 62. You will notice that there are five different changes that you can pick from for step 2. Check off just one of them and know that one change makes a difference.

Passing It On

Inspire a few other women by either buying them a nontoxic gift or telling them about your new discoveries. Word spreads fast, and it is so important to get your mother, your aunt, your sister, and your best buddy on board. I love to buy my girlfriends a bottle of nontoxic nail polish. It gets them asking questions, and one thing leads to another!

Savasana

We are going to do the "corpse" pose during every step of the program, as it will help you to develop mindfulness and give you a good rest. It is the pose that is typically practiced at the end of every yoga class. Wait until the house is quiet and you can carve out ten minutes of time. Make sure that there are no phones that will disturb you. Grab a face cloth or hand towel and rub a couple of drops of your favorite essential oil into it.

Lie down on the floor with a pillow under your knees, close your eyes, and place the towel/face cloth over your eyes. Take five really slow breaths. On each inhale, breathe in peace; on each exhale, breathe out a smile.

Chapter Three

STEP 3: Your Green Temple

Your body is your temple. You only have this one, so you've got to treat it with love. I have only just leaned to be really kind to myself. With the media constantly telling us that we have to look a certain way in order to be sexy or loved, it gets very boring. We force ourselves to go to the gym in order to sculpt our bodies and lose weight, but let's face it, it's not much fun. Moreover, we get home and have to deny ourselves the goodies that we should be allowed to enjoy. Can you imagine if an alien came down from Mars and saw how we punished ourselves—running like rodents on treadmills and forcing ourselves to stay out of the freezer compartment by telling ourselves that we are hideously fat. It's insane, and the Gorgeously Green program is going to change all of that for you.

If you follow the daily program in this chapter, you will get all the exercise you need to look and feel fabulous. Since I stopped punishing myself at the gym and took up a regular yoga practice, I have honestly never looked better. People often don't believe me when I tell them that all I do is yoga. They have the notion that it's just about stretching and breathing, which is not the case. There are many different kinds of yoga: Hatha, Iyengar, Ashtanga, and Anusara, to name a few. Most of these traditions will give you a seriously good workout. I have studied many different schools of yoga and teach a blend of them all. The Gorgeously Green practice is a "flow"-style program, meaning that you will move from pose to pose, raising your heart rate and training yourself aerobically.

You do not have to go to the gym. Remember that driving to the gym is a waste of your precious time and your money. And think about the amount of fossil fuel that is burned into the atmosphere getting there. I'm going to teach you an exercise program that you can do without even leaving your house. Once you've got the hang of this routine, you may even cancel your gym membership.

Okay, so you want to get into great shape. This is how with a three-pronged approach to fitness:

1. Flexibility
2. Aerobics for a healthy heart
3. Weight-bearing exercise to combat osteoporosis

To get into shape with yoga, you need to put aside only fifteen to 20 minutes a day. I do it as soon as I get out of bed, and it wakes me up really fast (better than caffeine actually).

You can take it slowly at first. When you feel confident that you know the routine, you can really go at quite a vigorous pace. All you need is a yoga mat, which you can buy at most large health food stores. The Gorgeously Green girl may be interested in either the Earth Lover's Yoga Mat or the Natural Rubber Yoga Mat, both available at *www. gaiam.com*.

You've never been formally introduced to Emerald. She will show you the Gorgeously Green yoga routine.

First, spend five minutes looking over the practice. The poses are pretty simple. Then you can place the book at the front of your mat to sneak a peak when you need to.

A fun way of learning the practice is to get your loved one to slowly read out the instructions while you negotiate the poses. My close friend, Melina, promised her husband that he would be required to read them through only once and never again. He reluctantly obliged, but they ended up having such a laugh that he decided he wanted to join in as well.

The Breath of Life

People get very worried and confused about the breathing in yoga. I always have students who think they've got it all wrong. It's actually really simple. As you are reading these words, just allow your breath to become a little deeper. Lengthen your inhale to a count of three slow beats, and then do the same with your exhale. Have your lips lightly closed. As you breathe in, imagine the breath going up your nose and down the back of your throat. Relax your face and shoulders. Close your eyes now, and practice three or four of these slow yogic breaths. It's amazing how something as simple as deep breathing can change the way you feel completely.

Once you start your practice, make sure you are breathing in this deep and restful manner. It will come naturally to you as you learn the poses.

This is a fantastic sequence because you can take it anywhere. I practice it in hotels, backyards, beaches, and living rooms. I even taught it to a client in her bathroom—granted it was the size of my bedroom.

It's an all-round fitness sequence that will train your strength, cardio, and flexibility. Get this down, and I promise that your days in the gym are numbered.

SALUTING THE SUN

Sequence 1

Mountain Pose

This is the blueprint for every other yoga pose and is an excellent opportunity to check your posture. Stand with your feet together, arms down by your sides.

- ✾ Stretch and elongate your toes.
- ✾ Hug your leg muscles onto your leg bones, feeling the muscular energy.
- ✾ Point your tailbone down toward your heels.
- ✾ Lift your heart up toward the sky and gently draw your shoulders back.
- ✾ Close your eyes and take 2 or 3 slow, deep breaths.

Standing Forward Bend Pose

To transition from the previous pose, on an exhale, take your arms out to the sides and fold forward from your hips. Once in the pose:

- ✾ Bend your knees if you need to.
- ✾ If your legs are straight, lift your kneecaps.
- ✾ Make sure that you have equal weight between your heels and the balls of your feet.

Mountain Pose with Arms Extended Up

On an inhale, extend your arms overhead with your palms facing each other.

- ❀ Relax your shoulders.
- ❀ Straighten your elbows.
- ❀ Reach your fingertips up toward the sky.

Straight-Leg Lunge Pose

On an inhale, step your right foot as far back as you can.

- ❀ Make sure your front knee is directly above your heel at a right angle.
- ❀ Look down to the floor in front of you to avoid craning your neck up.

Plank Pose

Hold your breath as you step your left foot back to meet the right foot. You are now in the mountain pose but horizontal (like a straight plank of wood).

- Lift the back of your knees toward the sky.
- Tuck your tailbone under and lift your belly.
- Soften between your shoulder blades.

Modified Push-Up Pose

On an exhale, drop your knees to the floor, then your chest, and finally your forehead.

- Keep your elbows close to your sides.
- Don't worry if it feels weird—your tush should be up in the air!

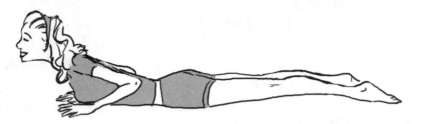

Cobra Pose

As you inhale, slide from the previous pose forward into the cobra.

- ❀ Slide your shoulder blades down and back away from your ears.
- ❀ Press your tailbone down into the floor.

Downward-Facing Dog Pose

Use the muscles in your belly (yeah, right!) to haul yourself back as you exhale into this pose.

- ❀ Spread your fingers.
- ❀ Draw your sit bones up and back.
- ❀ Draw your heels down toward the earth.
- ❀ Take 3 or 4 long, smooth breaths.

Straight-Leg Lunge Pose

On an inhale, swing your right leg forward between your hands into this lunge. If it doesn't make it all the way to the top of your mat, shove it forward with your hand. The first few times might feel a bit clumsy, but you'll get the hang of it.

❀ Your knee must be directly above your ankle.
❀ If this is challenging, come up onto your fingertips.

Standing Forward Bend Pose

As you exhale, bring your left leg forward to meet the right and fold forward from the hips.

❀ Try to have your fingertips in line with your toes.
❀ Bend your knees if you need to.

Mountain Pose

To come back to this original pose, inhale and take your arms out to the sides and use the belly muscles to lift your torso up.

❀ Back in mountain pose, it's time to recheck your posture.
❀ Keep your tailbone down toward your heels.
❀ Gently draw your heart up and your shoulders back.
❀ Soften your face, breathe deeply, and smile!

Well Done! You have completed one round of the sun salutation. Do at least two rounds of sequence 1 to start, and work up to four rounds.

Sequence 2

This is almost the same as sequence 1 but with a couple of modified and added poses. Give it a go.

Mountain Pose

Take a few moments in this pose to become still. Close your eyes and deepen your breath.

Mountain Pose with Arms Extended Up

As you inhale, sweep your arms out to the sides and up. Your palms should face each other.

Standing Forward Bend Pose

As you exhale, sweep your arms out to the sides and fold forward from your hips. Place your fingertips on the floor, in line with your toes. Bend your knees if you need to.

Straight-Leg Lunge Pose

As you inhale, step your right leg back into a lunge. Make sure your left knee is directly above your left ankle.

Plank Pose

Hold your breath as you step your left leg back to meet your right. Tuck your tailbone under and try not to let your hips sag down toward the floor.

Push-Up Pose

As you exhale, bend your elbows, keep your legs straight, and lower your shoulders until they are level with your elbows. Make no mistake—this is a tough pose that requires arm strength, but you'll gain strength by doing it! To make it easier, grip your elbows tightly against your ribs.

Upward-Facing Dog Pose

On an inhale, you are going to slide from the last pose into this one. The trick is to slide forward without your knees touching the floor.

- ❀ Draw your shoulders down and away from your ears.
- ❀ Lift your inner thighs up toward the sky.

Downward-Facing Dog Pose

Now you need to use all your belly strength to lift your nymph-like torso and exhale back into the downward-facing dog position.

- ❀ Lift your shoulders up and away from your wrists.
- ❀ Extend your inner shoulder blades up toward your waist.
- ❀ Take 5 slow breaths.

Standing Forward Bend Pose

On an inhale, jump or step your feet back in between your hands so that you land in the forward-bending pose.

Mountain Pose

On an inhale, come back up to the mountain pose. Stand absolutely still and take 3 slow breaths.

Congratulations. Now you've done sequence 2. Try to practice it twice and again work up to four cycles. When you get up to speed, I suggest doing both sequences three times. (If you get any pain in your wrists, stick to sequence 1.)

Standing Poses
Warrior 1 Pose

This pose is great for leg strength and tight shoulders.
Stand with your feet 3½ feet apart and turn your right foot out 90 degrees and your left foot in 60 degrees so that you have to turn your whole body over to the right. Bend your right knee so that it lines up with your middle toes. Extend your arms overhead with your palms facing each other.

- Stretch your arms up as high as you can toward the sky.
- Keep your back heel grounded into the earth.
- If you feel stable in the pose, try taking your head back and bringing the palms of your hands together. Look up at your thumbnails.

Switch sides.

Extended Side-Angle Pose

This pose will not only work your ankles, calves, and thighs, but you will also get a great side stretch.
Stand with your feet 3½ feet apart and extend your arms out to the sides.
Turn your right foot out 90 degrees and your left foot in 45 degrees.
On an exhale, bend your right knee to a right angle and place your right hand on the outside of your right foot. (If you have trouble reaching the ground with your hand, grab a chair or an

ottoman to put your hand on.) Extend your left arm all the way over to the right.

❀ Press the outside edge of your left foot heavily into the earth.
❀ Make sure your right knee is in line with your middle toes.
❀ Feel one line of energy from the outside of the left foot to the left fingertips.

Switch sides.

Triangle Pose

This is a delicious pose that will strengthen your legs, open your hips, and lengthen your spine. It is a favorite of almost everyone I teach.

Stand with your feet $3^1/2$ feet apart and raise your arms out to the sides. Turn your right foot out 90 degrees and your left foot in 45 degrees.

As you exhale, stretch your right arm all the way to the right and really lengthen the right side of your waist, then let your hand drop onto your shin or ankle (wherever it feels comfortable). If your neck is not too tight, look up at your left thumbnail.

❀ Lift your right kneecap to stabilize the joint.
❀ Press the outside edge of your left heel into the earth.
❀ Extend the left fingertips up into the sky.

Switch sides.

Warrior 2 Pose

This pose will strengthen your legs considerably. If held for 10 full breaths, it will also open tight hips and teach you to focus. As the goal of yoga is to calm and still the mind, this is a good pose to practice through simply observing the breath. Notice that when you get tired of holding the pose, your breathing will become more shallow and quicker. Train yourself to slow it down in the face of a challenge— it's a great lesson for everyday life.

Stand with your feet 3¹/₂ feet apart. Turn your right foot out 90 degrees and your back foot in 45 degrees. As you exhale, bend your right knee to a right angle, making sure the knee lines up with your middle toes. Extend your arms out to the sides, stretching through your fingertips.

❀ Push your right heel into the earth.
❀ Make sure that your right knee is directly above your right ankle.
❀ Gaze over your right fingertips.

Switch sides.

Hero Pose

This pose has a number of benefits: it will stretch your thighs and keep your knees young and vibrant; it also helps with spider veins and will open your shoulders. Make it a daily pose.

Come down onto your hands and your knees. Bring your knees together and your feet a little wider than hip-width apart. Sit down in between your feet. If it's too painful for the knees, grab a folded blanket or towel to place under your sit bones.

Take your left arm out to the side and then swing it up your back (fingers facing up toward your head). Reach your right hand up and then behind you to link with your left fingers. If you can't reach, use a belt.

✻ Sit up straight, lengthening the spine.

✻ Press the outside edges of your feet into the earth and take 3 or 4 slow breaths.

Switch arms.

Bridge Pose

This is fantastic for your back and shoulders. Lie on your mat with your knees bent and your feet hip-width apart. Interlace your fingers underneath you and roll gently from side to side, wriggling your shoulders underneath you. While exhaling, lift your hips up toward the sky. Take 10 slow, deep breaths.

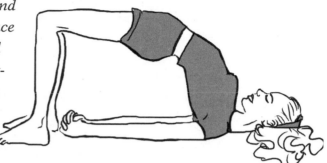

* ❁ Press the inside edges of your feet into the earth, keeping your knees pointing over your toes.
* ❁ As you inhale, feel your chest gently expanding toward your chin.

Simple Twist Pose

This is a personal favorite that I practice whenever I am irritated, tense, or tired. Lie down on your mat with your knees drawn into your chest. Roll gently from side to side to massage your lower back. Let your knees drop toward your right elbow and spread your arms out in a T-shape.

* ❁ Take a few long, slow breaths.
* ❁ Try to ease both shoulders into the earth.
* ❁ If your left shoulder is way off the floor, take your knees down lower.

Switch sides.

Seated Forward Bend Pose

This pose stretches your hamstrings and your back. It can be challenging, so go slow at first. Sit with your legs outstretched in front of you. Flex your feet and press your thighbones down into the mat. Reach for your feet (if you can't, get a belt and hook it around the ball of your foot). Hold the sides of your feet if you can and bend your elbows up toward the sky.

❀ Let your head and neck release down toward your thighs.

❀ Breathe deeply into the back of your body.

Thread Needle Pose

If you suffer from tight shoulders and a tight upper back, this pose is for you. Start on your hands and your knees. Thread your right arm under your left arm and slide it across the floor all the way over to the right, until your right shoulder blade is resting on the floor. Take 5 slow breaths. Switch sides.

❀ Relax your facial muscles.

❀ Relax your fingers.

Arm-Strengthening Time

Part of your weekly fitness plan includes weight-bearing exercises, which are necessary to keep your bones strong. Use small weights (2, 5, and 8 pounds) and do a lot of repetitions. You can buy dumbbells at any large store with a sports section or check out your local thrift store or www.craigslist.org. *Honestly, I do these just twice a week, and it does the trick. I sometimes carve out 15 minutes on the weekend and even do them while I'm chatting with my husband or watching my daughter play. Invite a girl-friend over to do it with you and go for a frozen yogurt afterward—whatever it takes. It's a small price to pay for strong, healthy bones. Emerald will now show us four simple exercises.*

Start with 2 pound weights for all of the following exercises. When you get stronger, you can move up to 5 pounds and 8 pounds.

Deltoid Lifts

Stand with your feet hip-width apart and slightly bend your knees. Extend your arms out to the sides. When you exhale, control the weights as you bring them down and together in front of you. Raise them up when you inhale. Repeat 10–15 times.

❀ Keep your tailbone tucked under.
❀ Gradually increase the repetitions.

Extended Bicep Curls

Stand with your feet hip-width apart and your knees slightly bent. Extend your arms out to the sides. As you exhale, bend your elbows and squeeze the weights in toward your shoulders. When you inhale, extend the arms out fully. Try doing 10–15 repetitions.

Traditional Bicep Curls

Stand with your feet hip-width apart and bend your knees slightly. Make sure your tailbone is tucked in to avoid overarching your lower back. Hold the weights with straight arms down in front of you, and when you exhale, squeeze them into your body. It's important that you practice this very slowly and pause for 3 beats at the top of each squeeze.

Start with 10 repetitions and build up to 3 sets of 10.

Chair Triceps

If you practice these regularly, you will see a difference in your arms in no time.

Sit on a chair. Place your hands on the edge of the seat with your fingers facing forward. Draw your sit bones about 2 inches away from the seat and then dip them down toward the floor. Try to keep your back as close to the seat of the chair as possible. Go for 8 repetitions and work your way up to 15.

Gorgeously Green Behind!

Firming and toning or even sculpting my bottom is pretty high on the priority list. I can do all the yoga or cardio I want, but if this area is lagging behind, I don't feel right about myself! Fortunately, there are two extremely simple exercises that you can do in the comfort of your living room.

Squats

The most effective exercise for lifting and tightening your bottom is a good old squat. I know—the mere thought of squats makes most of my clients feel in need of a stiff drink, but do them we must if we want to be followed around by something we're proud of!

* Stand with your feet a bit wider than hip-distance apart and slightly turn out your toes.
* Exhale as you sit into the squat and take your arms out straight in front of you.
* Lower down until your thighs are parallel with the floor.
* Inhale to come up.

Begin with 15 squats and work you way up to three sets of 15.

Lunges

The lunge is as effective as the squat for tightening. Lunges will tone and sculpt your hips, thighs, and "saddle bags." Very important!

Stand with your feet together and your hands on your hips. Step your right foot forward and bend the knee until the thigh is parallel to the floor. Make sure that your knee is directly above your ankle.

❀ Make sure your knee points toward your middle toe.
Try 8 lunges on the right leg and then 8 lunges on the left.

Fabulous Abs

Whether you want a six-pack or even a vaguely flat tummy, it's important to do abdominal exercises at least three times a week. We need to have strong abs to support our lower back. It is vital, so don't just think about it—do it!

The following exercise can even be done in front of the television or with extremely loud rock music blasting (for some reason it helps!).

❀ Lie on a comfortable surface and put your legs up on a chair (as shown).
❀ Interlace your hands gently behind your neck.
❀ Keeping your elbows wide and looking up at the ceiling, bring your chest up toward your thighs as you exhale.

Start slowly with abdominal exercises, because when you get tired, you will start to tense your neck muscles. Begin with 10 and work your way up to 20.

Kitchen Yoga

On mornings when you don't have time to even get out the mat, try the Gorgeously Green kitchen yoga practice. While the kettle is boiling and the toast is browning, you can be doing these fabulous poses to stretch out your lower back and hamstrings. These two poses will take you all of four minutes, so no excuse. If you've got kids, they can join in or laugh at you (as my daughter does!).

Supported Forward Bend Pose

I practice this pose every morning while I am waiting for the kettle to boil. It's quick, easy, and will open your hamstrings and hips.

Stand about 3 feet away from the countertop (facing it) and place your hands down firmly on the counter. Draw your sit bones back toward the wall behind you. Make sure your thighs are firm. Also make sure that your ears are in line with your upper arms.

To open your hips, place your right foot just above your left knee. Flex the foot and slowly bend your left knee. Take 5 slow breaths. Switch sides.

Bed Yoga

If you are having a really tough morning and can't even get out of bed, try Emerald's bed yoga to get you moving.

Simple Twist Bed Pose

Sit cross-legged and straighten your spine as much as you can. Place your left hand on the outside of your right thigh and put your right hand behind you (fingertips pressing into the mattress). Deeply inhale, and as you exhale, twist all the way to the right. You can use the pressure of your left hand pressing against your right thigh to create a deeper twist. Keep your chin slightly tucked in. Switch sides.

Thread Needle Bed Pose

We already covered this pose in our regular practice, but it feels fantastic to do it in bed. If you are not alone in the bed, it can be a bit suggestive to say the least, given the position of your bottom!

Start on your hands and knees and then thread your right arm under the left, sliding it along the bed until your right shoulder blade is in contact with the mattress. Breathe deeply. Switch sides.

Get a Move On!

We have to add one more thing to get your heart rate up. You can pick walking, hiking, or cycling, as all can be done outside where you can connect with nature. Even here in Los Angeles, I can manage to find a bit of greenery for inspiration. If you have any hills near you, use them. Get your bottom up to the top three times a week. It doesn't matter what time of day—just do it. If you are walking, you need to walk at a good pace for twenty minutes and then you're done. In the cold months, you can even power walk in the mall. My mother-in-law lives in Georgia, where it is sometimes freezing in the winter, so a group of women get together and stride through the mall at a frightening pace on a daily basis. Not the greenest surroundings, but at least they are moving and it doesn't cost anything. I am lucky enough to live near the Hollywood Hills, where there is a dog park that boasts an extreme incline. It can be a bit daunting to see some of the lithe actresses decked out in microshorts and a bikini top, but the steep hill is worth it.

Cycling is great aerobic exercise, and you can run errands or shop at the same time. The Gorgeously Green girl needs a bicycle for exercise and transportation, so if you haven't already got one, you know what to ask Santa Claus for this year.

Also bear in mind where you park when you go shopping. I find myself getting livid if there are no free spaces near the store. Not very green of me! First off, I could be letting older people have those spaces; second, I could add to my twenty-minute daily walk if I parked farther away. I've become so lazy. I do blame it on our culture, which promotes having everything at the click of a switch. My mother is my inspiration, because she is in her late sixties and is in great shape. She has never been to the gym, but she always takes the stairs two at a time and spends much of her day walking the dogs or doing manual work in the yard. Her body is healthy and lean, and she pretty much eats what she wants.

Hydration

You've heard it before and you will hear it again—drink lots of fresh water daily. If you want to check out what is up with your local tap water, go to *www.nrdc.org* and look at "What's on tap?"

The Gorgeously Green Girl needs to always have her reusable water bottle at the ready. I use one of my colorful metal Sigg Bottles (*www.mysigg.com*).

I have just started using the Vitalizer Plus (*www.rgarden.com*), which changes the molecular structure of the water and transforms it into "living" water. It looks like a fancy blender, with a very attractive glass jug, and it uses magnetic fields to transform your regular water into the dynamic, highly oxygenated water of a stream or fountain. My husband thinks I'm nuts, but I swear it makes me feel more vital!

Meditation

I am addicted. I have been practicing transcendental meditation (TM) for fifteen years now, and it's the only way I find a really blissful feeling naturally. When I'm tired, stressed out, or insane, it is the only thing that soothes me. Meditation is tailor-made for neurotic women like myself. There are tons of different techniques you can do. I like TM because it's simple and it isn't affiliated with any specific religion or philosophy. Anyone can do it. You can take a course, which typically consists of four hour-long sessions. It is pricey but definitely the greatest gift I have ever given to myself and was worth every penny. Go to *www.tm.org* to find out more. Or simply sit in a comfortable chair, making sure your back is upright and your feet are firmly planted on the floor. It's a good idea to set a timer for five minutes so you don't have to keep peering at your watch. Close your eyes and begin to observe your breath. Mentally follow each inhale and each exhale. If you find your attention wandering (which it will), just bring it back to your breath. When the timer goes off, take a few seconds to allow your mind to become absolutely still, absolutely silent, and then gently open your eyes. There doesn't have to be anything mystical about it. Good meditation is very simple.

If you want to get a little more serious about the whole thing, buy an eco-meditation cushion for yourself at *www.naturalhighlifestyle.com*. This cushion is great because you sit cross-legged on it. (I like to place it on a folded blanket so that my ankles are resting on something soft.) This position encourages good posture, as your spine will naturally lengthen. When we sit in a chair, we tend to slump!

Task

Start a little exercise journal or put up a chart on your fridge door. Commit to doing just one thing a day, then write down in your journal or your chart what you did. It will give you a great sense of accomplishment. Your one thing could simply be getting up off your chair now and doing a yoga pose, or walking around the block. People often ask me if I do yoga every day. The answer is yes, and oftentimes all I will have done is two of the bed yoga poses. I can be very sluggish sometimes, but my body cries out to be moved every day so I'm beginning to listen.

Pick One

Even if you managed to do just one of these things, pat yourself on the back. You'll need to revisit this chapter a few times before you get the yoga down. Don't feel you have to cancel your gym membership right away, but think about it. Above all, enjoy every bit of exercise you do. It should be a joyous experience—life is too short for it not to be.

Savasana

By now you should be getting used to the savasana pose. I resist it because it feels lazy, like I'm not doing anything. That is the whole point. If you are like me, you rush around in a frenzy most of the day, so it is really challenging to lie down comfortably and nurture your body with the breath. Ah—it sounds so good, I'm going to do it right now. Try to increase to eight slow breaths today, and remember to breathe in peace and breathe out a smile.

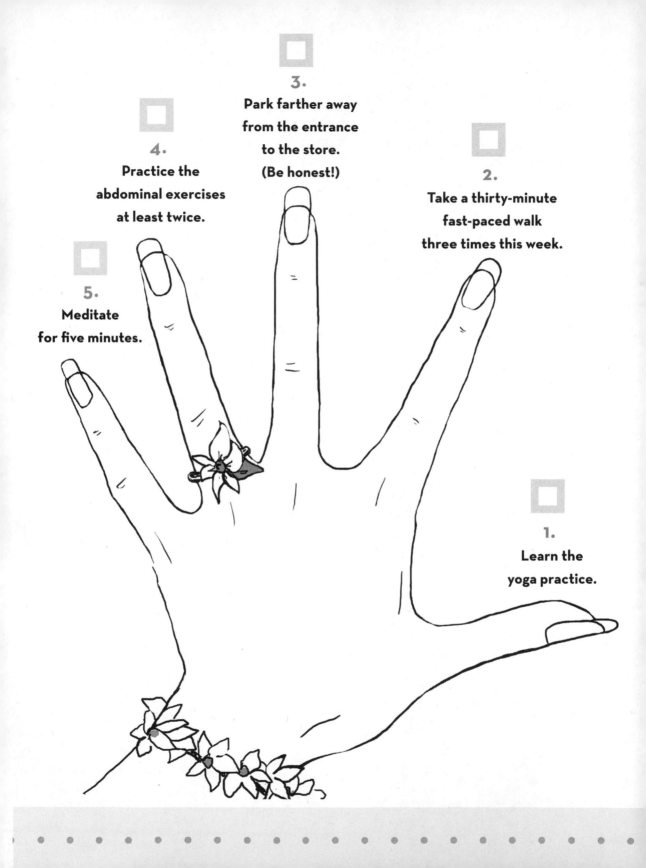

3.
Park farther away
from the entrance
to the store.
(Be honest!)

4.
Practice the
abdominal exercises
at least twice.

2.
Take a thirty-minute
fast-paced walk
three times this week.

5.
Meditate
for five minutes.

1.
Learn the
yoga practice.

Chapter Four

STEP 4: Soulful Shopping

Consume, Consume, Consume

Even the word *shopping* is appealing to me. I love it. Whether I am shopping at a megamart for my daughter or at an expensive funky boutique for me, I get a kick. My husband asked me the other day if I could get through a week—did I say *week*?—I meant a day—without "consuming." I was furious. How dare he criticize my shopping habits? After all, everything I buy is absolutely essential for the family. "We *need* things," I shrieked back at him. He had touched a button, because deep down inside I knew that we didn't need *all* the stuff. It's a tough habit to kick, though. We sure are a consumer culture. I want it, and I want it now!

My six-year-old is a wannabe consumer. She rarely watches television, yet living in a big city, she can't get away from the ads. I'd have to home-school her and live in an Amish community if I wanted otherwise—speaking of which, when I was pregnant, I swore to my husband that I wouldn't spoil our child and that a few wooden toys would have to suffice and blah, blah—cut to a room full of enough plastic to fill a toy store. It's not easy, I admit, but I'm learning to be tougher now, because I want her to be thankful for the simple things in life. I have to practice what I preach, so here's how I do it.

When I go shopping, I pick up a new saucepan or a pretty sheet set and take a few seconds to ask myself if we can make do without it.

Nine times out of ten, the item is put back on the shelf. The beauty of this exercise is that I get to walk away feeling great about myself. It is empowering to make a choice about every item rather than unconsciously filling up the cart. Try it—you will feel so light and wonderful walking away from the store with just the essentials.

I've had to redefine the word *need* for myself as well. I find myself "needing" a lot of personal things—this season's high heeled boot; or I'll realize that I can't possibly be seen in last year's skinny jeans when all the models and cool people are wearing bell-bottoms. I get it that the fashion industry deliberately changes the "must have" jean style every year so that we have to fork out for the latest design, but I've had to train myself to say, "Can I actually live without this?" Sometimes I have to repeat the question three or four times for it to really sink in. To my annoyance, the answer is almost always a resounding *yes*. People must think I have a screw loose in the store, because this dialogue is often out loud!

Window-Shopping

I've noticed that my friends and I rarely window-shop. We are used to seeing something and immediately buying it. Why wait when you can whack it on your credit card and pretend the transaction never took place? Instant gratification feels good for about half an hour. It's like a coffee rush—a jittery high followed by a droop in energy and spirit. The solution is to return to good old browsing.

Take yourself off with a girlfriend just to look and fantasize. If you see something you absolutely cannot live without, put it on hold for a couple of days so that you can really think about it. A lot of stores do full refunds, which always tempts me to buy a bunch of stuff quickly so that I can have a big trying-on session at home. In becoming green, however, I have had to change that little habit, as it is a total waste of fossil fuel and precious time.

My friend Kim, who is superconscious of the environment and superbeautiful, was telling me the other day that she goes back on her trusty bicycle at least ten times to look at an item that she is thinking of buying. She'll try it on with different outfits and in different moods, even at different times of the day, before deciding. "Don't the sales assistants pressure you?" I asked. "Yeah!" she replied, "but they can't *force* me to buy it!" I wondered if she worried that it would be sold if she waited, but she assured me that if it was meant to be hers, it would still be there waiting for her. I can take a leaf or two from her book.

If you don't live near any good clothes shops, you can spend hours browsing online. Although you don't get to touch the garment, you can often get a 360 view of it. If it's a "must have," you can order the item and try it on in the comfort of your own home.

There are loads of things we can do while we are on step 4 to reduce our heavy impact on the environment. Evaluating shopping habits is one of the biggies, because there is so much waste, and most of us don't want to think about where it all goes. Sure, we do a bit of recycling, but that isn't enough. So let's get on with it and see what we can do to help.

A Win/Win Situation

Commit to trying the "Can I live without?" exercise for a few weeks and save a surprising amount of money. The first two months I tried it, I was amazed when my credit-card bills came in. After another month of minimal consuming, I felt justified in buying a necklace that I had been salivating over for months. Created by a local artist in one of my favorite boutiques, this piece of jewelry was one of a kind, and the price reflected that. I never thought I would be able to afford it, but having saved on all the usual stuff I had been buying, I could afford the necklace. I will treasure it forever because it was made with love and care. That is soulful shopping. So reducing what I consume on a daily basis doesn't mean I have to go without—on the contrary!

Living in a consumer society like ours, it is hard to imagine living in abject poverty. It's chilling to realize that 20 percent of the highest-income people in the world account for 86 percent of total private consumption. Many of us are in that 20 percent bracket.

I would rather not dwell on the idea that our heavy-duty consumption has such an enormous impact of the environment, but it clearly does. From plastic to fuel, we need it, want it, and use it at the expense of our precious planet. The fantastic news is that we can begin to consciously consume by buying products that help, not harm.

Soulful Shopping Exercise

Out of all the things that you have purchased in the past few years, what items do you most treasure? Where did you buy them and what do they mean to you? Make a quick mental list or look around your home. It could be a vase or a candle or a bottle of perfume. I bet the items that mean the most to you were made in a special way and were given and received with love.

Looking around my kitchen, I can see an odd pair of wooden salad servers sticking out of my utensil jar. They always make me smile because they are uneven and clearly made from a peice of wood that had serious limitations. I purchased them from an old toothless man on a roadside in Argentina. He told me that it took him a day to carve each one, and he asked a pittance for them. I wonder what he was thinking as he chipped away all day long. There is something wonderful about things that are made slowly. Many of us are are in such a frenzy to get everything done quickly that we forget the details, the textures, and the smells.

Now make a list of five items that you have thrown away over the last six months—clothes, shoes, boxes, cell phones, toys, whatever. Next to each item, write how you disposed of it. For example, I threw away an old plastic alarm clock in my recycling bin. I don't know where it ended up and wasn't even sure that it should have gone in that particular bin. I also wanted to dispose of some old children's toys, but even Goodwill didn't want them, so they again ended up in the recycling bin. Suffice it to say that none of these items were purchased on a "soulful" shopping spree.

Repeat the exercise for the items you love, use, adore, and will never give away. It could be a piece of furniture or a special mug—whatever gives off a soulful feeling. One of my five items is a very expensive wooden hairbrush that I bought for Lola in England. It reminds me of when I was a child. If she takes care of it, she'll use it for years to come. How did you feel when you bought these items?

The Dreaded Three R's

The sustainable movement goes on about the three R's: reuse, recycle, and reduce. I'm fully up for the first two. I'll reuse whatever I can: shopping totes, water bottles, and plastic bags. I'm also pretty good at recycling now, even the hazardous waste, which is a pain in the neck because you have to make a real effort to get it to the right place. Reducing, however, gets stuck in my throat. I am used to trying to get more! More bang for my buck. If I can get two for the price of one, bring it on! The very word *reduce* makes me want to rebel. I want what I want and I want more of it.

But in recent years, I have found that it is much easier to reduce than I thought it would be. The huge positive is that when I reduce my shopping trips and general consumption, I get really excited on the few occasions that I do shop. It is sad that for many of us it is routine to buy clothes and cosmetics whenever we want them, so there is nothing to look forward to anymore. One day, I bought my daughter some new arts-and-crafts supplies, and she was totally nonplussed. I was horrified, because when I was a kid, it was thrilling to have anything new—a book or crayons was a big deal.

You may be one of those extraordinary women who don't like shopping, especially for clothes! One of my oldest friends, Ophelia, can't think of anything worse than having to traipse around boutiques, trying on clothes and shoes. She would rather look at art or sit for hours in a bookshop. If you are like her, you will find it a lot easier to go green than the rest of us. I marvel at another friend, Fiona, who spent all her hard-earned money on one exquisite antique chair—ugh! To think that my trendy dress will be gotten rid of inside a year, while she'll be sitting her dainty bottom on that chair when she's ninety.

Fix It!

When something breaks, we just run to the store and grab another, instead of taking the time to fix the item or looking in a thrift store or Ebay for a replacement. I have learned very late in life that there is something deeply satisfying about getting things fixed. The other day, my vacuum started making very strange sounds, so I went online to find a local repair store. The toothless repair man, Ronny, treated my ten-year-old Dirt Devil like a precious artifact and told me to come back the next day and it would be as good as new. Granted, the repair probably cost the same as a new one from a large discount store, but I saved a bunch of fossil fuel and packaging while helping to keep Ronny in business. It felt great.

There is a massive backlash against consuming, and many communities are coming together to put their money where their mouths are. One such group is in San Francisco and is an array of professionals who vowed not to buy one single new item in 2006. They believe that a consumer culture is destroying the world, and they call themselves The Compact. They are allowed to buy only secondhand items from thrift stores, Craig's list, and freecycle.org. I would love to be able to join this merry band or organize my own group, but I am not quite there yet. Apparently, the members go through withdrawal symptoms at first— ugh, perish the thought. It would feel amazing, though, to think that I was doing something so incredibly positive. The amount of money I would save would be enough to take me and my family on a seriously fancy vacation—okay, I might have to consider it, but one month would be a better goal for me to start with. Did I say a month? Actually, a day would be a good starting point.

Go Without for One Day

Try going one day without consuming. Make sure you have all the basics, including gas in the car, and see how it goes. Remember our "day-without" includes no newspaper, no coffee shop, no nothing—don't even consider opening your wallet or shopping online.

What if there is a really good sale on? Even that, I'm afraid, will have to wait. It's fun to do this with a bunch of your friends: you all agree on a day and then check in that evening to see how it felt. I did this with my Gorgeously Green Girls' Club. It was much harder than we thought. We picked a Tuesday; however, Kim forgot that she had a facial booked on that day, Gina had to buy a flea collar for her new puppy, and the only day my hairstylist was in before leaving for vacation was, of course, Tuesday! After rigorously checking our planners, we decided to attempt the following Friday, and it was a resounding success. Admittedly, I was itching to go out for my daily latte, but I saved four dollars by making it at home! Gina, who is stuck in an office all day, was thrilled that she had declined the Starbucks run and made herself a cup of herbal tea instead.

You may decide to go for the challenge of a no-shopping *week*. If you do this, it's a really good idea to have at least one mate to cheerlead when you're having a moment of weakness. It actually feels great. I used up packets of rice that hadn't been touched in a year and got pretty creative with my condiments. The most amazing thing was the amount of extra time I had on my hands. I typically never, *ever* have time to sit down in the course of a day, let alone read a magazine; however, that week I devoured two fascinating novels. I had no idea how much time and money my daily shopping routine consumed.

LITTLE QUIZ

DO YOU EVER:

- ❀ Consider what the grave site of your purchases will look like?
- ❀ Think about where your clothes come from and how they were made?
- ❀ Think about who made the items you are buying?
- ❀ Buy something that you never use or wear for a couple of months before tossing?

Take Time to Think

I often buy something because it's the "hot" thing of the season and I can't go without it, or it's on sale. These are my worst mistakes. The hot item is so out in a matter of months, and the sale item is totally "what was I thinking?" I am slowly learning that it is more economical and environmentally friendly to pay a little more for beautiful, classical pieces that will last me a lifetime. I still wear a creamy cashmere cardigan that belonged to my grandmother and carry an exquisite Kelly bag that I had palpitations buying in London twenty years ago—but they're classic.

We rarely think about how far our products have come when they are shipped to us, whether they were made in a sweatshop environment, if the workers were being treated fairly, if we displaced a local business owner with a large chain retailer, how the product was created, what type of materials were used, and how by-products were disposed of. Now, that's a lot to think about, I know—but if anything struck a chord, explore it further. For me, it's the sweatshop thing, because going green is about taking care of our environment, which doesn't just mean our physical planet; it also means animals and human beings.

Sweatshops

You may have noticed that many of the labels inside your clothes say that the garment was made in China. Does this automatically mean it was made in a sweatshop? It probably was, as you can be sure that if a garment was not made in a sweatshop, it will clearly say so on the label. What has this got to do with going green? Taking care of our environment means the planet *and* its inhabitants. The wonderful thing about going green is that we become aware of the well-being of every living thing.

Sweatshops exist everywhere—in China, Africa, Mexico, and even in the United States. A sweatshop is an unpleasant workplace that violates the law, so workers really suffer: there may be an absence of a living wage, poor working conditions regarding health and safety, verbal/physical abuse, and often extreme fear and intimidation. A friend of mine, Samantha, who is a local organic designer, told me about some of the conditions she has actually witnessed firsthand in Los Angeles—for example, bathrooms locked so that workers can't "waste time" using them, or if someone really needs to go, he or she is told to "hold it."

It begs the question of who is to blame for this appalling situation. Many of the big-brand companies deny knowledge of what is going on. They hire contractors and subcontractors, so it's easy for them to turn a blind eye; however, they have the power to investigate and make sure that their operations are responsible from top to bottom. Most companies don't do this because they obviously want to find the cheapest labor that they can.

With this newfound knowledge, I try to avoid supporting companies that use sweatshops. It certainly takes the joy out of finding bargains in a cheap fashion outlet. I'm not sure I want to wear a summer dress that has been sewed under extreme duress.

So who are the worst offenders? You can bet that every big brand that doesn't say otherwise is a culprit. What's a Gorgeously Green girl to do? Most of us have to continue shopping at these big box stores because it works for us financially and geographically, but we are not powerless. On the contrary, we have a voice, and it needs to be heard. My daughter is obsessed with a particular kind of doll that I know is made by a huge corporation with unsavory business practices. I wouldn't buy her one out of principle, but then one rainy afternoon a large box arrived in the mail from Auntie Kay—and my daughter was literally crying with joy as she pulled out the grinning doll. So I signed onto this great Web site (see below), and sent an e-mail to the manufacturer saying that I needed them to manufacture its toys in a responsible manner or I would boycott it entirely. The truth is that I will have to go there now, apparently quite often, because this doll, Charlotte, needs "bunches of clothes," according to my extremely privileged little girl.

I suggest going to *www.sweatshopwatch.org*. This is a brilliant Web site where you can join in the fight against a particular brand that is doing dirty business. This organization is not afraid of naming the worst culprits. You can scroll down and not only find out who they are but what you can do to help them stop their unfair practices. Always remember that you are extremely powerful because they want you as a customer. That one e-mail makes a difference.

Go to the following Web sites to purchase sweatshop-free basics:

- *www.thegraincollective.com*
- *www.sweatfree.org*
- *www.nosweatapparel.com*
- *www.tonicshirts.com*
- *www.americanapparel.net*

I've also discovered that many of the fantastic organic clothes designers springing up during this green revolution sell clothes that are made locally and responsibly. They are typically very open about where and how their garments are made. You will pay a little more, but it's a small price for something that benefits the people who made the clothing. It's just not fair that most of the big-brand designers have CEOs on multi-million-dollar salaries and at the bottom of the food chain there are workers who can barely afford to eat. Let's force them to change!

Fair Trade

Now let's take a step beyond how the garment was put together and think about whether the people who produced the cotton to make our cute little shirt were treated fairly as well. This takes us into the realm of fair trade. We want to make sure that the cotton producers get a fair price for their crop. Organic often goes hand in hand with fair trade, and I'll go into this a bit later.

According to **Coop America** (*www.coopamerica.org*), fair trade is "an alternative trading system that creates opportunities for farmers and artisans who are most vulnerable and most disadvantaged by conventional trade." Fair trade ensures that the farmers get a fair price and that sustainability is practiced. It also ensures that workers, especially women, are empowered.

Chocolate and coffee have been a huge point of focus for fair trade, because most of the world's cocoa and coffee beans are grown on small family farms and are the main source of income for family farmers in areas like the Ivory Coast in West Africa. You can buy the following crops with a "Fair Trade Certified" seal: tea, chocolate, sugar, rice, vanilla, and fresh fruit.

An organization called **Trans Fair USA** is an independent third-party certifier of fair-trade products. They have an excellent Web site, *www.transfairusa.org*, where you will discover that many fair-trade products are stocked in the large stores in which you shop. Go to the site and click on "Fair Trade in Stores" to find out the specific stores and items. It's important to remember that each time you purchase just one fair-trade item, you're telling the store that you want to buy these items because you are a conscious shopper.

Fair-Trade Coffee and Chocolate

Some big companies use child slaves in the harvesting of cocoa beans. Many work twelve- or fourteen-hour days with no pay, little food and sleep, and frequent beatings.

Bearing this in mind, you *always* want to buy fair-trade chocolate and coffee. Fortunately, they are easy to find and often have the bonus of being organic. If your local grocery store doesn't stock these fair-trade items, have a go at the manager and tell him or her to get with the program.

Look for a "Fair Trade Certified" label to make sure you're getting the real McCoy. Check out these Web sites:

❀ *www.greenmountaincoffee.com*
❀ *www.chocosphere.com*
❀ *www.taraluna.com*

Second Skin

Clothes are our second skin. They express who we are and can be an utter delight. We should never feel guilty about wanting to adorn ourselves with beautiful fabrics and accessories. That being said, we need to buy clothes that are made with love for the earth. What does this mean? Garment production can wreak havoc on the environment: pesticides, chemicals, and carbon emissions are all to blame. Mercifully, we can partially get around this by buying natural, organic, and locally made clothes that are every bit as fabulous as anything you will see on the runway.

Do bear in mind that there isn't a 100 percent perfect solution. There is so much to consider: Let's take the life of a canary yellow cotton skirt that I recently bought. Assuming the cotton was organically produced, I get a star; another if it was not made in a sweatshop. But now comes the murky business of dyeing the fabric. Dye is very toxic unless it is vegetable dye, and vegetable dyes typically create sludgy earth tones that aren't everyone's cup of tea. Instead of bright yellow, I would have gotten a dreary shade of mustard. The solution for many organic designers is to use low-impact dyes that are not *as* bad—but it's still dye that can pollute our water supplies. Moreover, the dyeing process uses a lot of water, and only some of the dye houses are equipped to recycle it. Then I have to factor in the fossil fuel that was burned in getting the cotton to the factory, the dye house, the shop, and then home to my closet—my carbon imprint isn't looking quite so good, and there I was feeling oh-so-smug about my fabulous *organic* purchase.

We don't want to drive ourselves crazy with all this carbon imprint detail, and eventually many of the negative aspects of production will change. For now, adding the odd organic item to your wardrobe is a very good place to start. I feel so sexy when I wear soft organic cotton clothes that empower the people who make them.

Retail Therapy

When you've saved a bit of cash, you may want to get Gorgeously Green by checking out some of the superchic eco-lines I have discovered. No need to get in the car—just shop from the comfort of your home, which actually brings up the question: Is shopping online eco-friendly? After weighing up the pros and cons, I've come to the conclusion that it is.

Although shopping online involves a lot of packaging and shipping, according to Joseph Rom, author and executive director of the Center for Energy & Climate Solutions, shipping ten pounds of packages by overnight air—the most intensive energy delivery mode—still uses 40 percent less fuel than driving round-trip to the mall, and ground-shipping by truck uses only one-tenth the energy of driving yourself.

The Internet also avoids the need for commercial building space, which has a heavy impact on the environment, and it reduces traffic congestion. So remember that each minute spent driving to the mall uses more than ten times the energy of a minute spent shopping online when using ground-shipping.

I understand that it's not every girl's cup of tea to shop for clothes online, since not being able to try things on can obviously be a total pain. You may be lucky enough to live in a big city where organic and sustainable shops are springing up all over the place. In that case, hop on your bicycle or a bus and away you go!

Living here in Los Angeles, the shops that sell really great organic clothes are spread very far apart and many carry a limited selection, so I'm lessoning my carbon footprint by buying online. The great news is that the green movement is forcing big retailers to carry organic clothes, towels, and linens, not only to save face, but also to keep up with customer demand. If you are going to one of these enormous stores for all your basics, it makes eco-sense to shop for everything under one roof.

I am obsessed with lovely clothes, and it is the one area where I won't compromise. I was astonished to find that major celebrities like U2 singer Bono's wife, Ali Hewson, has designed beautiful garments that are completely organic and made in the United States. You'll pay a little bit more than you would at the big-brand stores, but the clothes will last much longer (my cheap clothes look terrible after only two washes!).

Remember that you vote with your dollars. Organic clothing will become more reasonably priced if we spend our dollars on it. A friend of mine has just created a fabulous organic clothing line. She said that because of demand, the price of organic cotton is going down. Let's keep demanding it so that the prices will match those of the bigger stores. Think about it—if just 10 percent of everything we bought was eco-friendly, we'd put billions of dollars into the green economy.

Why Organic?

I used not to bother with the organic clothes thing. I sort of understood food, but surely it wasn't going to harm my skin to wear a nonorganic T-shirt. It may not harm your skin directly, although that's debatable, but what will harm you are the chemicals that are used and developed every year to deal with the pests that can destroy the crops. If the chemicals are strong enough to kill the pests, the chemicals are strong enough to kill animals and seriously harm people. Moreover, they pollute the air, water, and soil. Many pesticides are known carcinogens. Enough said. Gorgeously Green is all about caring for you and your fellows.

Eco-Community

As I have been living in the green space for the past few years, I have met some amazing human beings who really want to make a change. I am humbled by their commitment to only use products that will have little or no impact on our planet. Each of these men and women has a story about how they got to a place in their life where they needed to live their deeper values. Having personally gotten to know some of these individuals, I want to wear their clothes even more, not only because they are beautiful and organic, but also because they were made with good conscience and love. When I wear clothes that have been made with a deep understanding of the interrelatedness of all things, it makes me feel fantastic. Eco-conscious clothes have good juju!

One such story is about a great company called **Sameunderneath** (*www.sameunderneath.com*). The owner, Ryan Christensen, says, "I want to change the way people look at each other." Their logo "represents something larger than words; it is a symbol for education, truth, and progressive thinking." How cool is that! The clothes are made from sustainable bamboo and are silky soft. Ryan's wife is the designer.

Patagonia (*www.Patagonia.com*) is a large international company with incredible ethics. They primarily sell hip and functional sports and casual wear and have been in the forefront of the sustainable clothing movement for years. They have awarded $25 million to environmental groups across the globe. Every item you buy will have a tag with their 1 percent pledge on it, meaning they send that amount to varied groups. I love the Common Threads recycling program that they started in 2005. Customers can bring in old clothing and Patagonia will recycle it. The CEO, Casey Sheahan, says, "We hope to expand the worldview of recycling beyond just aluminum cans, newspapers, and bottles. We're aiming to make clothing a recyclable recourse." Now you know where to go for your sports togs.

ITS TRUE: A conventional cotton T-shirt uses 150 grams of pesticides— that's a whole cup of sugar!

The Good News

According to the Organic Exchange, a nonprofit trade association, organic cotton sales are seriously growing, so much so that they are expected to reach more than $2 billion by the end of 2008. Organic cotton, however, still makes up only 1 percent of the cotton produced in the world. Large retailers like Wal-Mart, Target, and Victoria's Secret are carrying or are about to offer organic lines, and Nike is one of the largest retail users of organic cotton in the world. You'll find that these lines are only marginally higher in price, so you don't have to remortgage the house to go eco-chic.

Gorgeously Green Picks

Fashion—For the latest eco-licious style tips and fashion trends, visit *www.gorgeouslygreen.com*. Simply type the password that you see below into the search bar. Password: Knockout.

Casual Everyday Items

❀ I adore **Loomstate** (*www.loomstate.org*). It makes all kinds of casual wear—great jeans, bashed-up denim skirts, and cute T-shirts. You can look for bargains at www.amazon.com. The company has also designed a special Green line for Barneys of New York.

❀   **Stewart + Brown** (*www.stewart+brown.com*) obtains its cashmere exclusively from cashmere herders in a remote region of Mongolia, providing the nomadic herders with an income. The company makes fabulous tops—T-shirts, long-sleeved shirts, and knitwear—all very chic and beautifully made. Also at *www.amazon.com*.

❀   A Los Angeles–based company, **Del Forte** (*www.greenloop.com*) makes the most fabulous-fitting jeans out of organic cotton—love them.

❀   **Under the Canopy** (*www.underthecanopy.com*) has an underwear and nightwear line that is to die for! Soft, dusky pastels in fine-ribbed organic cotton. It also makes bed linen and bathrobes, which make wonderful gifts, and it has a great selection of tops and bottoms.

❀   **Water Girl** (*www.watergirlusa.com*) is an offshoot of Patagonia and is devoted to helping the environment. It uses 100 percent organic cotton and has an extensive sportswear and swimwear line. I am in love with a couple of the company's bikinis.

❀   **Nau** (*www.nau.com*) is an interesting brand-new company with a high-concept design. It already has four or five stores across the nation. I strongly recommend you visit its awesome Web site, where you are asked to submit inspiring stories and you learn about the company and why it is committed to sustainable business practices. The clothes are everyday, outdoor/office, cool and trendy pieces that are reasonably priced.

❀   **The Grain Collective** (*www.thegraincollective.com*) is a really interesting company that sells fabulous basic shirts for men and women that are made out of bamboo and organic cotton. Check out its cool Web site to learn more about what these inspiring dudes are up to.

❀   Look for the **American Apparel** (*www.americanapparel.com*) Sustainable Edition to find reasonably priced basics.

❀   **Blue Canoe** (*www.bluecanoe.com*) is a really great company for office basics, great classical T-shirts, and a good line of sensible underwear.

❄ **No Sweat Apparel** (*www.nosweatapparel.com*) is where you need to go for boots, work clothes, pants, and T-shirts that were totally not made in a sweatshop.

❄ At **Hemp Sisters** (*www.hemp-sisters.com*), check out this company's hemp beanie, and its scarves and gloves are a winter must. They are reasonably priced and make great gifts.

❄ **Rawganique** (*www.rawganique.com*) is a fabulous company that carries one of the largest selections of certified organic hemp. Instead of cranking up your heat in the winter, purchase a couple of sets of its organic thermal fleece long johns.

❄ **Stella McCartney** (*www.stellamccartney.com*), daughter of Paul, has followed in her late mother's footsteps as an activist who promotes animal- and eco-friendly living. She has teamed up with sportswear giant Addidas to create a fabulous line of yoga clothes. They are superstylish—you will pay a bit more, but it's Stella McCartney—hello!

Funky/Fabulous

❄ **Undesigned** (*www.undesigned.com*) is owned by a native Angeleno, Carol Young, who has designed a series of beautiful and functional pants, dresses, and skirts. Carol uses bamboo and a lot of organic cotton. She makes everything herself in a small studio behind her store, and she has an adorable little terrier called Dora, who keeps watch. I'm in love. You can easily order her clothes online. They run pretty true to size.

❄ **Prairie Underground** (*www.prairieunderground.com*) is a wonderful Seattle-based company created by Davora Lindner and Camilla Eckersley. Their collection is very unusual—funky and fun. Whenever I wear my Prairie Underground dress, everyone wants to know where I got it.

❄ Ali Hewson and her husband, Bono of U2, have teamed up with designer Ronan Gregory to create the most beautiful clothing line called **Edun** (nude backwards) (*www.edunonline.com*). The collections are stylish and elegant. Her attention to detail makes each piece something you will treasure for years.

❀   Samantha Robinson and Karen Kananen created **Raw Earth Wild Sky** (*www.rawearthwildsky.com*), a line of easy-to-wear beautiful organic pieces that are also affordable. Their practices are ethical and sustainable from top to bottom. They care as much about the machinist sewing their clothes as they do about the gorgeous buttons and unusual trims. Many of the garments have rough, unfinished edges, which Samantha explains is "great, because if it's too long, you just cut off the bottom—no need for the added cost of going to a tailor!"

❀   **Peligrosa** (*www.peligrosaknits.com*) has comfy cashmere knits to die for. Everything is sustainable, from the low-impact dye to the coconut buttons.

Reusable Tote—Be a trendsetter and save the planet when you choose to ditch both paper and plastic. Take advantage of the special offer to receive your FREE ChicoBag—the trendy reusable tote that turns your shopping from gray to green. Visit *www.gorgeouslygreen.com* and type in the password that you see below into the search bar. Password: mychicobag.

❀   **Sworn Virgins** (*www.hoopladc.com*) makes the most fabulous bamboo dresses. They are soft, sexy, and work for day and night.

❀ How do you make an eco-friendly pair of sunglasses? With wood! And that is exactly what **I Wood Design** (*www.iwooddesign.com*) does. So if you want to emulate a Hollywood starlet, splash out and get yourself a pair.

❀ **Two Bees Cashmere** (*www.twobeescashmere.com*) was founded by Whitney Tremaine in 2003. I love her light, cashmere tops, which are great for layering.

Ecoture

❀ Where do the eco-stars shop? There are a few couture designers who are committed to going green. British designer **Deborah Milner** (*www.deborahmilner.net*) has designed an exquisite collection of gowns that are completely eco-friendly. She has visited the Yawanawa tribe in the Brazilian rain forest and learned about their eco-friendly methods for harvesting dyes. She is committed to sustainable and fair-trade ingredients. Milner has teamed up with the personal care giant, Aveda, which presents her globally.

❀ **Stella McCartney** (*www.stellamccartney.com*) has designed a line of sexy couture shoes with a leather-like plant derivative. You can find her shoes in most of the big, fancy department stores. Her clothes are mouthwatering; however, I would probably have to remortgage my house to dress in Stella. I'm a great believer in creative visualization, though, and I can *soooo* easily see my little feet in a pair of her eco-sandals.

❀ **Deborah Lindquist** (*www.deborahlindquist.com*) has designed red carpet–worthy frocks for celebrities and Gorgeously Green gals! She makes a lot of clothes out of old and recycled fabrics. I'm in love with her recycled cashmere cardigans and dresses.

❀ The talented **Linda Loudermilk** (*www.lindaloudermilk.com*) has created the most stunning couture collection I have ever seen. Her jeans are incredible and totally worth saving up for. Check out her Mission Limited Edition lines, where she brings a pressing environmental issue to the fore through really cool jewelry and T-shirts.

Oh—If I Really *Must* Buy Them!

I know many of you girls detest shoe shopping—it's so boring, and who cares about what we put on our feet, anyway? If you happen to be one of those bizarre females who actually likes to purchase shoes, you need to realize that you, too, can do your part to protect the environment. You need to look for a company that doesn't use the process of tanning shoe leather. This is a softening process that not only uses chromium (very toxic) but is also very energy intensive. Look for a company that uses recycled leather or that sells vegetable-tanned shoes and is chrome-free.

❀ Look for **Simple**'s Eco-Sneak (*www.simpleshoes.com*)—it's simply the best tennis shoe available and is totally eco-friendly.

❀ **Terraplana** (*www.terraplana.com*) is a British company with great ethical practices and shoes. It uses vegetable-tanned and chrome-free leathers and a bunch of recycled materials.

❀ **Moo Shoes** (*www.mooshoes.com*) is based in New York City but also has an excellent Web site. It is the first cruelty-free shop in the city, and all its shoes and purses are vegan.

❀ **Charmone** (*www.charmone.com*) is what you may want to be saving your pennies for. Gorgeous, dressy eco-shoes that would make even dedicated Jimmy Choo–wearers switch allegiance.

For the Babies and Kids

Now this is where I really have to be held back, as I am a soft touch for beautiful children's clothes. Being a first-time mom with Lola, I was very silly in that I bought all those adorable little baby dresses that lasted a minute. When I was growing up, we were dressed in hand-me-downs, with huge hems, and we were thrilled to get them. Each dress had a story: first it belonged to Aunt Irene in Denmark, then her daughter Helen, who cut a hole in the back with kitchen scissors, then Helen's little sister, and finally *me!* Nowadays, in our horribly disposable society, we tend to buy cheaper clothes and then chuck them away if they have a few stains on them. The Gorgeously Green mom needs to get smart.

Unfortunately, it's unavoidable not to dispose of baby clothes, because they can rarely be handed down due to the spit-up and poop factor, so try to do with as few of these items as possible. Do try to buy organic, especially for tiny babies. Their skin is so delicate that you don't want any harmful chemicals near it. You definitely want to avoid fabrics that are "no iron," as they are often treated with chemicals that I know you would rather not have sitting on your baby's paper-thin skin.

I'm lucky because my daughter wears a school uniform. It is the most awful, itchy nylon fabric imaginable, however. I'm trying to muster up the courage to tackle the headmaster about it, but since Lola has just started the school, I need to pick my moment wisely. It's a treat for her to pick out her weekend and holiday clothes, and I still try to make sure that the few items I buy are organic and good quality. I don't mind paying a bit extra, because I want to be able to hand these pieces down to friends who may need them. I couldn't believe it the other day when a friend of mine turned her nose up at a bag of clothes someone had given her—"ugh, sloppy seconds," she said—so I was the lucky one who went home with a fabulous authentic flamenco dress for Lola, which was stuffed in the bottom of the bag. If my friend had bothered to look, she wouldn't have let that one go.

Lola's best friend, Lily, is always fabulously dressed, and virtually all her clothes are purchased from the local thrift stores. Her dad is an avid collector of weird and wonderful memorabilia, so he spends a lot of time scouring the aisles of Goodwill. Obviously, he has a great eye for kid's clothes, too.

Here are my favorite companies:

❀ **Nina and Tom** (*www.ninaandtomfamilyfashion.com*), a lovely husband-and-wife team, were inspired by their own children to create an eco-friendly collection of fun, educational T-shirts for babies and kids. They hand-print every shirt with water-based dye, use organic cotton, and have the garments made responsibly in the United States.

❀ **Hanna Andersson** (*www.hannaandersson.com*) is a Swedish company that has a great online store, so credit cards at the ready, girls. A portion of every Hanna purchase is donated to support children in need. It gives yearly grants to hundreds of schools and nonprofit groups serving children across the nation. The company also uses the Oko-Tex standard, which is an ecological certification process that tests garments for more than a hundred harmful substances.

❀ I absolutely love **Rawganique**'s (*www.rawganique.com*) beautiful organic clothes for babies and kids.

❀ **Under the Nile** (*www.underthenile.com*) makes all of its children's and babies' lines out of 100 percent organic Egyptian cotton. They are simple and *sooo* soft.

❀ If nothing else, I make sure that my daughter sleeps in organic cotton. I buy the most fabulous organic long johns with a classic stripe from **Garden Kids Clothing** (*www.gardenkidsclothing.com*).

❀ For fabulous funky tie-dye sleepwear, check out **Lapsaky** (*www.lapsaky.com*).

❀ **Green Babies** (*www.greenbabies.com*) is one of the leading companies that specializes in organic baby and children's clothes. It has been around for years and creates really beautiful designs, especially for little girls.

❀ To avoid my child sleeping in a toxic cocktail (most mattresses made before 2008 use a toxic flame retardant called PBDE), the only safe alternative is to go for an all-organic mattress. **Eco Baby** (*www.ecobaby.com*) is the only company I know that regularly tests its materials and will provide the results to you.

If you prefer to shop at a major retailer for your children, ask the managers of the store if they carry any organic lines (many of them are starting to). If they don't, tell them how important it is to you, as a loyal customer, that they start stocking items that are environmentally friendly and safe for your kids.

For the Pets

Given that 63 percent of U.S. households have a least one pet, it's worth seeing if we can make any positive changes in this area. The most important item to avoid is a conventional flea collar, as it will likely contain extremely toxic chemicals that are not only harmful to humans but even more so to the animal on whose neck it is wrapped around. Remember that children will often put their faces up close to a pet's neck. Flea powders, lotions, and "bombs" should be avoided.

❀ Homeopathic herbal flea and tick collars can be purchased at **Holistic Family and Pets** (*www.holisticfamilyandpets.com*).

❀ Flea 'n Tick B Gone is a great alternative to flea powder and can be bought at **Sixwise** (*www.shop.sixwise.com*).

So now for the fun stuff:

❀ **Skooper Box** (*www.skooperbox.com*) is a biodegradable container for scooping the poop.

❀ **Poop Bags** (*www.poopbags.com*) is the eco-version.

❀ Make sure your little pooch or kitty plays with eco-friendly toys made out of hemp or recycled goods at **Ecoanimal** (*www.ecoanimal.com*).

❀ If you want to buy an eco-cat collar, you will find an dorable hemp and organic cotton one at **Green Kitty** (*www.greenkitty.com*).

❀ A friend of mine's puppy apparently loves her cool polar fleece bed from **Bone To Pick** (*www.bonetopick.com*).

❀ This is what I'm going to buy for my mother's black pug—an organic kimono from **Sckoon Organics** (*www.sckoonorganics.com*).

❀ **Heidi's Homemade Bakery** (*www.heidishomemadebakery*) makes organic doggie treats look good enough for humans.

❀ You can buy **Animal Spirit**'s truffles for two (*www.downbound.com*), meaning one for you and one for your dog!

Thrift Stores

The other day at dinner, a good friend of mine invited along her client, who was astonishingly gorgeous—not just her energy but also the way she was dressed. I immediately wanted to know where she had gotten her dress, shoes, and coat. She smiled and told me that she shops at only thrift stores. She is obsessed with vintage. We all looked on enviously as she told us how she picks out shirts or dresses that she loves and then takes them to her local tailor to alter so that they fit her perfectly. How original, innovative, and green. She'll never bump into someone wearing an identical dress—speaking of which, I bought a coat on sale from a major chain store a couple of years back. I loved it and still do; however, every time I wear it, I see at least two other people with the same coat. Needless to say, I've now gone off wearing it. I haven't the heart to throw it away, so I may dye it or "thrift store" it. Another "I told you so" from the husband—ugh!

So if you have time this week, go to at least one thrift store and let your imagination soar.

Take Care

Taking great care of every possession you own is the greenest thing you can do. Cheap mass-produced clothes don't last long however well you care for them. I don't think they are designed to withstand more than a few machine washes. You are supposed to get rid of them and then buy more. Your new organic cotton, hemp, and silk clothes, however, will last for years and years if you treat them well.

Dry-Cleaning

This is a huge environmental issue. Regular dry-cleaners should be avoided at all costs for two simple reasons: First, they are horrible air polluters. Second, the chemicals they use can be carcinogenic for you and your family.

Once I understood the horrors of a chemical called perchloroethylene (which the government is phasing out because it knows it is dangerous), I legged it to the nearest environmentally friendly cleaner I could find. Luckily, in Los Angeles there are quite a few choices. Go online to find the nearest in your area. You'll definitely pay a bit more, but it's your health. A bit more on the hideous perchloroethylene—perc for short—it's the sharp, sweet-smelling odor on your freshly cleaned clothes. It can also be found in shoe polish. The U.S. Environmental Protection Agency has found that emissions from freshly dry-cleaned clothes cause levels of perc to rise in the home. It accumulates in fatty tissue and breast milk.

For cleaning, I go to a business in a cute red brick building that prides itself on being green. George, the owner, is always there with a smile on his face. He cares about his work and creates an environment that is quite lovely: there is always classical music playing, and the ladies who work for him float happily around, clearly proud of their workplace. It actually smells pleasant compared with the last place I went, with its acrid chemical fumes and blistering heat. The owner (don't know his name) never smiled at me in the three years I went there. He had a permanent scowl—not unsurprising, given the man was daily pumping toxic pollutants by the dozen into the blue California skies. It bothered me that I only lived half a mile away from his vile establishment, but as my husband pointed out, if you live in a big urban sprawl like Los Angeles, these pollutants are everywhere.

Wet-Cleaning

This is very safe, and we will see a lot more wet-cleaners springing up as people demand better and safer care of their clothes. Regular dry-cleaning is as it sounds. The clothes simply have chemicals poured onto them. I find that gross, because they never get really clean. I much prefer the idea of the wet-cleaning where the garment gets a proper wash but in a very delicate manner. Nowadays, I dry-clean only if I absolutely have to. If the label says "Dry-Clean Only"—*only* being the operative word—then it will have to go. Note that if a garment says "Dry Clean" without the "Only," you really don't need to go to the expense.

Check out a cleaner near you that offers either wet-cleaning or a liquid carbon dioxide cleaning, because it's much safer for you and the environment. To find a wet cleaner, go to *www.nodryclean.com*. To find a liquid carbon dioxide cleaner, go to *www.findco2.com*. Be wary of many cleaners who claim to be environmentally friendly or green, as this is often a bit of a white lie. You need to grill them and find out exactly what they are using. Here are some of the dodgy methods to look out for:

Hydrocarbon is not at all green. Hydrocarbon is made from fossil fuels and pollutes as much as regular petroleum. Some cleaners claim that it is organic, but this is totally misleading.

Solvair is a machine that replaces perc with glycol ether, which is a toxin. These machines rinse your clothes with liquid carbon dioxide, so the cleaner may tell you they are just a "liquid CO_2 cleaner," purposely leaving out the Solvair part of the equation.

Greenearth is a method that replaces perc with soloxane or D-5, which is similar to the ingredients found in deodorants and shaving cream. The Environmental Protection Agency has noted that D-5 may be a carcinogen.

With this information in hand, ask your local environmentally friendly cleaner which process is used. If you are not satisfied with the cleaner's answer, move on. I am well aware that many of you girls may not find a good liquid CO_2 cleaner in your neighborhood—if this is the case, pick your poison or hand wash instead! I always used to have my cashmere dry-cleaned until my mom came to stay recently. She was appalled at how much they charged and insisted that a girl is much better off hand washing her cashmere anyway—thanks mom! A great friend, Natasha, insists that she gets the best results for her cashmere by machine washing and then a low tumble dry. She says that cashmere retains its original shape much better that way; however, it makes me a little nervous, so I'll stick to the rinsing and wringing and hanging outside to dry.

Ask your dry-cleaner not to pack up your clothes in plastic—again a total waste of a polluting resource. If they refuse (one of the ones I went to did), just tell them that you'll have to take your business else-where. If you are worried about the unlikely event of your clothes get-ting dirty or dusty on the way home, take along a garment bag.

Hand Washing

Whenever possible, I hand wash. It's a bit of a pain but quite gratifying because of the physical energy you will burn. This is the hard manual work that got my mom into shape when I was growing up. I wait until I have three or four sweaters and bras and then I fill a bathtub with two or three inches of water and a little detergent. Don't use too much, as you will be forever rinsing. I swish and squeeze to remove the grime and then start the rinsing process.

A great tip for wet sweaters is to put them in a large dry towel, roll up, and twist the towel as hard as you can. It really helps to have some-one help you. On the weekends, I put my man to good use! (Better still—get him to do the whole thing.) This removes all the excess water so that the sweaters are ready for laying flat to dry.

Gift Giving

One of the most exciting ways in which you can inspire your friends to go green is to buy them eco-friendly gifts. I either make gifts (see page 269) or I go to some of my favorite ethical companies. When a close girlfriend's birthday is coming up, I always ask if she needs anything. Some people are really embarrassed to tell you; however, if you offer some suggestions, you will almost always get an enthusiastic response. "Oh yes! I really need some organic sheets," or "Oh yes! I always forget to buy a reusable coffee mug!"

Here are some good girlfriend gift ideas and where to get them:

Everyone loves to receive a gift that benefits the people who made it, as well as the planet. I'm passionate about an organization called **A Greater Gift** (*www.agreatergift.com*). I sent a close friend, Belinda, a gorgeous cushion embroidered with a tree. She went nuts over it and was so moved by the fact that she could visit this organization and find out exactly who made the cushion. This company promotes the social and economic progress of people in developing regions of the world.

I love to buy organic bed linen and recycled tableware for gifts. I almost always go to a company called **Vivaterra** (*www.vivaterra.com*), where they have a beautiful selection.

For reusable stuff (cups, bottles, and bags), you will find absolutely everything you need at **Reusable Bags** (*www.reusablebags.com*).

Introduce your girlfriends to solar by purchasing either a solar rainbow maker or a solar cell phone charger at **Real Goods** (*www.realgoods.com*).

For yoga gifts, go to **The Y Catalog** *www.TheYCatalog.com*, as 10 percent of its profits go to a worthy cause, plus they have supercool yoga gear that is designed by the goddess-like yoga teacher, Shiva Rea.

A really lovely gift is an aromatherapy diffuser. I suggest an electric one over the models that use candles. They use very little electricity and are safer. I once got into a horrible fire with the candle variety; some oil dripped onto the candle and formed a fireball, which blew up in my face. I guess you'll definitely be going for electric now! There is a great selection at **Aroma Thyme** *www.aromathyme.com*.

A very cool girlfriend/boyfriend/any friend gift is a solar-powered backpack from **Reware** *www.rewarestore.com*. They come in a bunch of different colors and will enable the sun to power all your gadgets.

Jewels

By now, most of us have heard of blood diamonds, and many of us are steering clear of buying these little rocks from their evil traders. Blood diamonds are associated with terrorism, environmental damage, and human rights abuse. All the diamonds that Brilliant Earth and Green Karat sell are from Canada, and they use recycled gold. Traditional gold mining is horrible for the environment, as it devastates large areas, displacing local people and poisoning their water. Here are some companies that respect the workers and the environment:

❀ **Earthwise Jewelry** (*www.leberjeweler.com*) creates beautiful pieces with conflict-free diamonds, fairly traded gemstones, and environmentally conscious metals.

❀ **Brilliant Earth** (*www.brilliantearth.com*) and **Green Karat** (*www.greenKarat.com*) specialize in conflict-free diamonds.

Gold and silver can be horrible for the environment, too. The extraction of these metals causes toxic waste. The open-pit mines are appalling to look at. I have found a couple of great companies that use recycled silver:

❀ **Moonrise** (*www.moonrisejewelry.com*) practices sound mining, fair labor, and ethical sourcing. Its necklaces are beautiful.

❀ **Jennifer Northrup**   (*www.zanisa.com*) creates exquisite bracelets from vintage forks.

❀ **Brian Bentley** (*www.porterhousecrafts.com*) makes cuff bracelets out of recycled flatware.

❀ **Harriete Estel Berman** (*www.harriete-estel-berman.info/jewelry/ jewel.html*) is a metalsmith who makes the most amazing bracelets out of old tomato soup cans and the like. She is pricey, but her bracelets are art pieces.

❀ **Maize Hutton** (*www.maizehutton.com*) designs cute recycled silver earrings at a very reasonable price.

❀ **Kirsten Muenster** (*www.kirstenmuenster.com*) designs one-of-a-kind pieces from ethically sourced materials. If you are thinking of a special girlfriend gift, this may be the place to go.

There's a great fair-trade company called **Fiema** (*www.fiema.com*) that supports a women's cooperative in Ghana. Some of the bracelets are made from recycled plastic containers or recycled glass. They are stunning to look at and very unusual.

Go to **Great Green Goods** *www.greatgreengoods.com* and find some of the most extraordinary recycled jewelry you have ever seen. I love the silver bracelets that are made out of cutlery and the necklaces made from beads that are created from old magazines.

If you feel as passionate as I do about workers in this industry being treated fairly, sign the "No Dirty Gold Pledge" at *www.nodirtygold.org*.

Shopping Changes You Can Make Right Now!

❀ **Shop online.**   But avoid next-day air, because it uses five times the fuel of things sent by ground.

❀ **Purchase in huge amounts.**   It's all about saving on the packaging. Buy a large gallon size of olive oil and the biggest bags of granola you can find. You can always decant them into smaller jars when you get home.

❀ **Bulk food bins are the way to go.**   Most major health food stores have these bins, and they are fabulous because they are way cheaper and greener. If you want to be supergreen, reuse plastic bags from home to fill. A tip is to make sure you have plenty of glass jars and containers at home. Personally, I don't like having unruly bags hanging around in my cupboards. I prefer to store in glass, rather than plastic. You can purchase a great set of pyrex storage containers at *www. shopworldkitchen.com.*

❀ **Choose organic.** Buying products made from organic ingredients is not only healthier and safer for you and your family, but it also helps to protect the groundwater, farmers, and wildlife.

❀ **Share.** Before making a trip to the grocery store, call a couple of neighbors or friends to see if you can shop for them. They can e-mail you a list and it'll save them a trip. It'll be their turn next time! Alternatively, carpool with a couple of girlfriends and enjoy a good gossip on the way.

❀ **Always bring reusable totes to the store**. A great tip is to bring along two or three reusable plastic containers, too. That way, I can save on time, money, and extra packaging at the deli/bakery country. Just have them weigh your salami or cheese and get them to put it straight into your container. They'll put the price sticker on the outside of your container; when you get home, you put it straight in your fridge. Do the same thing when buying a sandwich.

❀ **Save your produce bags.** Save those flimsy produce bags to bring along to your next shop. That way, you'll save time and fossil fuel. It's a pet peeve of mine to have to locate the roll then fiddle around trying to find which end actually opens!

Plastic Containers

I use plastic sparingly nowadays because recent studies have shown that many plastics contain a dangerous toxin called Bisphenol A . (BPA) is a hormone-disrupting chemical that can mimic hormones in your body and has been linked to obesity, prostate cancer, and breast cancer.

BPA can be found in the following:

❀ Beverge cans
❀ Canned food containers
❀ Plastic bottles and containers
❀ Dental fillings and sealants

BPA can leach out of containers when you do one of the following:

❀ Heat containers or bottles
❀ Fill containers with hot liquids
❀ Put acidic foods in containers

It's hard to avoid BPA, but we can minimize our exposure by avoiding the above three actions.

Poop—Yes, Poop

Buy recycled goods whenever you can. It is one of the most important things we can do because we will create more demand for these kinds of products, so recycling will become more efficient and a bigger industry.

At the moment, many of the large recycling companies complain that there is not enough consumer demand, so let's change that right away—and a good place to start is by buying poop! There are many fabulous products available that absolutely do not smell, I promise.

❀ **Great Elephant Poo Poo Paper Company** (*www.poopoopaper. com*). My daughter is tickled pink by the name. It's also a great Web site for kids because they can learn all about the history of elephants and read interesting and fun facts.

❀ **Elephant Dung Paper** (*www.elephantdungpaper.com*). This company works tirelessly to help save the elephants in Thailand. Go to its Web site to read about the founder's moving story.

❀ **Sheep Poop Paper** (*www.creativepaperwales.co.uk*). This company's Web site takes you through the step-by-step process of how this extraordinary paper is made.

❀ **Terracycle** (*www.terracycle.net*). Buy some incredibly effective worm poop fertilizer for your lawn at this company's Website.

Paper, Paper Everywhere

Although it's obvious that we need to use recycled paper whenever possible, it's not always that easy to find. Mercifully, large office supply stores like Staples now stock 100 percent recycled printing paper, and it's no more expensive that the regular stuff.

I love good stationery and am so thrilled that we can now indulge in beautiful paper without harming the environment. Go to one of the following Web sites and order plain recycled paper or cards:

❀ *www.paperorganics.com*
❀ *www.twistedlimbpaper.com*
❀ *www.acorndesigns.org*

Another lovely idea is to buy paper that has seeds embedded in it. You can purchase Grow-a-Note seed-embedded paper from the **Greenfield Paper Company** (*www.greenfieldpapercompany.com*).

Refuelling

I need a few coffee/tea stops during a busy day. I look forward to my vanilla latte midmorning. For your coffee stops, buy a reusable mug. All the major coffee shops have a great selection. Mine is emerald green, and I adore it. It is also easier to carry around than paper cups, which often leak or spill midsip.

Also buy a reusable water bottle. I try to steer clear of plastic bottles because of the risk of biphenyl A, leaching. Most bottled water comes in plastic that has been designed for a one-time use only, so don't refill. The best choice is stainless steel. My favorite bottle is the **Sigg** water bottle (*www.reusablebags.com*), which is made of lightweight metal. There are dozens of cute designs and sizes to choose from. I love that I don't have to deal with empty water bottles rolling all over my car floor anymore, which can be very dangerous if one of them happens to find its way under my brake pedal!

TIP: Scrub out your stainless steel water bottle with on old tooth-brush, hot water, and baking soda, once a week.

Tote in Style

I always used to think that reusing plastic bags was a bit creepy. I'd see those touchy/feely types in Birkenstocks pulling out a dirty canvas bag at the grocery store—ugh. Things have changed. It is now supercool to be seen toting your used bags. It is simply the smartest thing you can do. The real problem is remembering them. I always intend to use them, but I get to the store and they are waiting in my kitchen, or I park far away from the store, get to the cashier, and realize they're sitting in my trunk. A tip is to put them on your passenger seat so that they are right next to your purse. You always have to drill a new habit in, but once you've done it for a month or so, it will become second nature. My husband bought me the cutest grocery bag at *www.blueq.com*, which always gets a lot of compliments. It has illustrations and dialogue from the old *Dick and Jane* books all over it.

Another of my favorites is made out of old juice boxes (*www.ecosys.com*). The totes are made in India, and the trade supports over two hundred local families. My daughter picked one out for me that is covered in juicy red apples—I love it!

The Gorgeously Green Chico Bag is a tiny four-inch pouch that opens up into a large tote (eighteen by eighteen inches). When you're done, you stuff it back into its little pouch that can fit in your pocket or your purse. I highly recommend getting two or three and always keeping them in your purse; that way, if you forget all your other totes, you'll be fine. The bags come in fabulous bright colors, and you can even attach them to your key chain. They also don't get dirty like the canvas totes, so you can avoid the down-at-heel look if you so desire!

Paper or Plastic—No Thank You!

We are faced with this question most every time we reach the cashier at the grocery store. I always used to think that paper was probably better, since you could recycle it, but now I've changed my mind. They are both horrible for the environment and should be avoided at all costs.

Plastic bags are made from petroleum derivatives, so the manufacturing process is unsustainable and extremely polluting. They will live for thousands of years in a landfill, as they do not biodegrade, and they are a menace to marine life. In the garbage process, millions escape and end up in our rivers and oceans, choking and killing many creatures. Never throw your plastic bags in your curbside recycling bin. For the most part, they are not recyclable curbside and become a menace at the recycling plant, where they clog and break machinery. Check out your local grocery store. Many cities have now mandated that stores must have a recycling bin near the entrance or in the parking lot, so the bags can be taken to an appropriate facility.

Paper gets even more complicated. Until recently, I felt very pleased with myself when recycling paper. I had a vision of all of it being carted off to a lovely clean facility nearby, where good-hearted men in hemp shoes sorted it out and then sent it over to more hemp-clad individuals who would recycle it into the eco-paper I always buy. Not the case where I live. Apparently in Los Angeles, most of our paper is shipped to China, where the recycling process is not only costly but seriously polluting (the regulations aren't so strict over there). How ghastly—ships that pump out their carcinogenic fumes in Long Beach Harbor, then travel thousands of miles of burning fossil fuel, and finally, more carcinogenic fumes are puffed into the Asian skies. Moreover, the production of paper in the first place involves pulping, which involves the gassing off of dangerous chemicals during production, and then it has to be repulped when the paper is recycled. I'm probably better off chucking my paper into the regular trash after learning about this process.

I always feel so pleased with myself/smug when I have remembered my shopping totes. I was in Trader Joe's yesterday and the very cute cashier began to applaud my eco-friendly bags to the fury of the woman waiting in line behind me—he went on and on about how cool it was for me to care about the planet and even gave me a little card to fill out that would enter me into a drawing to win $25 of free groceries. "It's Earth Day," he gushed, "and we like to applaud customers with a conscience." I began to feel like the nasty classroom goody-goody, as the woman behind shot me poisonous looks. She clearly needed a stack of paper *and* plastic to carry the contents of her overstuffed cart home. I was doubtful that even those double plastic-inside-paper bags would be strong enough to carry her gallon of milk, two watermelons, and the rest. I hate to be a smarty-pants, but canvas is infinitely stronger than even the double combo, and you don't have to wait while the baggers do the laborious stuffing inside thing.

I have purchased a Simplehuman Profile Can (a small trash can; go to *www.kohls.com*) for my kitchen for two eco-reasons: (1) paper or plastic grocery bags (when I forget my tote) fit perfectly into it, so at least they get a second use; (2) having a smaller trash can has helped me to reduce my daily waste. It just makes me think more about not buying packaging, as I simply have nowhere to put it.

It's all about remembering! Write a note on every mirror in your house and put those totes by the front door, on your car seat, your partner's car seat—whatever it takes. Keep in mind that plastic bags are not even the tip of the iceberg. They have become a symbol of eco-awful.

The Grocery Store Line

Trying to shop to fit into the "twelve items or less line," I'll even shed a few items on my way so that I'll qualify—or try batting my old eyelids at the cashier if I'm one or two over the limit. Problem is, this type of shopping uses more gas, time, and tailpipe emissions, since you need to go to the store more often. Instead of aiming to get out of the store fast, do a massive shop in one session. Sure, it's dull waiting in line, but I make a game of it by looking at other people's food choices. I am very nosey and love to amuse myself by making up stories: Is she having a romantic dinner tonight? Or, he's out to impress his girl with that fancy piece of goat cheese and an expensive bottle of wine.

Instead of trying to get out of the store fast, try to do a massive shop in one session and let your imagination soar as you stand in line.

ITS TRUE: At least half of the pollution that comes from transporting your food is from your drive to the store. The other half is from commercial transportation.

- -

A Highly Inconvenient Truth

It's ironic that with all the modern-day convenience products, life has become so very inconvenient. The amount of trash I have to get rid of is annoying and frightening. While taking a sustainable living course a few years back, I had to weigh my trash every day, *all* of it. Even when I was seriously trying to reduce the amount of packaging and waste that came in and out of my home, I couldn't get away from the hideousness of the gargantuan pile that got spirited away to the landfill on a weekly basis.

- -

Task

See if you can spend an entire day being superaware of the waste that you may be adding to the landfills. It's amazing how immune we are to waste because we are so accustomed to packaging. The other day, I went to the drugstore to buy a few things like dental floss and toothpaste. When I got home and put the items away, I had an entire plastic bag full of cardboard and plastic packaging. So I added considerable waste to the planet with this tiny shopping trip. The only way to decrease packaging is to try to buy big.

At the end of one day of shopping, fill as many used grocery bags as you need to with packaging and take a good look at what is going into the landfill or the recycling container. It makes me feel better to know that my packaging can be recycled, but even that process requires energy for the machinery. Your increased awareness is all that matters.

If you go on a shopping spree this week, see if you can resist most of the bags that the salespeople want to pack your goodies in. It's tough for me because I love to see a new shirt being lovingly wrapped in silky tissue and placed in a colorful bag with fancy handles. I justify it by telling myself I will reuse the bag, but if it's paper, it won't withstand too much reuse. Take the bag in the first store, but when you go to the next one, pack your item with your previous purchase. And say no to tissue paper! It's much cooler to ask for your new bra and panties to be packed alongside your organic apples in a tatty old canvas tote—trust me!

You could also pick one day of the week that is your designated no-shopping day. Remember that everything counts, so keep your wallet firmly shut!

Pick One

Now it's time to check off the one change that you are going to do for this step.

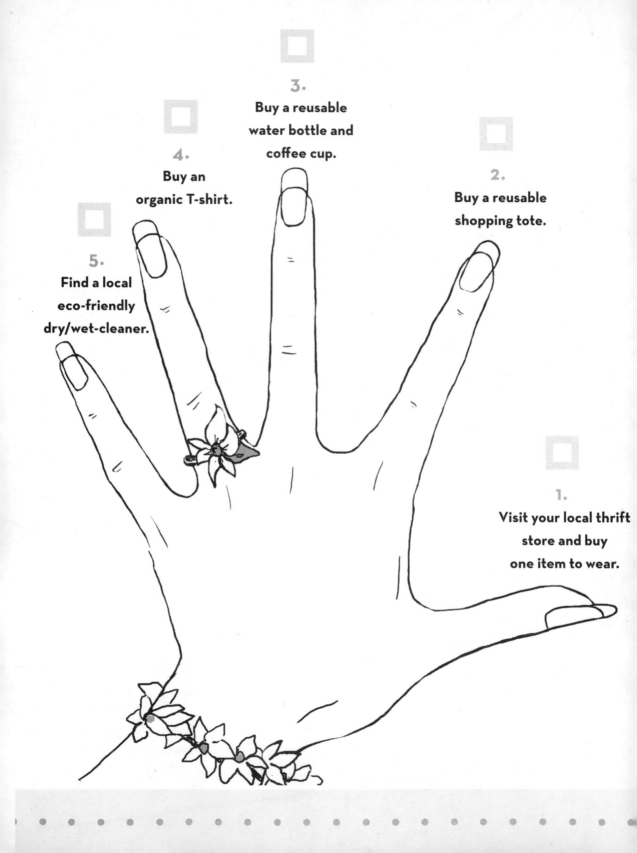

3.
Buy a reusable
water bottle and
coffee cup.

4.
Buy an
organic T-shirt.

2.
Buy a reusable
shopping tote.

5.
Find a local
eco-friendly
dry/wet-cleaner.

1.
Visit your local thrift
store and buy
one item to wear.

Savasana

Yes—another one of those corpse poses is required. How easy that you just get to lie on the floor with your arms and legs outstretched, and you can say you've done yoga today! The misunderstanding about yoga is actually that people think it is not doing any good if it's not unpleasantly hard. Get into position and remember to use cushions to support a dodgy neck and your lower back. Take five very slow breaths—listen to the sound. Then draw your awareness like a scan, starting at your toes, all the way up your body, noticing any areas of tightness or gripping. Let go. Take a few moments to reflect on the new choices that you are making and on some of the actions you have taken in this step, even if it's just reading this chapter. Breathe in peace and breathe out a huge smile.

Chapter Five

STEP 5: Your Palace: Creating the Home You Deserve

Your home should be a palace fit for the green queen that you are fast becoming. My home is a sacred place. I love to get inside and close the door on the world. It makes me feel good to know that I have a safe space to go.

I'm beginning to understand that making my home safer isn't just about installing an alarm system; it's more about making sure that it's a nontoxic zone. In the last chapter, we talked about how dry-cleaning brings hazardous synthetic chemicals into the home; in this chapter, you will discover that there are many toxic culprits.

I absolutely refuse to use anything in my home now that could be even remotely toxic. I have a husband and a child who I want the best for—our health comes first.

Making the change to nontoxic cleaners was not easy for me. My husband calls me Howard Hughes because I'm obsessive about cleanliness, particularly in the bathroom and kitchen. I love gleaming surfaces and I even like the smell of bleach. I used to get manic with my antibacterial counter spray every morning. I thought I was doing the right thing by zapping all the germs and bugs so that we wouldn't catch any nasty viruses. I didn't realize that I was causing more harm than good and that the toxic fumes were infinitely worse.

Having made the decision to switch, I had to get my lovely

housekeeper on board. I'm lucky enough to have the long-suffering Patti come once a week to help me out while I am working. The poor woman has a constantly streaming nose and watery eyes from the allergies she's developed—unsurprising given her close contact with these harsh chemicals every day of her life. I got so passionate about the whole thing that I told her she needed to convert every household she works in to a nontoxic one. She raised her eyebrows, knowing that most of her clients wouldn't go for it, but in my home she'll at least have one day's respite.

Polluting Your Home and the World

The most important thing to realize is that not only do most cleaning products hurt you, but they can seriously harm the environment. They are flushed down our drains, into the storm drains, and finally into our precious water supplies. Many cleaning products contain petrochemical components that are harmful to people, animals, and the environment. They degrade slowly, build up in the environment, and are toxic to aquatic life. Production of these products also requires a massive amount of energy.

There is a lot of talk about running out of water in the not-so-distant future. It is not so much that we will run out of water but that we will run out of *unpolluted* water. Seventy-three different kinds of pesticides have been found in groundwater, which is potential drinking water. It becomes more of a reality when we realize that half the world already has a massive problem with finding fresh drinking water right now. Moreover, the planet is warming up by a significant amount every year. According to researchers at Scripps Institution of Oceanography at the University of California, San Diego, and at the University of Washington, global warming will reduce glaciers and storage packs of snow in regions around the world, causing water shortages and other problems that will impact millions of people. We can make a huge difference by not only conserving water but also by becoming aware of what we flush down our drains on a daily basis.

The Gorgeously Green Solution

Don't worry—you can still have a gleaming palace with eco-friendly household products. I will show you how. I remember visiting a model green house a couple of years ago (the eco-home). It was on an old clapboard house on a college campus, surrounded by a fully native yard. The thing that struck me was how dingy it looked inside. It also smelled a bit stale. I noticed a large box of baking soda in the bathroom with a scrubbing brush that looked as if it had seen better days. The living room was filled with unattractive recycled furniture. Most of the cooking was done in a solar oven outside. Apparently, the oatmeal cookies that were served took two hours to bake. The director, Hilary, offered me one from a scratched plastic container, but it looked highly unpleasant so I politely declined! I came away rather depressed. I understood what they were trying to do, but I knew there had to be a better way. To add insult to injury, it was a hot day, and Hilary clearly eschewed the use of deodorant. It is lucky that the experience didn't put me off the whole thing for life.

The Gorgeously Green solution is the opposite. I want your bathroom as squeaky clean and shiny as you do and your home to smell as wonderful as mine does. Let's start with the hub of the house.

The Kitchen, Laundry, and Overall Cleanup

I spend a huge amount of time in my kitchen. When I'm not slaving over the stove, I'm feeding my daughter, talking on the phone, checking e-mails, or just chatting with friends. I can't relax unless it's clean and relatively tidy (almost impossible with six-year-old madam spreading her mess into more unchartered territory as the day progresses).

Under the Sink

I'm not going to get you to start label reading again. Cleaning products are very simple. Virtually all of your regular cleaners will have to go unless you absolutely know they are nontoxic. We are so used to that strong under-the-kitchen-sink smell that it seems almost natural; however, you are smelling fumes. They are volatile organic compounds (VOCs), which are petrochemicals that give off gases at room temperature. Moreover, their production contributes to greenhouse gas emissions. So you see the term "organic" isn't always a positive thing—it depends on the chemical formulation. When I talk about dangerous chemicals, I am usually referring to *synthetic* chemicals, which have been created in a lab. A basic chemical, such as water, is obviously completely harmless.

To start with, chuck all of your bleach/antibacterial sprays. These "antibacterial" products contain the chemical, triclosan, which degrades quickly when it's exposed to chlorinated tap water, producing dangerous by-products. Triclosan also decomposes into chlorine by-products when it is exposed to high temperatures, so it is in effect rendered useless as a germ buster if you are cleaning with very hot water. Now, these "hospital-strength" virus and germ busters have been truly busted. Fortunately, there are some brilliant alternatives.

Why Not Bleach?

Chlorine bleach is a poisonous gas. It is a hazardous chemical. Never mix it with acid- or ammonia-containing cleaners, because it gives off a highly toxic gas.

When it disappears down the drain, it produces organochlorines, which could be carcinogenic; studies have shown that chlorine bleach could also contain immune system, reproductive, and neurological toxins. It is corrosive and can seriously irritate the skin, eyes, and lungs (which I have actually seen happen to the aforementioned Patti).

Why Go Phosphate-Free?

Buy dishwashing and laundry detergents that are phosphate-free. Phosphates are added to make detergent more effective, but they also cause a lot of trouble. The problem starts with something called algae bloom, which loves to consume phosphates when they drain into our lakes and rivers. Algae gorge themselves, reproduce, and then die. Next up are the microorganisms, which feast on the dead algae, reproduce, and end up stripping the water of oxygen. Eventually, the river or lake dries up. Not a great situation for a planet that needs to conserve its clean water supplies. Years ago, phosphates were eliminated from many cleaning products but not from dishwashing detergents—except, that is, the Gorgeously Green ones.

There are many phosphate substitutes that are added to detergents, liquid soaps, and water softeners to improve cleaning action. Unfortunately, they are not biodegradable and are suspected carcinogens.

Other Hidden Chemicals

Glycol ether (2-butoxyethanol) is often found in window cleaners and floor cleaners that have a strong pine/citrus smell. This chemical was classified as a hazardous air pollutant under the U.S. Environmental Protection Agency's Clean Air Act. High-level exposure to this toxic chemical can cause serious health effects such as nose, throat, and lung irritation, dizziness, headache, and lung/liver damage.

Laundry detergents sometimes contain alkylphenol ethoxylates (APEs)—I encourage you to try pronouncing that one out loud! This chemical is used for stain removal and can damage your immune system and disrupt your hormones. It could also be contaminated with the carcinogenic 1,4-dioxane, which can penetrate the skin.

I'm not going to get any more scientific here, I promise. It just needs to be understood that those innocent-looking products that advertise with images of angelic children bouncing through summer meadows are often filled with chemicals that the Gorgeously Green girl would turn her nose up at. It's also hard to see which of your favorite products contain them because manufacturers are not required to list them on the package.

Be wary of crafty labeling, which is designed to mislead you. When a cleaning product pronounces itself "nontoxic," "hypoallergenic," or "natural," you should be thinking, says *who*? These claims are never verified by a third party, so they are meaningless. Aerosol labels promising "no CFCs" are very silly because chlorofluorocarbons were banned from all aerosols in the seventies.

Finally, don't automatically think a product is green when it boasts that it is "biodegradable." A more credible label will tell you how many days it will take for the product to biodegrade—three days or a century!

Gorgeousy Green Tried-and-Tested Absolute Favorites

There are so many fabulous alternative household cleaning products out there, some of which smell so yummy that you'll want to bathe in them. When you are searching, bear in mind that not all eco-products are supereffective. I've done the testing for you, so take your pick:

Cleaning Products—To get updated on the newest and grooviest eco-cleaning products and household goodies, visit *www.gorgeouslygreen.com* and type in the password that you see below. Password: Dazzle.

Mrs. Meyers (*www.mrsmeyers.com*). I am obsessed with these great products that are formulated with essential oils, which make them smell absolutely wonderful. I love the geranium lemon verbena all-purpose liquids. You can dilute them with hot water for your kitchen floor and walls. A little goes a long way.

Orange Glo (*www.greatcleaners.com*) is brilliant for virtually all countertops. Go online and order three or four, because you will go through them quickly. Buying in bulk saves money and energy.

Citrus Magic 5 in 1 (*www.citrusmagic.com*) is a really strong cleaner for stains, carpets, grills, grease, glue, and even outdoor furniture.

Ecover (*www.ecover.com*) is a tried-and-trusted company with the best Ecological Limescale Remover. You can find it in most Whole Foods stores or order it online. Its dishwashing liquid is also excellent and won't leave residue on your glasses.

❀ **Citra-Solv** (*www.citra-solv.com*) is one of the few eco-friendly dishwashing detergents (along with Ecover) that really works. (There are many green ones that are totally ineffective.)

❀ **Bon Ami** (*www.bonami.com*) is top of the list for all your scrubbing needs (no chlorine, perfume, or dye).

❀ **Orange Guard** (*www.orangeguard.com*) is a miraculous pest-control product for ants, roaches, and fleas.

❀ **Daddy Van's All Natural Beeswax & Lavender Furniture Polish** (*www.pristineplanet.com*) is an absolute must for the Gorgeously Green girl. You will never look back.

❀ **Seaside Naturals All Natural Non-Toxic Dusting Spray** (*www.pristineplanet.com*) is what it claims to be and does a very good job for your quick-shoot-around-the-house dust!

❀ **Lifetime Bathroom Cleaner** (*www.greenfeet.com*) is an eco-friendly product that does a great job and smells fabulous.

❀ **Shower Kleener** (*www.greenfeet.com*) will take care of your tiles beautifully.

Toilet Cleaners

Don't ever buy a conventional toilet cleaner, as it is very likely to contain naphthalene, which is a suspected carcinogen, as well as a mixture of chlorine bleach and other dangerous chemicals.

If you want to save money and don't need fancy bottles, just pour a cup of distilled white vinegar into the toilet bowl every couple of weeks, leave it for about ten minutes, and then flush.

If you want something a little more sophisticated, try one of the following:

❀ **Mrs. Meyers** (*www.mrsmeyers.com*) does a wonderful toilet cleaner in lavender!

❅ Try **Ecos Toilet Bowel Cleaner** (*www.ecos.com*), too.

What about the Germs?

We are a germ-obsessed society. Many argue that with all our antibacterial everything, we are killing the germs that we need for our immune systems. Because of the overuse of antibacterial agents, new strains of viruses and germs are coming alive—same sort of deal as the overuse of antibiotics.

I see all the mothers of my daughter's friends constantly charging after them with fistfuls of antibacterial wipes. One mother even gave her child a midday bath as soon as she got home from preschool. I've done pretty much the opposite. I was the terrible mom who picked up the pacifier from the grocery store floor and stuck it right back in Lola's mouth. She got sick less than any child I know! My parents explained to me that children actually need germs to build a strong immune system. The best bet is to let go of all those wipes (which is more wasted paper and packaging), and just make sure you wash your hands as often as you can remember during the flu season.

It's worth mentioning that most antibacterial handwashes contain some very worrying ingredients. In analyzing one brand, I counted fourteen ingredients that could be harmful to your health. A good old bar of soap is a much better choice.

Remember the villain of the piece is triclosan (mentioned earlier), which is certain to be in most handwashes and wipes. Aside from being harmful to your health, critics postulate that it's causing some really serious drug-resistant bacterial strains to emerge—scary stuff. The best alternatives for wipes are as follows:

❅ **Ecover** (*www.ecover.com*) caters to your every eco-need.

❅ **Earth Friendly Baby's Eco Baby Wipes** (*www.ethicalbabe.com*) are my personal favorite, as they smell so good and are supersoft.

❅ **Clean George Hand Sanitizer** (*www.cleangeorge.com*) is the best-ever hand purifier. It actually moisturizes your hands like lotion, while keeping the germs at bay. It is also alcohol-free.

Scrubbing

Green enthusiasts promote the usage of baking soda and lemon juice as a good all-round cleaner. Unfortunately, I can't get past the image of the dingy bathroom in that eco-home I visited. I do use it for my wooden cutting boards because I like the idea of lemon juice cleaning a surface that food will be on tomorrow. Check out the way the baking soda fizzes when you pour on the lemon juice! I also soak my cutting boards once a week with vinegar to kill any bacteria that may be lurking. As listed earlier, try Bon Ami if you need something to scrub at tough stains or the grime in your sink. Bon Ami is a mild chlorine-free powder made with natural minerals. I use it for cleaning my oven as well. (Don't even think about regular oven cleaners, as they contain chemicals that can damage your kidneys, liver, and digestive tract.) You can buy Bon Ami at most major health food stores or go to *www.bonami.com*.

It's not a great idea to use cellulose kitchen sponges, as they are minibacteria incubators. According to Ellen Sandbeck in her fantastic book, *Organic Housekeeping*, "Scientists collected and tested sponges and dish rags from one thousand kitchens and five American cities. They found dangerous bacteria, including *E.coli*, salmonella, pseudomonas, and staphylococcus, which can cause food poisoning, living on two-thirds of the sponges tested." I use clean dish towels or rags and toss them in the wash pile every day.

Polishing Wood

Conventional spray polishes can contain a plethora of toxic chemicals, including morpholine, which is a skin irritant and can form into carcinogenic nitrosamines. I used to love my dusting sprays and was horrified upon hearing about their toxicity. I now use olive oil with a few drops of lemon or lemongrass essential oil. I love "green" cleaning as it never fails to save me money!

Sexy Cloths

I try to be really green and use old tea-towels, T-shirts, and even underpants for dusting. I must admit that I found myself dusting the television the other day with a pair of my husband's old Calvin Kleins. That being said, a microfiber cloth is a good investment, as it will pick up rather than push around the dust and, of course, it is reusable. You can find microfiber cloths at most hardware stores.

Method (*www.method.com*), which is sold at Target, is a great microfiber mop that also doubles as a floor duster, with disposable dusting cloths that are compostable!

Goo Be Gone

I don't think I'm alone in having a child who really enjoys defacing every available surface with stickers. Lola went through a phase of sticking those annoying little "Hello Kitty" white heads with a pink bow over every conceivable surface in her bedroom. I now try to fish around in those horribly *non*-eco-friendly party bags and confiscate them before she notices. If you haven't had to deal with the chewing-gum-on-brand-new-booster-seat scenario, you're lucky! For all those sticky nightmares, try rubbing an ice cube over the mess. It's often miraculous.

Goo Gone Spray (*www.alwaysbrilliant.com*) is a pretty good bet for the toughest removals.

Moths Be Gone

Never use mothballs. They contain chemicals that are carcinogenic. Instead, make sure that your stored sweaters and woolens are really clean, as moths like dirty, sweaty clothes—and my husband wonders why they always target his closet!

Buy some lavender and cedar wood essential oil and put a few drops of each into a little spray bottle with some water. Mist over clean, stored clothes.

Mozzies Be Gone

Nearly all mosquito repellents are highly toxic. Citronella is the miracle essential oil to put them off. Buy a small bottle of citronella essential oil and then buy a lamp ring. All you have to do is put the lamp ring on top of your compact fluorescent lightbulb (CFL), add a few drops of oil, and you're set. If you are sitting outside, add a few drops of this oil to your favorite moisturizer instead of using insect repellent spray or lotion. It's great for kids and babies, too.

The Absolute Worst of the Lot

Get rid of air fresheners immediately. Fresh air—hello! They cause the dirtiest, most dangerous air you could breathe. Many of them contain formaldehyde, a carcinogen; phenol, which could cause major skin problems; and petroleum distillate, p-dichlorobenzene aerosol propellants, which could cause nausea, diarrhea, and liver and kidney damage if ingested. Not to mention the fragrance that produces the sickly faux flower smell of these ghastly sprays—yuck.

The best way to deal with unwanted bathroom smells is to light a stick of incense. Also, **Citrus Magic** (*www.citrusmagic.com*) air freshener is really effective. Lola and a friend sprayed an entire can over themselves a week ago because they wanted to smell "fabulous" for a party! Thank goodness it wasn't the toxic stuff!

You could also simmer some cinnamon and cloves or a few sprigs of fresh rosemary in a saucepan for ten minutes. When you are done, let the water cool and throw it on your plants.

Eight Must-Have Products for the Gorgeously Green Girl

If you have time, you may want to save lots of money and make your own cleaning products. It's actually incredibly easy and fun, and it will not make your home look or smell like a dingy hippie commune. I use a mixture of the store-bought eco-cleaners and my own. Most importantly, you can save a lot of money.

Stock your cupboards with the following eight products and you can clean just about anything:

1. **White vinegar**—*see the section on vinegar.*
2. **Baking soda**—*eliminates odors and is a good scrubbing powder.*
3. **Borax**—*removes dirt; is antifungal and a possible disinfectant.*
4. **Hydrogen peroxide** (3 percent concentration)—*nontoxic bleach, antibacterial agent, and stain remover.*
5. **Lemon juice**—*grease cutter and stain remover.*
6. **Liquid castile soap**—*all-purpose cleaner, grease-cutter, and disinfectant. Castile means that the soap is vegetable-based and not animal fat-based.*

7. **Olive oil**—*makes great furniture polish.*
8. **Essential oils of lavender, geranium, and tea tree**—*antibacterial and add a great smell to your home.*

Tea Tree Oil

I have a passion for this strong-smelling essential oil from Australia. It is a natural solvent and is brilliant for cutting grease while killing germs and bacteria. They actually swab down hospitals with it in Australia. It also has a variety of health benefits: I put it on sores and cuts; in shampoo for dandruff; on bleeding gums; and dilute it with water for a mouthwash.

Be careful that you're getting the real thing—it comes from the *Melaleuca alternifolia* plant. There are at least one hundred fifty species of the Melaleuca plant, but only the alternifolia one has the healing properties that you need. So check the label. Also, take a whiff before buying, as it should have a very strong smell. You want to make sure it hasn't been diluted. Buy organic if possible. Most large health food stores and many drugstores now stock it. You can also buy it from *www.mountainroseherbs.com*.

Vinegar

Vinegar deserves a paragraph of its own because it is one of the best cleaners. It can sometimes bring to mind the gloomy eco-house, but it is so effective that I have gotten over it. I chuck a cup in the main body of the dishwasher for every other cycle and use it as a drain cleaner with boiling water. Drain cleaners are the same as oven cleaners—avoid them. I also clean out my washing machine with vinegar (run it through a cycle once a month).

Vinegar is the best window cleaner I have ever found. I have tried every tip and method for my windows. I have a large picture window in my living room that birds like to use as a bathroom. Everything leaves a smeared effect except a water/vinegar (half and half) solution. I use old rags from torn-up T-shirts. You can also clean your microwave, kettle, eyeglasses, and lunch boxes with this wonder substance.

Fun Floors

Okay, if you do your own housework, floor cleaning is without doubt the hardest and most tedious job of the lot. Here are my two tips to make it more fun.

1. Be smart and buy a really good vacuum. You get what you pay for. It's an investment, since a top-of-the-line vacuum will last a lifetime and make the job so much easier. My friend Ronnie at the vacuum store says that most of the cheaper models create even more dust, as they haven't got good enough filters. He said if you go for a cheap one, make sure you leave the house for twenty minutes when you're done, as you don't want all that "rubbish" in your lungs! For what it's worth, he recommends any of the **Miele** models (*www.miele.com*).
2. Buy a pair of floor sweeper slippers. from **Hi-Dow** (*www.hi-dow. com*). They are fantastic. Mine are baby pink with the mop thing on the soles. I get a cardio workout while I polish, and we've got a lot of wood floors!

Gorgeously Green All-Purpose Spray

As most conventional all-purpose sprays are made up of a concoction of potentially hazardous chemicals, I have chosen to make my own. It is ridiculously easy to make and I have two or three large spray bottles on the go, all the time. It's brilliantly effective at cutting grease, germs, and grime; it smells wonderful and will save you a lot of money. You can use this spray on just about everything: fridge, countertops, walls, doorknobs (for germs), toilet seats, sinks, and so on.

32-ounce plastic spray bottlei

2 cups water

1/2 cup distilled white vinegar

I teaspoon pure castile soap (peppermint is my favorite)

3/4 cup hydrogen peroxide

20 drops tea tree oil

20 drops of lavender or lemongrass essential oil

Simply fill a large 32-ounce plastic spray bottle with the water. Add the vinegar, castile soap, hydrogen peroxide, tea tree oil, and lavender or lemongrass essential oil. Lavender is lovely for the bathroom spray and lemongrass for the kitchen, so make two separate bottles at the same time. In the hot summer months, I add about 10 drops of citronella essential oil to the spray, as it is an excellent insect repellent.

This spray is suitable for acrylic, ceramic tile, wood, marble, and granite.

Gorgeously Green All-Purpose Heavy-Duty Cleaner

If you need a really strong cleaner for tiles, walls, and doors, try this excellent brew: Fill a bucket with really hot water. Add a squirt of dishwashing liquid, half a cup of baking soda, and 20 drops of tea tree and lavender essential oils. You are saving water by using the bucket rather than running water.

More Trees?

Every time you tear off a few sheets of paper towels, remind yourself that you are helping to cut down forests. I don't want to guilt-trip you— actually, I do! The green girl needs to do one of two things: either switch to 100 percent recycled paper or just use old cut-up towels and rags and throw them in the washing machine when you have a full load. I must admit that giving up paper towels is one of the hardest habits to kick. It's so much easier to mop up my cutting board with paper and chuck it. I don't relish the idea of having to wash out a cloth that is ingrained with tomato seeds and cheese gratings. Yes, it's more work for sure, but saving the world sometimes requires a bit of elbow grease.

TIP: Keep a large bag or an empty trash can full of old rags. Keep one or two of them handy in the kitchen every day and use for all mopping up and wiping. At the end of the day, chuck them in the washing machine, but wait until you have a full load.

IT'S TRUE: If every household in the United States replaced just one roll of virgin fiber paper towels with 100 percent recycled ones, we could save 544,000 trees (National Resources Defense Council).

Final Cleaning Tips

The best-ever silver cleaner is toothpaste, but if you can't face the smell or don't believe me, you can always try putting a large pot of water on to boil, add 1 teaspoon of both salt and baking soda, and immerse the silver in the boiling water. Turn off the heat and leave for sixty seconds, then polish with a dry cloth. Or try the **Twinkle Silver Cleaning Kit** (*www.drugstore.com*).

If you need to polish shoes, avoid regular polishes, as they are highly toxic. Use either olive oil or the inside of a banana skin. The latter leaves a residue that you need to vigorously polish off, but it's worth the work to get a sweet-smelling shine.

Greener Plastic

Toxic chemicals such as dioxin and benzene can be released into the environment during the production of certain types of plastic, and some types leach chemicals in the landfill. Choose your plastics wisely not only to protect the planet but also your health.

Always pick plastics labeled with number 1, 2, 4, or 5; avoid those labeled with number 3, 6, or 7 (in the chasing arrows on the bottom of every container). However, even with the "better" plastics, you can still get chemicals leaching into food. The Institute for Agriculture and Trade Policy has issued a "Smart Plastics Guide" that includes the following guidelines:

1. *Avoid using plastic containers in the microwave. Use glass or ceramic containers instead.*
2. *Try not to use cling wraps, especially in the microwave.*
3. *Avoid plastic bottled water, if possible.*
4. *Discard old or scratched bottles. Water bottles with numbers 1 and 2 on them are for single use only.*

Be especially careful with plastic baby products, particularly baby bottles. You want to avoid number 7, which is polycarbonate and has the ubiquitous bisphenol-A that can leach into the milk or water. Evenflo and Medela make bottles from safer plastic, and you can be sure to get a safe bottle from Green to Grow (*www.greentogrow.com*). A fantastic organization called **Healthy Child Healthy Planet** recommends using bottle nipples made of clear silicone, because they hide less bacteria than the yellow rubber ones and are heat resistant. It's worth spending a little time browsing *www.healthychild.org* as they have a ton of information about keeping your baby's environment safe.

Whiter Than White

I want my white sheets and towels to be blindingly white. This is not easy for the green goddess, because if you are committed, you are not going to want to use bleach or any laundry powders that contain chlorine bleach/bleach alternatives. The cleaning product manufacturers call these whitening agents "optical brighteners." This is because the blinding blue/white that we see is really just a special effect created by certain chemicals that absorb ultraviolet light and emit it back as blue light. So understand that whiter does not nescessarily mean cleaner. That said, a lot of people really want the white, regardless. There are two natural alternatives: one is to add half a cup of lemon juice and the other is to add a couple of scoops of **Oxo Brite Non-Chlorine Bleach** (*www.ecos.com*).

If you have hard water, it's a really good idea to add a cup of borax to every load. It will help the detergent to work more efficiently. You can buy borax at most large grocery stores and all health food stores. My favorite laundry detergents, both of which smell amazing, are:

❀ **Mrs. Meyers Laundry Detergent** (*www.mrmeyers.com*). The lemon verbena and geranium smell so good that you'll want to bathe in them.

❀ **Oxy-Prime Powdered Laundry Detergent** (*www.oxyboost.com*) really works on whites and is nontoxic and contains no phosphates. It is effective at all temperatures.

❀ **Method Laundry Detergent** (*www.methodhome.com*), which you can find at large chain stores including Target, Kmart, and Sav-On. It smells great and does a very good job.

My family thought I needed help when I told them last week that I was going to switch to "soap nuts" for our laundry. I gingerly held out two little brown nuts that come from the "soap tree." ("For real!" as my daughter says.) The presentation met with a stony-faced silence by my husband and uproarious laughter from my daughter—she wanted to plant them. Undeterred, I stuffed the washer with a grubby white load and threw in the nuts. The result was a fresh-smelling, snowy white bundle of towels and underpants—so there! **Maggie's soap nuts** (*www.maggiespureland.com*) come in a cute little muslin bag in which to put them for washing.

Go green with your fabric softeners, too. I use softeners only for towels. **Sun and Earth Ultra Fabric Softener** (*www.sunandearth.com*) is a really great product.

If you want to save your pennies, add half a cup of baking soda to the rinse cycle and feel the difference!

Not So Hot!

I always used to think that if I used the hot-water setting, my clothes would get cleaner. I now realize this is not the case and that even the cold setting's water is slightly warm. I use the warm setting for whites and mixed loads and the cold setting for dark loads.

Simply changing to the cold/warm setting instead of the hot will make a big difference in your utility bill and your impact on the environment.

Don't Burn Your Clothes

My husband swears I have ruined all his clothes in the dryer. It's not true, although there has been a bit of shrinkage, I'll admit. A few years ago, my mum sent him some very expensive pajamas from England. One evening, I heard terrible cussing from our bedroom, and my husband appeared in what on first glance seemed to be a pair of stripy clam diggers. "Yes?" I demanded defensively. He just stared at me. I tried to blame it on our housekeeper, Patti, but he wasn't amused.

Since becoming Gorgeously Green, I try not to use the dryer at all in the summer. Living in southern California, I air-dry virtually everything, which saves me even more on the energy bills. I grew up with washing lines in the English countryside, so it is very nostalgic for me to bury my face in freshly air-dried laundry—slight difference in the L.A. smog, but oddly enough, a similar fresh smell. I strongly suggest buying any kind of outside drying device that takes your fancy. You would be amazed by the amount of choices available: you can get a basic retractable washing line, a fancy drying rack, or even a contraption that looks like a massive umbrella and spins around in the wind. If you live in an apartment, be like the sexy Italians and buy a small wooden drying rack, then set it by an open window or on a balcony. The huge bonus is that your clothes will last so much longer. Over time, the dryer ruins clothes. Check out **Urbanclothesline** *www.urban-clothesline.com* for a fantastic selection of drying devices.

I do have to iron a bit more now that I air-dry; however, I find it quite therapeutic with the right music playing and a good friend to have a gossipy chat with. A good tip is to whip your things in before they get completely dry; then you can smooth and fold without having to iron or put them in the dryer for a quick fluff.

If you don't mind your towels being a bit scratchy—which I love—air-dry whenever possible, because they take the longest in the dryer. It's also prudent for the Gorgeously Green girl to buy smaller bath towels. Those massive bath sheets use a terrific amount of water in the wash. My husband, all six foot four of him, wasn't thrilled when I presented him with a smaller-than-usual new organic towel. "What the . . . ," he moaned, holding up the almost napkin-size towel. "This will dry my arm if I'm lucky!" I'm glad to report he is now used to them and is secretly pleased that it has saved us a good deal of money.

I never use drying sheets—those awful flimsy little things that you put in with your drying load. They are a total waste of paper and money and are often filled with synthetic chemicals. You don't need them.

My husband is thrilled about my old-fashioned laundry techniques. His T-shirts have never looked better. That being said, he is a little concerned about the new outdoor decor—dish towels, shirts, and underwear strewn over hedges and bushes (better than drying racks). I sometimes agree to take them in before entertaining!

Energy-Saving Stuff

White Goods

We are talking about all your kitchen and laundry room appliances here. Let's change our white goods to green goods. If you are moving or considering buying a new kitchen appliance, you would be very wise to check out the energy efficiency of the model you are considering. I recently purchased a new washing machine and went for one that was a little more expensive, because I knew it would save money in the long run and be better for the environment.

Look for the energy star sticker on the appliance. Mercifully, the Department of Energy introduced a labeling program that tells you which appliances are energy efficient. For more information, go to *www. energystar.gov*. These stickers also apply to smaller appliances like blenders, so if you are thinking of replacing anything, go energy efficient.

If it's time to buy a new electric kettle, try to buy an energy-efficient one and make sure that you fill it only with as much water as you need, because they use an enormous amount of power—between 1,800 and 3,000 watts, which is enough to power fifty ordinary lightbulbs or two hundred seventy energy-efficient ones.

If you're getting a new fridge, make absolutely sure it is energy star rated, as this appliance guzzles the most energy. It's also worth mentioning that a side-by-side fridge is the worst for conserving energy. The one with the freezer on the top or bottom is much better.

When buying a clothes dryer, gas dryers are much more energy efficient than electric. Same deal with ranges and ovens.

Cleaning the coils of your fridge is a huge energy saver—ugh! I know it's a pain, so you might want to palm this delightful job onto someone else. My husband saw me coming a mile off with that one and suddenly had some rather urgent work to do on the computer! You may need to get someone to help you pull the entire fridge out so that you can get to the back of it. Mine are sort of at the bottom front and equally hard to get to. Some fridge coils are encased within the fridge itself so that you can't really see them. If this is the case, make sure that you vacuum and clean really well around the bottom front of your fridge, as this area can become dusty and clog up the vent leading to the coils.

Make sure you don't set your fridge and freezer too high. Try a couple of degrees lower and see if it still does the job. It's really important to check that the seal on the door of your fridge is doing what it should. The seal tends to wear out over time, so check by inserting a dollar bill and see if it slides down—if it does, time to arrange a visit from your local dealer, or if you are a handy girl, you may be able to purchase a new seal online and put it in yourself.

Energy zapper that it is, remember to turn off the fridge and leave the door open when you go away on vacation. It will also give you the opportunity to defrost the freezer if you don't have a self-defrosting one.

Don't run your dishwasher or washing machine until they are full. We've heard it a million times before, but trust me—it makes a big difference in your energy bill. These two appliances make up a large portion of your home energy consumption. Frankly, it is a relief not to have to run them every day, because I detest unloading the dishwasher—as does every other member of my family; and doing laundry comes in a close second.

IT'S TRUE: An energy star–rated washer uses only twenty gallons of water per load, whereas a conventional machine uses forty.

Wrap It Up

Wrapping your hot water heater can save a lot of energy and money. First, check whether your heater has a high R-value of insulation (needs to be at least R-24). If you can't figure this out, just see if your tank is warm to the touch. If it is, it means that you should insulate it. You'll save almost 10 percent in water-heating costs, and it's easy to do.

Contact your local utility company. It may sell insulating jackets at low prices and install one for you. Alternatively, go to your local hardware store and find the guy or girl who can show you what to buy and how to do it.

IT'S TRUE: Eighty to ninety percent of energy for washing clothes goes into the heating of the water.

More Personal Suggestions for Saving Energy

This is so awfully obvious, but I have to mention it. During the winter months, draw your curtains as soon as you can. It will prevent the cold from coming in and you won't have to whack the furnace up to such high heat. Particularly draw curtains in the bedroom to get it all cozy and ready. On this note—ever used a hot water bottle? In England, it's a staple, but not in southern California. We do, however, get some seriously chilly nights here, so I have found that shoving a hot water bottle in my bed a while before I turn in for the night puts a huge smile on my face. Check out the **Vermont Country Store** (*www.vermontcountry store.com*).

Another personal warming option is to purchase an herbal wrap that you can put in the microwave and wrap around your neck at the office or at home. **Heat Makes Sense** sells an aromatherapy shoulder wrap that is wonderful (*www.heatmakessense.com*).

The last idea is extraordinary—a heated bra. It hasn't actually been released for sale yet, but look out. It's been created by the lingerie giant, Triumph, and is set to be the new eco-sexy item for winter. It has pads in it that are made out of eco-friendly gel. You microwave and shove them in, giving you warmth and a much needed (for some of us) larger cup size.

Do-It-Yourself Audit

I have recently purchased a supercool gadget for measuring your energy consumption. It's called the Owl Wireless Energy Monitor looks like a high-tech alarm clock and is very simple to install: you just click part of it onto the cable that runs from your electricity box and then stand the alarm-clock thing in your kitchen (or wherever you want it). It will show you exactly how much electricity you are using in dollar amount. It thrills me no end to switch off a light and see it whizzing down a few more cents per hour. It is quite amazing how much the price goes up from simply switching on my kettle. Given that I make twenty thousand cups of tea a day, I'm switching to iced tea. Purchase it at the **Ethical Superstore** (*www.ethicalsuperstore.com*).

Save Even More Money for the Fab Things

Honestly, I'd rather my dollars go toward a new purse than fill the coffers of my local gas and electric company. The beauty of deciding to cut down my energy usage is two-fold: (1) I don't feel the difference; (2) I'm off to get the new cool organic shirt I want and perhaps some shoes while I'm at it! It's so simple to do:

1. Set your air conditioner to 78 degrees. If you're too hot, strip off!
2. Set your heating thermostat to 68 degrees in winter. Turning down just 1 degree cuts your fuel consumption by 10 percent (think shoes!).
3. Switch all your bulbs to CFLs or LEDs—the curly-looking ones that last ten times longer than the regular ones.
4. Flick off lights even if you leave a room for a few minutes.
5. Unplug all appliances after use—even a phone charger drains electricity. Purchase a Smartstrip (*www.homeusa.com*), which has a surge protector that turns off connected devices when you turn off your computer. It also works for your television.

Get Switched On

You may have heard of previously defined CFLs. They are the ones that look curly. They have three major benefits:

1. They use much less electricity.
2. They reduce pollution. Realize that every watt of electricity you use creates pollution.
3. They last much longer.

Remember that changing just one seventy-five-watt lightbulb to a compact florescent bulb cuts roughly 1,300 pounds of global-warming pollution, lasts fifteen times longer, and saves money.

Some people get a bit put off by the bright white light of a CFL. The color temperature of light is rated in degrees Kelvin, so if you want a more yellow light, go to the 2,700 Kelvin range.

CFLs contain a small amount of mercury, so they should be disposed of in your hazardous waste box.

Light-emitting diode (LED) lightbulbs are even better than CFLs, as they last more than ten years. When they wear out, they just start getting dimmer; they also contain no mercury. They are more expensive, cannot be used with dimmers, and are not so easy to find, but if you do happen upon some, grab them. In the long run, you will save more money. Some holiday lights and flashlights are now using LED bulbs.

Check out the online store **Best Home Led** lighting (*www.best-homeledlighting.com*).

The Olden Days

The other day, my six-year-old daughter, Lola, looked up at dinner and asked me if I had been invented way back in history! Amused as I was, she's got a point. Things were so different thirty years ago when I was growing up in England. We didn't use so much energy and we certainly didn't consume so much. We didn't have paper towels or plastic wrap. Everything was stored in bowls with a plate on top or in plastic containers. It was certainly a much greener way to live, and I find myself reverting to many aspects of that lifestyle.

TIP: Instead of using plastic wrap, put a plate or bowl on top of your leftovers before putting in the fridge.

Reminiscent of those "olden days" is the use of cloth napkins. I never use paper napkins anymore. It seems much more civilized to use the real thing. Lola was thrilled with a recent purchase—on one of my retail relapses, we found a beautiful silver bunny napkin ring. If you must use paper napkins, at least make sure they are made of recycled paper.

IT'S TRUE: If every household in the United States replaced just one package of virgin fiber napkins with 100 percent recycled ones, we could save 1 million trees (Natural Resources Defense Council).

TIP: Buy a bunch of cloth napkins when you go shopping. You can toss them in the washer every couple of days. You can color code, getting a different color or pattern for every family member, so each keeps to his or her own!

I've stopped using my microwave unless I urgently need to defrost things. I don't like the thought of those rays altering the molecules in my food. I also don't stand near it when it's in use, so the rays won't alter *my* molecules either! It is yet to be proved that they are harmful, but again,

I'm not taking any risks, and we got by without in the olden days. Moreover, my microwave is a 1970s model and is probably rather dangerous!

Recycling

This is a huge deal. When many of us think about going green, it's the first consideration; however, it can be confusing, and rightly so. If you are confused as to exactly what you are supposed to recycle in your area, I suggest getting on your trusty computer and looking up your city's Department of Public Works. Your city will have its own set of policies regarding recycling. Every single city in the United States now has a Web site. I have found that while some of these Web sites have a recycling link on their front page and are supereasy to negotiate, others will give you a phone number to call or link you to a separate site. The whole process should take you less than five minutes and then you are all set. The most important things you need to find out are:

1. *How to get a recycling bin (if you don't have one) or repair an existing one. Most cities will provide one if asked.*
2. *What recyclable items are accepted.*
3. *Which numbers (in chasing arrows) of plastics are accepted.*

If you have a recycling bin and can't face getting on your computer, I'll make the process as simple as I can for you. I was very confused until I did the research. Generally speaking, this is what you can and should put in your recycling bin:

- All clean paper (magazines, newspapers, and junk mail)
- Clean aluminum (rinse out all your cans and toss them in)
- Only plastic with number 1 or 2 in the chasing arrow (water bottles should have tops taken off them). As every municipality varies in which numbers they accept, call 1-800-CLEANUP: You simply enter your zip code and choose the "where do I recycle the following items?" option. You will be put through to a recorded message from your local Bureau of Sanitation, telling you exactly which numbers they accept.
- All glass, including green glass, wine and beer bottles

If for some reason your city doesn't provide recycling bins or a recycling service, you may have noticed that many large grocery stores now have recycling centers outside. You can also go to *www.bottlesand-cans.com* and type in your zip code to find the nearest center. I know it is annoying to have to bag it all up and take it there, but just think how Gorgeously Green it will make you feel. If you live in an apartment or condo, go have a chat with your building manager or homeowner's association about obtaining recycling services ASAP.

It amazed me to learn that 40 percent of the contents of a landfill is paper, and 13 percent of that is newspaper. Some people have asked me why they can't just toss their paper into the regular trash, as its biodegradable. The problem is that paper—and anything for that matter—needs air to decompose. Once the paper is in a sealed landfill, it will last forever.

Keep a separate recycling bin in or around your home. Make sure it is near the kitchen, or you may be tempted to just toss things in the regular trash can. The coolest must-have recycling bin ever is called the **Ecopod** (*www.ecopod.com*). It's a home recycling center. You toss in your aluminum cans and plastic bottles, step on a pedal, and see them come out completely flattened! Then you put your glass and other bits and pieces in the top bin. It's pricey but well worth the investment.

If you don't want to shell out for that, you can use any old bin, although aesthetics are important to me. My stainless steel kitchen bin had seen better days, so I scrubbed it up, got all of the rust off from around the lid, and bought another identical one. They sit side by side and actually look pretty cool. If you haven't got room for the side-by-side thing, stick a bin in your laundry room, hall, or garage. I use one for paper and the other for glass and cans.

I love the **SimpleHuman Profile Can** (*www.kohls.com*) that I mentioned before, because it is a perfect fit for your grocery bags and is very inexpensive. Since I have started using it, I have miraculously halved my kitchen trash. Don't ask me how—it just happens when you use a smaller trash can.

IT'S TRUE: Recycling a glass jar saves enough energy to light a 100-watt lightbulb for four hours. Recycling an aluminum can saves enough energy to run a TV set for three hours (*www.ladpw.org*).

So get a grip and recycle *everything* that you possibly can. It's amazing that much of what we normally throw away can be put to good use with just a little effort. You don't even need to throw food scraps away, because I will soon teach you how to compost.

Be Gorgeously Green and make the effort to rinse out aluminum cans and yogurt pots, because many of them can be recycled, but they need to be odor-free. Remove plastic tops from water bottles, as they melt at a different temperature. Remind yourself as you are recycling that is really does make a difference for little old you to do these small things!

Into the Landfill

There are some items that cannot be recycled, and its important that you don't throw them in the recycling bin. It will create more time, energy, and work for the recycling plant. Here's a list of what *not* to chuck in:

ceramic	stickers
Pyrex	used napkins and tissues
stainless steel tableware	waxed paper
lightbulbs	milk and juice cartons
rubber bands	laminated paper
full cans	fast-food wraps
spray cans	drink boxes
plastic with number 3, 4, 5, 6, and	wet or food-stained paper
especially number 7 (don't forget	
to check in with your Bureau of	
Sanitation)	

These items will sadly have to go straight to the landfill.

Special Treatment

Many items surprisingly fall into the "Hazardous Waste" category. You should know what these are and how to dispose of/recycle them properly.

adhesives
aerosol cans
air fresheners
batteries
CFLs
drain cleaners
drugs
electronics
fluorescent light tubes
furniture polish
kerosene/propane

lighter fluid
liquid cleaners
mercury thermostats
metal polishers
mothballs
nail polish remover
oven cleaners
rug and upholstery cleaners
rust removers
shoe polish
smoke detectors

To find out what on earth you can do with all this stuff, go to *www. earth911.org*. It's an excellent resource for everything to do with waste. You can click on "Household Hazardous Waste," then "Municipal HHW Services," and all you need to do is type in your zip code to find out where your local station is.

Drug Alert!

Before throwing away half-used medicines, check out a fabulous company called the **Starfish Project** (*www.thestarfishproject.org*). It will accept your used bottles of antibiotics, antifungals, antivirals, and antiretrovirals. The company takes all this stuff to developing countries where most people cannot afford to buy drugs of any sort. Also ask your local RiteAid about its safe-drug disposal programs.

Never throw old medications down the toilet, drain, or waste disposal, as they will contaminate our precious water supply. Treat them as hazardous waste.

E-Waste

Anything electrical that you want to get rid of is called e-waste. It's a murky area because it costs a lot of money to dismantle a computer or cell phone. Brokers buy this waste and sell it to developing countries with no regulations or environmental standards. As it costs about thirty-five bucks to dismantle a computer, many companies would rather get rid of them and not have to worry about the toxic pollution they will create.

It's amazing to think that the average life span of a computer is now just two years, and the average life span of a cell phone is less than two years. Hazardous e-waste includes the following items:

- Televisions and computers that contain cathode ray tubes (CRTs)
- LCD desktop monitors
- LCD televisions
- Plasma televisions
- Portable DVD players and LCD (liquid crystal display) screens

If these items end up in a landfill—and 4.6 million tons of them did in the year 2000—they leach toxic chemicals into the land or release them into the atmosphere.

The Gorgeously Green girl can do the right thing by purchasing from manufacturers like Nokia and Dell, which are currently leading the way in accountability; they have take-back programs to recycle their products responsibly. Nokia has eliminated toxic chemicals from all of its new cell phones, and they are also free of the highly toxic polyvinyl chloride (PVC).

Staples takes in computers, monitors, laptops, printers, and faxes. All brands are accepted; however, you will have to pay $10. The company responsibly recycles and disposes of e-waste for you.

If you have a computer that is under five years old that you want to get rid of, visit *www.recycles.org* or *www.pcsforschools.org*. Both are nonprofit organizations that will refurbish you computer and take it where it's needed most.

If you have an older computer or any other electronics that are taking up space in your attic, closets, or garage, go to *www.eiae.org* and click on your state. You can then scroll down to find the nearest electronic recycling company in your area. It is so worth taking the trouble to do this. Gorgeously Green girls never toss e-waste in the trash!

IT'S TRUE: Fifty to eighty percent of used electronics in the United States are shipped to India, China, and Africa (BAN—Basel Action

Network). If you are interested, *www.ban.org* lists recyclers that don't export waste.

If you are giving, selling, or donating your old computer, make sure that you have erased all of your personal information from your hard drive. You can get a techno-wiz to extricate it from your computer and have the fun of getting a hammer out and smashing the hard drive to pieces, or you can order simple and inexpensive software that will erase your secrets for good (*www.disk-wiper.com*).

A No-No

Never buy Styrofoam, as it cannot biodegrade. The coffee cup you drink from today will still be hanging around in a hundred years. If your local deli or office canteen serves your to-go sandwich in a Styrofoam container, ask them to consider using plastic or cardboard boxes instead. Alternatively, take your own reusable container when you go.

If you have foam or Styrofoam packing peanuts that you need to get rid of, try not to throw them in the trash, as they will end up taking up a lot of space in the landfill. Try to find a second use. They are great for drainage in the bottom of a plant pot, or just reuse them when you are mailing something breakable. You can go to *www.epspackaging.org* to find a Styrofoam drop-off location near you.

Plastic Chucking Made Simple

Every plastic container on the planet has a number on the bottom in the chasing arrow. This is a code for recycling and is very important. Bear in mind that most recycling centers only accept numbers 1 and 2. Always remove the bottle tops or pump dispensers, as they are often made from a different plastic and may not be recyclable.

I always try to buy containers with a number 1 on the bottom because I know that I can recycle them. They may be made into carpets, T-shirts, fiberfill, tennis balls, combs, car bumpers, furniture, and more!

It amazes me that everyone doesn't recycle water bottles. It's so easy and so necessary. Every year, one billion water bottles end up in the landfill—that plastic could have been used to make 74 million extra-large T-shirts, among other things! Know that many municipalities do not recycle number 3. Always check, as it is a pain in the neck for those good recycling people if they have to pick out all the stuff you shouldn't have put in there.

Milk Cartons

As waxed milk cartons cannot be recycled on account of the wax, try to buy bottled milk. I know—you've got to schlep to the store to give the bottles back, but know that the regular cartons are bulky items that'll just clog up those landfills. Same with shiny soy milk cartons—that stuff is known as aseptic packaging, which is not recyclable. If you must buy the cartons rather than the glass bottles, buy them in bulk— the bigger, the better, or buy milk in plastic with number 1 or 2 in the chasing arrow.

Easy Peasy

Buy 100 percent recycled trash and kitchen bags, plastic resealable bags, paper towels, and toilet paper. Never buy the regular stuff, because it's just cutting down more trees—simple as that. Many of the name-brand toilet paper companies still use paper made from virgin trees, many of which come from virgin forests. I wonder if they would switch to recycled postconsumer waste if millions of women refused to buy virgin paper. Make the change now and tell all your friends to do the same.

Junk Mail

I don't want one single page of it—most of us don't—so it is a shameful waste of this planet's dwindling resources. Time to get rid of it. Here are seven reasons to eliminate junk mail:

1. *It wastes 28 billion gallons of water for paper processing each year.*
2. *Most junk mailers use inks with high concentrations of heavy metals like zinc and magnesium in addition to high-gloss UV varnishes, which are difficult to recycle.*
3. *The result is more than 4 million tons of paper waste each year.*
4. *It costs $320 million of taxpayers' money to dispose of unsolicited mail each year.*
5. *It costs $550 million to transport junk mail every year.*

6. Landfill space is getting to the point that it disfigures rural areas and pollutes groundwater.

7. We each get about forty pounds of junk mail a year—more than a tree's worth of paper per family.

It's amazing to realize that the average person receives only 1.5 letters each week, compared to 10.8 pieces of junk mail (Native Forest Network). I took out a membership with an organization called Green Dimes and have found it to be really effective. It takes a few months to take effect, but the amount of my junk mail has significantly shrunk. I have heard good reports about all of the following: *www.greendimes. com*, *www.junkbusters.com*, and *www.exuberance.com*.

Alternatively, consider the following:

1. Major credit bureaus give out lists to credit-card and insurance companies. If you get those awful preapproved credit-card offers on a weekly basis, call 1-888-567-8688 and an automated system will take you off all major credit bureaus for five years.

2. Send a postcard to the Direct Marketing Association and it will stop 75 percent of national mailings coming to your home: P.O. Box 643, Carmel, NY 10512.

3. When buying a new appliance, be wary of those little manufacturer's warranty cards that you are asked to fill out and send back. They are used to collect names for mailing lists. Realize that your warranty is good anyway if you keep your receipt.

IT'S TRUE:

❀ **Every year, 100 million trees are chopped down for junk mail sent to American homes.**

❀ **Paper makes up a third of all the waste that Americans send to the landfill.**

❀ **More than nine large trees worth of paper are sent to each U.S. home, and the response rate is less than 2 percent.**

❀ **Our local taxes are used to dispose of this junk mail that we didn't even want in the first place.**

If you've got a bit of time on your hands, it's well worth going to the trouble to do the following:

1. *Contact all the catalogs you don't care for and tell them to stop sending you unwanted material.*
2. *Contact all of your banks and credit-card companies and tell them not to release your name, address, social security number, e-mail address, or phone number for marketing, mailing, or promotional purposes. The federal privacy law passed in 2000 says that you have a right to do this and that it must be honored.*

IT'S TRUE: Recycling 1 ton of paper saves 17 trees, 6,953 gallons of water, 380 gallons of oil, 587 pounds of air pollution, 3.06 cubic yards of landfill space, and 4,077 kilowatt hours of energy.

Closing the Loop

It's as important to buy items made of recycled materials as it is to actually recycle. The reason many recycling plants do not accept certain plastics right now is that there is no market for them. I loved the idea that my recycled yogurt cups might be going straight to the recycling plant to be smooshed into a lovely recycled doormat or fleece. *Not the case!* The recycling plant has to be able to sell our trash to a company that will do the smooshing thing if there's a market for it. If there's no demand for fleece made out of recycled yogurt cups, we'll never close that loop. So when the winter months come around, you know what to go shopping for!

The Bathroom

The bathroom is a refuge for many of us. It's the place I go to think or to work out a major problem. I spend a lot of time in that little room—relaxing baths, blow-drying my hair, and more!

We've already discussed nontoxic cleaning supplies, so at least we're not going to chemically pollute ourselves anymore. However, we do need to think about the chlorine in our shower. Chlorine bonds to skin and hair and can destroy their natural bacterial balance, leading to dryness, itchiness, and flaking. Because chlorine gas is released in hot water, you need to make sure that your bathroom is very well-ventilated.

I also recommend purchasing a chlorine filter from **Real Goods** (*www.realgoods.com*). The last thing to think about is shower curtains. My husband thought I had gone stark-raving mad when I changed ours on account of their being "dangerous." I had just done some research on regular vinyl curtains and was a little concerned. I found a great hemp shower curtain that dries out really quickly, and I love the fact that hemp is naturally antibacterial and mold resistant. Vinyl releases chemical gases and odors when the temperature rises; vinyl shower curtains are also not made with renewable resources, so they will sit in the landfill forever. To add insult to injury, they are difficult to clean. Call me crazy—but change your shower curtain. There is a great selection at **Health Goods** (*www.healthgoods.com*).

Towels

It's easy to go green with towels. Just make sure you buy 100 percent organic cotton or bamboo. Everyone is crazy about bamboo right now because it is a renewable resource and requires no fertilizer or pesticide to grow. The fabric is also extremely soft. Find a great selection at **Gaiam** (*www.gaiam.com*). If you want some really deluxe organic cotton towels, go to **Anna Sova** (*www.annasova.com*).

Bold Mold

I find that mold loves to work its way into the grout in my shower and around my tub. I deal with it by filling an old spray bottle with water and half a cup of tea tree oil. I spray everywhere, including the tiles, twice a week. If you have very bold mold that refuses to leave, try Oxy-Mold from **Mold Advisor** (*www.moldadvisor.com*), which has the Gorgeously Green seal of approval and really works.

Luxury Soak

I used to soak in a full tub of very hot water every single night. Not anymore, I'm afraid—with utility bills going through the roof, I have to ration myself and save the soak for a luxury spa type of night. Even when I do treat myself to a bath, I'm mortified by the gallons of barely used water that disappear down the drain—so much so that I'll often wait for the water to cool down and then haul buckets of water to pour outside on my garden at eleven at night. This is not my activity of choice, but what is a green girl to do? When I build my superduper eco-home in the wilds of somewhere, I will have a grey water system installed, which will make use of all that water without the dripping bucket scenario. A grey water system would use my old dish, shower, sink, and laundry water to irrigate my yard.

As water preservation is of prime importance, look for any kinds of annoying leaks, however teeny, and get them fixed now. One drop of water per second can add up to over one hundred fifty gallons a month.

A low-flow showerhead is a must. It can save you up to $300 a year on water bills. If you don't want to compromise on water pressure, purchase your low-flow showerhead from *www.oxygenis.com* (look for its Five Star Resort Spa Series).

It's also easy and inexpensive to install faucet aerators. They can cut your faucet water use by 50 percent. You can purchase them at your local hardware store and either get a plumber to install them or try to do it yourself by following the easy directions given at *www.h2ouniversity.com*.

IT'S TRUE: Switching from a bath to a shower saves 2,000 gallons of water a year.

Flushing

Don't be in a rush to flush. Each flush will use up a ton of water. Agree with everyone in your house not to flush at night—unless it's number twos. Remember that seventies hippie thing: "If its yellow, let it mellow. If it's brown, flush it down." You could opt for a compost toilet system. It's a system that turns your poop into compost for your veggies. I'm not quite there yet!

Make sure you have a low-flush" toilet, as you will conserve a huge amount of water. In 1992, the Department of Energy mandated that all new homes should install low-flush toilets, so if your toilet was installed after this, you are probably okay. That being said, there is a lot of controversy because of the double-flushing and clogging-up scenarios: apparently there are a gazillion complaints daily from owners of these water conservation toilets, so if you are one of these annoyed customers, you may want to upgrade. You get what you pay for, and it's worth going for a power-assisted model so that you don't have to flush twice.

If you have an old toilet, there are some very effective measures you can take:

1. Get a half-gallon container with water (an old milk or juice container would be perfect). Remove the label and fill it three-quarters full of water. Add a few pebbles or some sand or gravel; whatever you have on hand; then top it off with some more water. Replace the cap tightly and lower into your toilet tank. This easy tip will save you half a gallon of water each time you flush!
2. Buy a Toilet Tummy or a Frugal Flush Flapper (*www.cetsolar.com*). to reduce the amount of water you flush by 50 percent.

IT'S TRUE: Americans flush 4.8 billion gallons of water down the toilet every day. With a low-flush toilet, you will actually save 6 gallons of water every single time you flush.

Also check for leaks, which are very common. A leaky john can waste up to 100 gallons a year. Go to *www.cetsolar.com* to purchase Leak Detection Dye Tablets.

By the way, those blue toilet deodorizers are an eco-horror on a par with air fresheners. Don't even think about them.

Don't Be a Sponge

I always used to buy those natural coral-like sponges for my daughter, until I realized that I was robbing the ocean floor. I don't buy regular sponges from the drugstore, as they contain polyurethane, which is not good for you or the environment. Instead, I use organic cotton face cloths.

On Your Feet

Try a wooden bath mat in your shower or tub (*www.alsto.com*). It's more stylish and eco-friendly than plastic, and it helps deal with mold, mildew, and bacteria. Alternatively, you could try a natural cork bath mat (*www.realgoods.com*), which is naturally antifungal. Make sure that you get one whose manufacturer is a member of the Forest Stewardship Council.

The Bedroom

We spend half of our lives in our bedroom, so it is best to have a room that is toxic/pollutant-free. The air in my bedroom smells much cleaner since I have installed a huge air purifier. It's not the most attractive thing in the world, but it makes a big difference. Be warned not to get a white or cream-colored one. I made that mistake thinking it would look prettier in the bedroom, but it just got dingy and dirty really quickly. Most of them are completely quiet and use very little electricity. You get what you pay for, and it's another area that I wouldn't skimp on. The best models can remove pesticides, VOCs, formaldehyde, solvents, chlorine, and cleaning chemicals. The HEPA (high-efficiency particulate arresting) filter on the high-end models also removes allergens, smoke particles, and other pollutants; and the UV light will kill bacteria and viruses. The best one I've found to date is the **UV Air Purifier,** which is available at *www.realgoods.com*.

There are certain plants that eliminate household toxins, particularly formaldehyde, which is a cancer-causing substance that can be found not only in personal care products but also in no-iron clothes; drapes and fabrics; insulation materials, plywood, and particleboard used to build homes; paints; and especially medium-density fiberboard (MDF), which is used to make furniture and cabinets. Fill your bedroom with as many green plants as you can. Here are the top ten:

areca palm	*English ivy*
lady palm	*dwarf date palm*
bamboo palm	*ficus alii*
rubber plant	*Boston fern*
dracaena "Janet Craig"	*peace lily*

TIP: If you have a lot of light in your bedroom, go for the plants that have flowers or variegated colors. If your bedroom is a bit shadier like mine, stick to really dark green ferns or palms, because they are the only ones that will tolerate a lack of light.

Holy Smoke

I don't burn just any candles anymore. The fumes can be really toxic (reproductive toxins, neurotoxins, and carcinogens). Even those lovely smelly ones you were given as a special gift aren't necessarily safe. The only way you can be sure is to buy 100 percent beeswax candles that are unscented or candles made out of soy (*www.somethingwicked candles.com*).

A rather romantic idea is to purchase a body massage candle. You light it and wait for it to heat up into a soft, sexy massage cream (*www. jetaimefragrances.com*).

The sexiest bedroom scent is an essential oil called ylang-ylang. Geranium is also wonderful. Buy an aromatherapy stone—they are electric (use very little power) and very safe. Add ten or so drops of an essential oil and feel the aphrodisiac properties take over!

A Cloud

If you calculate how many hours of your life you are actually sleeping on your mattress, I would say that it is superimportant. It should not only feel as though you are floating on a cloud, but it should also be organic, because you don't want chemicals seeping up into you, destroying your newfound greenness. Mattresses can be chock-full of unpleasant chemicals, including stain and water repellents, which emit formaldehyde. Moreover, many mattresses are made from petroleum-derived nylon, polyester, and polyurethane, all of which can give off harmful VOCs.

Wool is a good choice for a mattress because it is fast-drying for the sweaty among us, it is mildew and dust mite resistant, and you won't go up in flames, because it's naturally flame resistant. You can find the best-ever wool mattresses at **Shepherd's Dream** (*www.shepherdsdream.com*).

If you're after a cotton mattress, go 100 percent organic. You will find beautiful hand-quilted mattresses at **White Lotus Home** (*www. whitelotus.net*). Find absolutely safe and eco-friendly baby mattresses at **Naturepedic** (*www.naturepedic.com*).

Ikea carries really affordable mattresses containing alternative flame retardants. **Sealy Posturepedic** (available at most mattress stores) is free of Teflon stain- and water-resistant treatment.

Luxury

I have a thing about nice bed linen. Whether it's for sleeping or romping around, it shouldn't ever be cheap and nasty. Polyester sheets fill me with horror. Not only are they scratchy and slippery, but they apparently have a weird electrostatic charge that attracts positive ions. Just to clear the ion thing up—negative ions are the ones we want around us. They give off a fresh, clean smell and charge the air with great energy. To add insult to injury, polyester is made with petroleum-based fibers, which the Gorgeously Green girl will want to avoid. Moreover, anything that has a no-iron finish is toxic, because it is covered in a resin that will never wash out. Unfortunately, my daughter's school uniforms are covered in so much of this awful stuff that they sort of stand up of their own accord. Call me precious, but I've had them lined with organic cotton. My next step is to tackle the head of the school!

Get organic linen sheets for the hotter months. You will feel as though you are sleeping in a superfancy hotel. Just remember to fold them before they are completely dry so that you don't have to iron. In the winter, I use organic flannel sheets. They are so snuggly. I can honestly say that since I switched to organic, I get a sounder sleep. Same deal with comforters, duvets, and blankets. Even if you can't afford to change it all now, consider asking for an organic wool comforter, covered in organic cotton for your birthday. You will treasure it for years. Wool will provide you with insulation and a completely sweat- and allergy-free sleep. It is also a natural fire retardant. Check out a company called **Nirvana Safe Haven** for organic, wool comforters (*www.nontoxic.com*).

If you suffer from allergies, get a wool pillow, because dust mites hate them. If you prefer something a bit firmer, go for an organic cotton one and feel the negative (good) ions floating around your head as you sleep.

For the yummiest organic sheets, check out one of the following:

❀ *www.gaiam.com*
❀ *www.goodnightnaturals.com*

When you make your bed in the morning, spray a little aromatherapy mist over your pillows and comforter cover. The most divine one I have found is the Mist by **My Beautiful Soap Company** (*www.mybeautifulsoapcompany.com*).

Multiple Chemical Sensitivities (MCS)

Because of the pollutants in our environment, many people suffer from MCS yet many go undiagnosed, thinking they just have to live with aches and pains. Daliya Robson, owner of Nirvana Safe Haven, was one such person. She grew up on a farm in Australia, which was regularly sprayed with DDT. As a little girl, she was surrounded by these dangerous chemicals and even ate tomatoes and peas covered with them. As a result, she grew up with terrible aches, pains, and allergies. At her wits' end, she was meditating on a beach one day, and the thought came to her: I will *not* let the makers of these toxins kill me! And so she started a Web site selling everything from nontoxic carpets to carbon-activated blankets. She is now recovered and has a fantastic amount of information for anyone who suffers from allergies or chemical sensitivities (*www. nontoxic.com*).

Pain in the Neck

If you pick one bed item to be organic and can't yet buy a mattress or mattress pad, buy a pillow, as you'll be breathing on it all night. I have had neck issues for the past few years and have tried every imaginable pillow to try to find relief. I am ecstatic, as I have a pillow that is not only completely soothing for my neck, but it is made out of organic buckwheat or millet hulls and eco-wool (*www.serenitypillows.com*). It is ergonomic, as its creator also had bad neck problems. I've never had such a scrumptious night's sleep.

Wide Awake

I avoid having too many electrical appliances by my bed. I refuse to have an electric alarm clock, as I hate the sound and the electronic digital display. I am in love with my **Zen Alarm Clock** (*www.now-zen. com*), which I have had for many years. It is battery-run, and the alarm is a beautiful Tibetan bell sound. It is gentle and soothing but still wakes you up. I have gifted many friends with this beautiful clock, and many say it's "life-changing."

Night Light

While we are on the positive/negative ion subject, consider getting a salt lamp (*www.thesaltoftheearth.com* and *www.mysaltlamp.com*). Okay, I know it sounds weird, but they are really pretty to look at, especially in a bedroom. A salt lamp looks like a large glowing stone and is supposed to balance out the positive/negative ions so that you can maintain some kind of natural air quality.

There have been scientific studies (I love scientific studies!) that demonstrate a salt lamp can increase the negative ion count by up to 300 percent. Some people put them by their televisions or computers. The bedroom will do for me.

Let's Talk About Sex!

There are two important things you can bring into the bedroom that will put a Gorgeously Green smile on your face. The first is a nontoxic sex toy. We have to get really savvy about plastic because harmful phthalates are added to make an item soft and squishy—you can see where I'm going on this one! So the answer is a phthalate-free toy. Fortunately, there are a few good ones on the market. I am thrilled to bits with a company called **Outrageous Toys**. They have a line called Passion Produce. Each vibrator is a different fruit or veggie—they light up like iridescent jewels. My favorite is the Red Raspberry—they even come in a mini–wooden crate with straw—a great girlfriend gift. You can purchase them at *www.amazon.com*.

While we're talking sex toys, I had a very embarrassing situation a couple of months ago: My in-laws were staying, and during breakfast, Lola ran in wielding a vibrator that she had found in a drawer. Now this was not any old vibrator—it was a huge hot-pink affair with a cumbersome remote control hanging from it (a gift from Melina, my best friend, in the United Kingdom). Standing in the middle of the kitchen, holding it up like an Olympic torch, Lola was burning with excitement: "What on earth is it, Mommy?" With a virtual double flip, I snatched it and ran back to the bedroom with Lola trotting behind.

"It's a toy," I said, stuffing back in a drawer. "What *kind* of toy, Mommy?" Totally flustered, I replied, "It's a baby toy!" Wrong answer. "A baby toy, Mommy? What kind of a baby toy? That is *soooooo* cute. Was it mine? Can I play with it?" I had to put an end to this tirade before facing the in-laws, so I definitely told her it was a *very* dangerous baby toy that she couldn't possibly play with because it could explode and kill someone. She never mentioned it again!

If you want to avoid a similar situation, I have discovered a very discreet line of vibrators. They are called Natural Contour. Resembling pretty pastel sculptures, you would never know. I love the "Liberte" in pale lemon. They are in-law and security-guy-at-the-airport-friendly. If you order one, don't forget to get the **Energie** (*www.drugstore.com*)— it is a Kegel barbell—yes you got it—a workout for your you-know- what. It's mint green and very heavy (it really is a weight and you have to do it sitting or lying down). By the way, if you can clench it standing up, you absolutely don't need it.

The Ferrari of vibrators, another eco-friendly one is called the **Lelo** (*www.lelo.com*). It is quite incredible: a teeny, silky device that fits into the palm of your hand. Instead of batteries, you plug it in to recharge. It's very energy efficient, even if it is used for hours on end! It has twenty-seven speeds. I love what is written on the little insert that comes in the gorgeous box: "The clitoris is the only feature of the human anatomy whose sole function is to convey messages on sensual pleasure. Use it wisely, often and with care."

Lube also needs to be addressed. You don't want to be coating any of your or your partner's precious bits and pieces with anything toxic. Many of the lubes available are full of chemicals or petroleum. I adore a cream called **Egyptian Magic** (*www.egyptianmagic.com*). It is made from honey and beeswax and totally does the job. If you can't get a hold of this wonder balm, the best way to go is sesame, jojoba, or almond oil.

So once you've got your candle burning, your salt lamp glowing, and your scrumptious sheets turned down, all that remains is your ylang-ylang essential oil. Dab a few drops into your palm and spread over your pillow. Sex toys at the ready and you are all set.

TIP: To make sexy-smelling sprays, fill a spray bottle with water and then add about twenty drops of the essential oil of your choice. Spray on your pillows before going to bed. If your room ever smells a bit stale, you can spray some on the curtains as well. It's a nice thing to do before you have company. I'll sometimes give the living room curtains a quick spritz before the doorbell rings.

Running Serenity

I love the sound of running water outside my bedroom window. Living in a noisy city, I need to have a few natural sounds to soothe my frazzled nerves. That said, I don't want to have to use yet another electrical appliance, so the solution is the readily available **Solar Fountain** (*www.serenityhealth.com*). I bought the most beautiful copper fountain that runs for free off the sun.

The Rest of Your Home

We've now gotten rid of all the worst offenders—except for bugs and creeping critters. Pesticides and insecticides must be avoided at all costs by the Gorgeously Green girl. They are horribly toxic, especially to pregnant women, babies, small children, whose internal organs are still growing and maturing, and pets.

Cayenne pepper is great for ants, and tea tree oil in a water spray is an effective measure against other creepy crawlies.

I've found a great nontoxic bug repellent called **Battle** (*www.battle thosebugs.com*). It's really effective for ants and roaches. A portion of the company's proceeds go to an organization that I support called Healthy Child, Healthy Planet.

I also like **Orange Guard** (*www.orangeguard.com*), which works for ants, fleas, and many other bothersome bugs.

Green Electronics

It sounds like an oxymoron, but many electronic companies are racing ahead to find a way to make their products eco-friendly. If you are about to purchase a new computer or TV, look for the most green model you can find. Ask the store about the different brands that adhere to a green policy. The electronic giant **Sharp** (*www.sharpusa .com*) has come out with the AQUOS, a television that uses half the amount of energy as a similar-size model (model LC20D42U). The company has also partnered with the Environmental Protection Agency and transport companies to reduce air pollution by increasing the efficiency of its transporting/trucking systems.

Television: Hold on to your old/current model. There is absolutely no need for you to get a plasma screen unless you really have to. They are not earth-friendly, as they use a crazy amount of fossil fuel to produce. In one room of our house, we have a small, ugly TV that no one seems to be bothered by because we're all used to it. I don't think it would bring me inner happiness to exchange it for a plasma model. Knowing I'm helping to save the planet does make me feel better.

Techno/must-have gadgets: Same deal with new DVD players, computers, and iPods. We tend to treat these items like disposable toys when the girl next door has a cooler, smaller, cuter model. Try to salvage what you have and refrain from purchasing the newest model with the bells and whistles, unless you can't live without it. Be proud of last year's model, and remember compassion is the new fashion. It is vital that you don't just sling your old gadget or phone in the trash can. It will make its way into the landfill and leach dangerous chemicals into the air, earth, and water.

The Big Solar Deal

The way to go for the Gorgeously Green girl is obviously solar. If you can afford to, you can power your entire house by the sun. My dream is to have my home be completely solar powered. I can only imagine how wonderful it would feel to turn on a hot shower and know that it wasn't harming the planet or costing me a penny.

Most of us cannot afford to make the switch. Even though there are great tax incentives, it can be very costly. You also need to have the space to install a lot of south-facing solar panels if you want to really decrease your energy bills.

I am thrilled to have discovered **Citizenrē Renu**. They will rent you a solar system that will provide as much of your electricity as possible. All you have to do is reserve your system and pay a nominal monthly rental fee (*www.renu.citizenre.com*).

A fantastic Web site for everything solar is *www.realgoods.com*. **United Solar** (*www.uni-solar.com*) offers solar options that are easy to integrate into a roof.

It's worth getting someone to give you a free quote for your roof—

you'll also learn a lot in the process. I couldn't afford the whole she-bang, so I started off with a solar-powered fan for my attic. I had no idea how much heat got trapped up there—heat rises, hello! This fan is a small solar-powered panel that has a DC motor powered by the sun; it exhausts all the hot air from my attic and obviously runs free of charge. It has made a huge difference—so much so, I rarely use my A/C, even here in Los Angeles. These Web sites give you some options:

❀ *www.sunrisesolar.net*
❀ *www.bigfrogmountain.com*

There are also some great solar gadgets available that are very affordable. Check out this solar charger for your cell phone and rechargeable batteries at Solio (*www.solio.com*). My husband bought me a wonderful solar rainbow maker. You stick it in a sunny position on a window. As soon as the sun hits, it makes tiny rainbows all over your room!

Handy Girl

If you are into a bit of home DIY, best to wise up to what's safe and what's not paint-wise. I love painting small rooms. My husband doesn't love that I call this a therapeutic activity. After seeing the last bathroom I did, he suggested that a handy man might be better the next time. Granted, there was the occasional paint blob on the granite tile floor and I had gone a little over the top with my fancy texturing sponge. I painted over the light switches, which apparently was not a good idea, but that being said, I did use nontoxic paint and he couldn't argue with that. My husband quickly hired a handyman last week when I mentioned that the kitchen needed a bit of a touch-up. I will be making absolutely sure that Enrique uses nontoxic paint and paint stripper.

Regular paints give off low-level toxic emissions even years after you have applied them. The source of these nasty chemicals is a variety of VOCs. Fortunately, you can now buy one of three safer alternatives:

❀ Natural paint, which contains nothing toxic (*www.greenplanet paints.com*)
❀ Zero VOC paint, which has very little of these toxic compounds

(*www.ecosorganicpaints.com*)
* Low VOC paint (*www.sagepaint.net*)

Paint stripper can be awful, as it contains methylene chloride, which is carcinogenic. Luckily, you can buy one that is water soluble and non-toxic at *www.citristrip.com*.

Home Renovations

If you are renovating or redecorating you home, there is no reason not to go green with every single detail. There are so many fabulous companies and resources available. It only makes sense to pay a little extra for materials that will not harm your family or the environment. I was shocked to discover that a beautiful chair I almost bought for my husband was full of toxic chemicals. There is an eco-alternative for absolutely everything you need, from carpets to curtains, from glass to grout—you'll find what you need to make a difference.

Did you know that carpets and much of your furniture gases off? I know that sounds a bit rude, but these items actually throw off toxic chemicals. Drapes and upholstery are typically treated with very toxic flame retardants and can also give off formaldehyde, which is very toxic.

* Avoid furniture that is marked stain resistant.
* Avoid all products that contain PVC.

Before decorating or renovating, go to *www.greenhomeguide.com*. This Web site will provide you with a lot of useful information, tips, and resources. I often window-shop at *www.wildflower.organics.com*, as the Web site sells exquisite furniture and linens. Go to *www.furnature.com* to find the most beautiful eco-friendly furniture.

Victory Garden

In World War II, everyone in the United Kingdom planted a victory garden, because good food was in such short supply. I love the idea of a victory garden for this era. We all need to eat fresh organic veggies, so why not plant them? It's inexpensive and great fun.

Time to get your gardening gloves on, girls! Whether you live in a small studio apartment or have an enormous backyard, I have some ideas for you—so no excuses.

There is nothing more delicious than a homegrown organic tomato and basil salad. Vegetables and herbs are fairly easy to grow and will save you a lot of money, as these items are pretty costly to buy organic, even in the summer months.

Every Gorgeously Green girl should have her own herb garden, no matter what. Even if you're not a keen cook, you can transform simple dishes into culinary wonders just by adding a handful of freshly chopped herbs. They are so easy to grow and maintain that a child of five could do it.

There is no excuse for you not to garden. If you have silk-wrapped nails, you can wear sexy gardening gloves, and if you live in a tiny apartment, you can go with planters and window boxes. It feels great not to have to pay a fortune for a small bunch of wilting herbs at the grocery store, most of which will be wasted anyway. All you need is a pair of scissors and a huge smile as you snip what you need.

Vegetables take a bit more work to cultivate, as you need to prepare really good soil and then look after them, which involves weeding, feeding, watering, pruning, and so on. I have come to love vegetable gardening. It provides an escape from the rigors of a stressful day. It is exceedingly more therapeutic than sagging in front of the TV and much more enjoyable than sorting loads of laundry.

As I live in a big urban sprawl, it's my way of understanding the interrelatedness of all things, which is imperative for me to do at least two or three times a week. It's truly the only way that I can really feel, on a visceral level, that we are not separate from nature. To realize how much care a simple plant needs to survive humbles me in the face of consumerism. It forces me to consider the amount of food I chuck away without even flinching. An hour in the garden encourages me to think twice about throwing away a couple of old carrots that have taken me months to nurture and grow. I'll find some way of incorporating them into a vegetable soup or stew or even carrot cake.

The other fabulous thing about gardening (if you have a yard) is that you will expend hundreds of calories. I don't get out of breath easily, but a few minutes of bending down and tugging at weeds or turning soil will get my heart rate right up there—infinitely more gratifying than the treadmill at the gym.

As fossil fuels will continue to go up in price over the next few years, I think that many more of us will be thinking about growing our own produce; good-quality food will undoubtedly become more expensive. Don't get overwhelmed with the idea. If you are not a gardener, start with one vegetable and see if you enjoy it. Depending on where you live, you could grow lettuce in the winter and tomatoes in the summer. Both can easily be grown in containers.

Off to the Nursery

Before you start gardening, go to your local nursery/garden center and stock up on the basics. The first thing to buy is a pair of fancy gardening gloves. One bare-handed dip in the soil will totally ruin your manicure, so don't even think about it. Even if you don't paint your nails, you'll get leathery old hands in minutes. I favor the kind that come up to my elbows, because soil has a funny way of creeping in where it isn't welcome, like sand on a beach.

If you are actually out in a yard, invest in a pair of crocs for the summer months or rubber boots for the winter. I have avoided them at my peril and have ruined all my favorite Birkenstocks. You have to sport something that you can actually wash off. Flip-flops work pretty well in the summer, but your shiny new pedicure may need a little more protection.

If you haven't already got good gardening tools, treat yourself to a really good trowel, gardening fork, and hand clippers. Don't be cheap with the clippers, as they'll fall apart after one season.

If you're a novice gardener, I suggest buying small seedlings (tiny plants) when they are available rather than seeds. Planting seeds is a little more labor intensive, because you have to germinate them first and then do the whole transplanting thing. In the "Supereasy Seeds" section on page 181, I will show you the few seeds that work brilliantly just by tossing them straight into the earth.

If you have the space, buy the biggest planters that you can afford. I love the old wooden whiskey barrels. If you live in an apartment with no outside area, get a window box—you'll be amazed what you can grow in it.

Good planting soil is a must. Make sure that it is completely organic.

Don't be persuaded into buying chemical fertilizers—you won't need them. If you want to add fertilizer, make absolutely sure that it is organic. There are so many good ones available that you won't have a problem finding what you need. Getting the soil right will not only grow more bountiful produce and flowers, but it will also help to keep the pests at bay. Plants are like us. If they get the right nutrients, they stay healthy and disease-free. And it all starts with the soil. I strongly suggest that you add a couple of large bags of worm castings to your newly prepared soil and some mulch. The worm castings will improve the soil texture and the mulch will keep the soil moist, which is ideal if you want to keep your worms happy. Lots of happy worms are key to a good garden.

The most complex part of growing an organic garden is learning how to control the pests. As you are no longer using pesticides, the good news is that you will encourage the beneficial insects, like ladybugs, to come back into your yard.

5 Tips For Your Organic Garden

1. Make you own insecticidal spray by filling a spray bottle with water and ½ cup of liquid castile soap. For more of a repellent, add three cloves of finely chopped garlic and let spray stand for an hour before spraying.

2. Use beer as bait for your slugs. They love it, so bury a small bowl of beer in the most visited area and watch them drink! Clean your trap out every two or three days.

3. Grow garlic around your plants as it naturally repels pests.

4. Mail-order beneficial insects like ladybugs and mantis.

5. Create a bird sanctuary with feeders, baths, and birdhouses. The birds will gobble up many of the pests and fill your garden with song.

You will find all sorts of wonderful organic gardening tips and advice if you visit *www.gardensimply.com*.

Herbs

Let's start with the herbs. First, make a list of the herbs that you want to plant. Here's what's on my list. I am lucky, because in southern California, I can have many of them year-round.

Rosemary—It's really easy to grow. You'll get a lot, and it works well as a decorative shrub.

Sage—Think of a dish of fresh ravioli with sage butter.

Mint—It's great for summer drinks and cocktails; however, make sure it's in a planter, because mint spreads like crazy.

Parsley—You need it for thousands of dishes, so plant loads.

Thyme—I always add this herb to soups and stews to make them extra special.

Bay tree—Bay trees are beautiful, easy to maintain, and the leaves flavor soups and stews.

Oregano—I use it for all Italian dishes, from marinara sauce to pizza.

Basil—I use basil wherever and whenever I can. I love it. Fresh pesto is heavenly.

You can plant all of these herbs in just two large planters or in your yard. Make sure you have well-prepared soil. While they take root, water them regularly. Summer herbs like basil and oregano like a lot of sun and warmth (just think Mediterranean). The rest can do fine in partly shady and cool climates.

Veggies

Now you are ready to buy your plants. Nurseries will stock only seasonal varieties, so see what they've got. Only buy things you know you will use, such as lettuce, spinach, tomatoes, basil, zucchini, and bell peppers. Last year, I got really ambitious and planted a grain called amaranth, which you grind and use to make bread. At the same time, I planted calendula, with the intention of making a medicinal tea. I don't know what I was thinking—*grinding* grains into flour! My husband got a lot of mileage out of that one.

I can't live without my tomatoes. I plant heirloom tomatoes and try new varieties every year. I also plant cherry tomatoes in containers, as they are supereasy and great for kids.

I also plant as much basil as I can fit in. I plant at different times during the summer months so that I'll always have an abundant supply. Sometimes I experiment with bell peppers, zucchini, and eggplant, all of which I love to eat and all of which are pretty easy to grow.

Because of the warm climate where I am, I have to be careful with "cool" crops like lettuces and cabbages, because we can suddenly get searing heat in the middle of February (especially with global warming in action). That said, it's trial and error with gardening and the fun of experimentation.

If you are going to be Gorgeously Green and have a go, I suggest you buy a brilliantly simple book about organic gardening called *The Vegetable Gardener's Bible* by Edward C. Smith.

Supereasy Seeds

If you are going to start your garden with seeds rather than plants, it will require a fair amount of commitment in that you have to mist the tiny seedlings as they grow indoors, because they cannot get too hot, cold, or dry; and then you have to transplant them into your garden. There are, however, a few seeds that you can put straight in the earth, and they are so easy to grow that a three-year-old could manage:

1. **Arugula** is an absolute must for every Gorgeously Green gal. Just make two or three long inch-deep trenches in the soil and scatter the seeds. In just three or four weeks, you will have these wonderful, peppery greens to add to your salads.
2. You can grow **mesclun salad mix** in a large window box or planter near your kitchen and eat the greens all year long. Say good-bye to those expensive and unhealthy bags of salad.
3. **Spinach** grows very quickly. You can just pick off what you need to add to salads.
4. **Radishes** are pretty easy. As soon as the winter months are over, throw in the seeds and they'll do their thing.
5. **Beets** are pretty hardy as well. I do germinate mine, as it gives them a head start. I put a little potting soil in each compartment of an old

cardboard egg carton, plant the seeds, and just make sure I water them every day. I then plant the whole thing in the soil, as the egg carton will biodegrade.

6. **Swiss chard** is so very easy to grow, and you'll have it ready to eat very quickly. I love to steam it and sprinkle it with a little toasted sesame seed oil and soy sauce. It's also great added to soups and stews and is chock-full of cancer-fighting vitamins and minerals.

The Gorgeously Green girl needs to buy organic seeds and plants. If your local nursery doesn't have a good selection, go to *www.dirtworks.net*. Get everything you need for your organic garden at this excellent site.

You can also order a really good free catalog from **Wild Garden Seed** (*www.wildgardenseed.com*). It's easy to read and has a little bit of interesting blurb about each plant.

Garden In a Tub

My favorite way to grow my salad is in a large wooden whiskey barrel. I keep it really close to my kitchen and plant half with mesclun salad leaves and half with arugula. I like the tub for these greens because they don't like too much sun, so I can move the tub, making sure it's always in the shade.

Children's Garden

One massive benefit of gardening, whether in a planter or a yard, is that we get to teach children about how things really grow. It's amazing to me that many kids just think vegetables appear by magic on their plates or on supermarket shelves. It's vitally important that they appreciate how much care and work is involved in growing something as simple as a carrot. If they grow their own, it's thrilling for them to eat the fruit of their hard work. It's the most effective way to get your kid to eat veggies.

Most children love cherry tomatoes and strawberries. Both can easily be grown in small planters, so it's a good summertime gift for your children, nieces, nephews, or friends. Some gardeners like to plant their strawberries in a hanging basket, as they look beautiful and the ground-crawling pests can't get to them.

I bought my daughter a planter, and she decided to do some artwork on it first, making it her own with some custom graffiti. I showed her how to plant the strawberry plant and taught her how to take care of it. We talked about how it was a big responsibility and that the plant would die without her attention and care. She never missed a day of watering it and was beside herself with pride when she could offer the juicy red jewels to her friends on play dates.

Greener Than Green

If you have a lawn and really want it to look picture-book green, please do not use regular commercial fertilizers and pesticides on it. You are not only endangering your health, but it's like passive smoking—your neighbors will have to pay a price as well. Find alternatives at *www. healthylawns.org*.

The most eco-friendly option for those of you who live in warm areas like me would be to rip up your lawn and replace it with native drought-tolerant plants. I have finally managed to persuade my husband to go for it. Our front lawn is going, and my new plants will attract hummingbirds and ladybugs—my neighbors can watch the wildflowers grow!

More Lawn Tips

Do not use a gas-powered lawn mower—it is hugely polluting. Electric or manual is the way to go. Check out the excellent selection at *www. ecomowers.com*.

Leaf blowers are ghastly. Not only is the noise enough to send even the most level-headed girl into a rage, but they also emit seriously nasty fumes that add to global warming. Pick up a rake—its great exercise.

You can save a lot of water and money by using drip irrigation in your garden. Replace your regular sprinkler head with a low-cost drip-watering emitter. Plug one end of a piece of drip tubing into the emitter and run the tube along the base of your plants, then secure the end of it with a rock or a stake. Spray sprinklers can be really wasteful; moreover, in the summer months, I'm beginning to see my water rates escalate.

Get Gorgeous, Get Composting

Girls like me are more interested in their compact than their compost. That said, I have discovered the joys of a pastime that I previously believed was strictly for the eco-nuts in rubber gardening shoes—I'm now one of them. Yes, I'm thrilled to say I have joined the club.

My husband was appalled when I arrived home with an enormous black composting bin one rainy Saturday morning. "Where on earth is that going?" he asked. "I haven't really worked that out yet," I said as I looked around our small manicured backyard. "Well," he said, "I'll leave that in your expert hands." Did I detect a note of sarcasm? I stood in the downpour, wondering if this monstrous bin would offend our summer brunch guests, staring at it as they tucked into their tofu scramble. Not a good idea.

I finally decided to wedge it down in a corner where it is almost out of sight. The only annoying thing is that I have to walk across our yard every time I want to empty the scrap bucket. I've become so lazy—so accustomed to everything at my fingertips. It is crazy that I worry about extra inches around my waistline and yet am miffed at having to walk fifty yards twice a day to my attractive bin!

I love composting. I'm thrilled that I don't have to throw out any food scraps. I can't bear the thought of my food waste adding to the already maxed-out landfills. So this is how it works. I throw all fruit and veggie scraps, tea bags, coffee grounds, egg shells, and bread into a cute little compost crock that sits on my counter. When it is full, it goes on its journey to the end of my yard, where it is emptied into the black monster. I cover each layer of old food with a bit of dirt, shredded newspaper or some dried leaves and make sure the whole thing stays moist (in the hotter months, I spray some water into the bin a couple of times a week). A few months later, all of that waste turns into odorless soft brown dirt, which is commonly known as compost. It seems to be a bottomless pit, because however much I put in just disappears.

There are a number of great composting bin alternatives now available. The main choice will be whether to get a spinning barrel or a regular bin design. The disadvantage with the spinner is that you have to wait until, it's full—you can't keep filling and spinning because at some point you have to let the whole thing sit and compost for awhile!

The advantage is that the materials will compost faster as the pile is being oxygenated via the spinning process. If you get the conventional black bin monster, like mine, you can go on filling it daily, but you do need to turn the compost once a week and add an activator. You can purchase all of the above plus accessories from **Real Goods** (*www.realgoods.com*). If you live in an apartment that has any kind of outside area, suggest getting together with the other residents of your building to share one.

You could also consider vermicomposting, which is a method that involves just dirt and earthworms. The compost is created really quickly, as the worms eat the scraps and produce the sweet-smelling mixture within days. There are really cool college campuses that use this technology to deal with all the cafeteria waste. There are also some supergreen dudes who keep worm-composting bins in their kitchen. I have to admit that I couldn't deal with having earthworms in my kitchen on any level. That being said, I am now using worms in my regular compost bin, and they are chomping up all that waste at a very pleasing rate. If you're worried about your compost bin smelling or attracting pests, worms are the way to go. They are really easy to get. Just go to **The Worm Farm** (*www.thewormfarm.com*), and this company will tell you exactly how many you need for your specific bin and will mail them to you. I promise you don't even need to touch one; when the bag comes, you just cut it open, turn it upside down, and the worms that are packed in earth will slide easily into your bin.

You can buy your compost bin at:

❀ *www.realgoods.com*
❀ *www.dirtworks.net*

Eighty Things You Can Compost

paper napkins	wood chips	old wedding bouquet	seaweed and kelp
freezer-burned vegetables	lint from behind refrigerator	spices	old herbs
pet hair	hay	pine needles	birdcage cleanings
Post-it notes	popcorn	leaves	paper towels
		matches	grass clippings

potato peelings

unpaid bills

weeds

hair clippings from
  hairdresser (can you
  imagine asking?)

stale bread

coffee grounds

wood ashes

sawdust

tea bags

shredded newspaper

egg shells

ATM receipts

houseplant trimmings

old pasta

garden soil

corncobs

Jell-O

aquarium plants

Sunday comics

Kleenex tissues

soy milk

tree bark

flower petals

pumpkin seeds

expired flower
  arrangements

white glue

citrus wastes

stale potato chips

old leather gardening
  gloves

wheat bran

nut shells

guinea pig cage cleanings

moldy cheese

shredded cardboard

apple cores

outdated yogurt

toenail clippings

pie crust

leather wallets

onion skins

watermelon rinds

date pits

olive pits

peanut shells

burned oatmeal

dryer lint

bread crusts

cooked rice

banana peels

wool socks

soggy cheerios

theater tickets

burned toast

animal fur

stale cookies

vacuum cleaner bag
  contents

greeting-card envelopes

peanut butter
  sandwiches

grocery receipts

cardboard cereal boxes
  (shredded)

produce trimmings from
  grocery store

dirt from soles of shoes
  and boots

The payoff is that you get to use your precious compost on your garden or in your planters. It is the best fertilizer available.

Task

Weed out all your toxic cleaning supplies. You may want to use some of them up or chuck them right out. Be sure that you do not chuck drain cleaner, air fresheners, or aerosol cans in the recycling bin or the trash, because they'll sit in the landfill for years and years.

Put these "hazardous waste" products in a box until you can get it together to take them to your local hazardous waste collection center. Better still, call all your neighbors and tell them you are doing a hazardous waste run. To find out where your local center is, go to *www.earth911.com* and type in the item you want to dispose of and then your zip code.

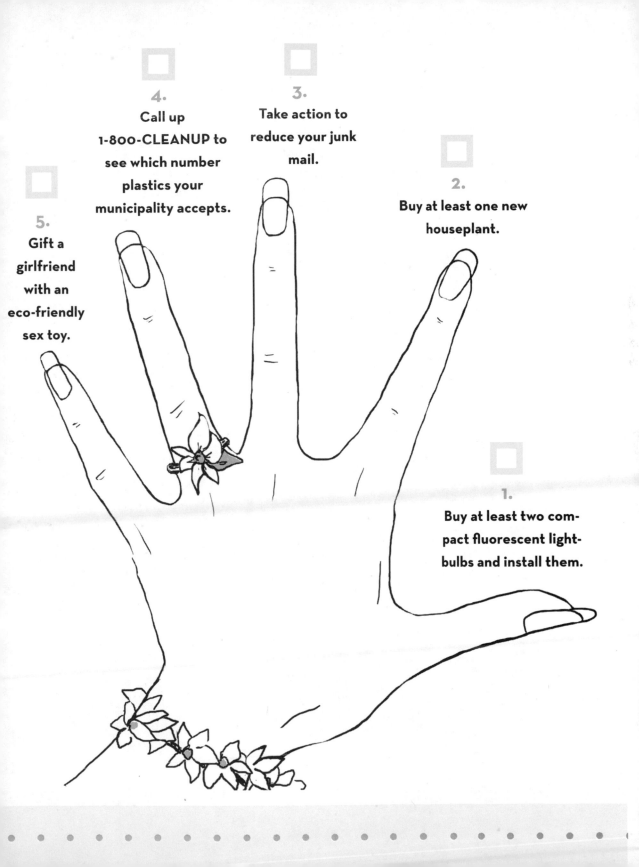

4.
Call up
1-800-CLEANUP to
see which number
plastics your
municipality accepts.

3.
Take action to
reduce your junk
mail.

2.
Buy at least one new
houseplant.

5.
Gift a
girlfriend
with an
eco-friendly
sex toy.

1.
Buy at least two com-
pact fluorescent light-
bulbs and install them.

Savasana

This is so well deserved. You have had a lot to think about in step 5. Lie down in your comfortable "corpse" pose and begin to focus on your breath. You should spend this time feeling really good about yourself for beginning to make these incredible changes in your life.

You deserve to have the best, as does everyone around you. Breathe in the new clean air and breathe out a smile.

Chapter Six

STEP 6: Every Last Bite

You Can Have Your Cake and Eat It, Too

I love eating almost as much as shopping. I am fortunate because I adore healthy food, not because of any virtue but because I want to feel great all the time. It is so simple—if I eat junk, I feel absolutely awful. The other day, I ended up at a kids' birthday party eating tacos, french fries, and chocolate ice-cream cake. I was starving, and the fries must have had something addictive in them, because I couldn't stop (notice I blame it on the food). Even before the party was over, I felt dreadful. I just wanted to go to bed for the rest of the day. It made me grateful for the beautifully fresh and nutritious food I have become accustomed to.

I was incredibly lucky that I learned to cook from my mother as I grew up. She is an extraordinary cook, in that she can make anything taste delicious. She is also a simple cook who always uses the best ingredients she can find. She will skimp and save on everything except food. She sent me away at the age of eighteen to study at The Cordon Bleu School of Cookery in London, where I learned from madames in little white caps, who poured butter and cream into everything and yet were as skinny as bean poles. Europeans tend to favor whole foods or "real" foods. I love Nina Planck's definition of real food in her excellent book, *Real Food:* "it's old, and it's traditional." She believes that it's the industrial and processed foods of modern times that create heart disease, obesity, cancer, and misery.

Eating healthily for me is not about denial. If I deny myself anything, I just want it more and more and more until I eventually cave in. If I feel that my jeans are getting a bit too tight, I just cut down on my portion size, but I keep on eating all the things I love.

Going green is about positive actions that we can take for the health of our body and our environment. The two often go hand in hand, organic food being a good example. I have traveled extensively in Europe and love that women seem to enjoy their food more than here in the United States. I've never seen a low-fat anything in Greece or Italy. We all know the French adore their wine, cheese, chocolate, and croissants, and you don't see as many obese women walking around Europe as you do here. If you don't believe me, go to Paris or read *French Women Don't Get Fat* by Mireille Guiliano. My motto is enjoy everything in moderation—my only caveat being that I only eat foods that are sustainable, and mercifully, most everything except for beef and some fish is sustainable.

Growing up in England, we consumed vast quantities of freshly baked bread, either covered in a thick layer of yellow butter or fried in a tub of lard. A day didn't go by without cheese, red meat, and golden syrup (similar to maple syrup). My favorite dessert was called "Spotted Dick," which was made out of suet (animal fat plus flour), raisins, and tons of the aforementioned syrup. It was always served with a generous bucket full of custard (cornstarch, sugar, and yellow dye)—yummy.

The redeeming factor was that most of our food was relatively unprocessed and unspoiled: Meat came from the local butcher, where the animals were grass-fed; veggies came from the local fields; bread from Bert Robinson down the road. There was something comforting about knowing where it all came from. It was local and seasonal. It was "real" food that didn't contain all the hidden sugars and chemicals of modern processed food. As a result, we were generally healthier, and obesity wasn't the major issue that it is today.

Thirty years later, it's a different story. Most foods have to travel thousands of miles to get to us, and therein lies the problem: they are chock-full of preservatives so that they can arrive in one piece and to prolong shelf life—never mind the horrors that go into producing them.

The Gorgeously Green diet is about enjoyment. Life is not worth living without delicious food. I must confess that I'll be sitting in a business meeting or teaching a yoga class and my mind will often wonder off into planning my lunch or dinner menu. One of my clients is a wonderful cook, and we spend every minute of our session salivating over recent discoveries. Even when she's upside down in a headstand, she'll be listing the ingredients of a must-try recipe.

I believe that the cells in our body are very intelligent. When our brain sends a signal to them that we are about to deny them nourishment, they will grab onto every bit of energy they can and store it, because they know they are going to be starved. The fat stores are activated and the dieter starts complaining that she only has to look at a cookie to gain weight. We need to send the message to our cells that they will always get what they need. We simply have to listen to our body and see what it wants. A case in point is when a girl gets pregnant. As soon as the second pink line showed up on my test stick, I felt nauseous and yet craved fat. Not olive oil, but nasty, fatty fat—french Fries, grilled cheese sandwiches, and pancakes. Why? It was because I needed some more padding on my hips and behind to support the growing bean. When I'm sick, I crave very specific foods. Our bodies are supersmart.

Whether you are vegetarian, vegan, or a full-on carnivore, you need to find a way that works for you practically and ethically. You may be considering stopping eating red meat or cutting out sugar, but my advice is to make gradual changes or you will flip out. If you eat red meat three times a week, try cutting back to once a week. If you eat chicken every day, cut back to twice a week.

My program is about making small lifestyle changes that are easy and comfortable. Granted, meat eating is not very sustainable. Let's take a minute here to define sustainable: it means being able to continue into the future. As far as meat eating is concerned, the rate at which we are presently consuming will not be able to continue into the future. Why not? Well, because there is a growing number of us on the earth and we've gotten used to eating meat almost every day. I remember when it was a huge treat to have a steak; and a roast chicken was reserved for a special Sunday lunch occasion. Today, every all-you-can-eat buffet offers chicken, turkey, and beef. Meat is in our in sandwiches, on salads, and is thought to be really good for us. It may be, but in small quantities. We don't need it every day.

IT'S TRUE: Seventy percent of all agricultural land in the world is used to raise farm animals. The rest is used to grow crops, a third of which is used to feed the animals.

Cows Contribute to Global Warming

It sounds a bit silly that chomping cows are responsible for almost 20 percent of global warming gases, but they are. If you factor in the transportation, carbon dioxide farm emissions, methane from deforestation, and nitrous oxide in the cow poop, it makes sense. It's not their fault, and to add insult to injury, most of them aren't treated very well either. Sorry—I can't justify a tender filet mignon anymore; I'll just have to face the ridicule of my family and carnivore friends as I tuck into my tofu steak.

I don't know whether you're a hamburger girl, but if you are, think about the fact that most of the meat between your buns comes from a devastated rain forest in Central America. Dr. M. E. Ensminger has written ten books about the raising of livestock. In his textbook *Animal Science,* he writes about how we have hacked down precious rain forests to create cattle pastures. Since most of our hamburger meat comes from South America, his words are pertinent to anyone who has walked through the yellow arches:

> *Is a quarter-pound of hamburger worth a half ton of Brazil's rainforest? Is 67 square feet of rainforest—an area about the size of one small kitchen—too much to pay for one hamburger? Should we form cattle pastures to produce hamburgers in the Amazon, or should we retain the rainforest and the natural environment? These and other similar questions are being asked too little and too late to preserve much of the great tropical rainforest of the Amazon and its environment. It took nature thousands of years to form the rainforest, but it took a mere 25 years for people to destroy much of it, and when a rainforest is gone, it's gone forever.*

Slowing Down

The great news is that if all of us reduce our meat consumption by only 10 percent, enough grain would be saved to feed 60 million people and help preserve what little rain forest we have left. So let's commit to cutting down this week. Now, obviously if you are vegetarian or vegan, good for you! We may all get there eventually, but go easy on us for now!

My husband calls me a hummingbird because I buzz around so fast that sometimes he barely sees me. I find it hard to stay still and I have a tendency to gobble my food. The phone is always ringing in our house (my husband swears all the calls are for me), and the "you've got mail" icon is constantly leaping up and down on my computer screen. The pace of life is fast. Most of my girlfriends describe their lives as busy, crazy, or chaotic. It is no wonder that shopping for food has become an inconvenience to be crammed into an already bursting-at-the-seams day. I understand the attraction of "convenience," food but I rarely enjoy it. Processed food doesn't taste great and feels awful in my body. The only answer is to slow down—and the area of my life that is most in need of the brake pedal is food.

In this step, we are going to take the time to shop so that cooking and eating will be a great pleasure rather than a chore. There is a wonderful movement that began in Italy called the slow food movement (*www.slowfood.com*). It's all about using beautiful, seasonal ingredients and slowing down enough to enjoy the preparation and consumption of our meals. I love the idea of slowing down so much that I have used the word *slow* for a Gorgeously Green mantra:

S—seasonal foods
L—local foods
O—organic foods
W—whole foods

SLOW. This is a reminder of the four simple things that we're trying out in step 6 so that we slow down and really appreciate our food in a way we never thought possible.

S—Seasonal Foods

It is just common sense. If we eat food that is eaten when it is supposed to be, it is delicious. You can't deny that a soft, ripe tomato (ideally an heirloom) eaten in the summer is a different animal to its hard, plastic-looking counterpart in the winter. Strawberries and raspberries taste horrible if they are not in season. Imagine eating a chilled slice of watermelon when it is freezing outside, or conversely, a steaming chicken potpie on a sweltering summer evening.

We Gorgeously Green girls have got to get with it! Produce that is eaten out of season is not kind on the environment: Fruits and veggies have to travel thousands of miles to get to us, burning huge amounts of energy to do so. They are gassed, injected, or sprayed with chemicals to prolong their life—yuck. Besides, fruits like peaches and even oranges become a huge treat if you have to wait for them.

L—Local Foods

If you buy locally, it's more likely than not going to be in season. I love farmer's markets with a passion. Since making my local one a regular Sunday excursion, I have learned exactly what I should be eating month by month. My favorite farmer is the salad woman. She waxes lyrical about the different varieties of lettuce she has, and she handles her bell peppers and radishes like precious jewels. Go to *www.ams.usda.gov/farmersmarkets/map.htm* to find a farmer's market in your area. Or go to *www.localharvest.org* and *www.csacenter.org*.

If you're a meat eater, it is really important to buy from local producers. Most of the meat in the United States is factory farmed, and these foul institutions are called concentrated animal feeding operations (CAFOs). I don't like them because they treat animals really badly, packing them in as tightly as they can and making it impossible for them to go outside or even get a glimpse of daylight. Their health is severely compromised due to these unnatural living conditions, and thus the farms become breeding grounds for disease. More than half of all antibiotics used in the United States are for factory-farmed animals. Moreover, many of the bacterial strains are becoming resistant to these too frequently used drugs—pretty scary stuff. Finally, because there is so much excrement in such a small space, the surrounding water supplies are often polluted, whereas the poop of a pasture-raised cow is a natural grass fertilizer.

Enough said. I certainly don't want to eat the flesh of miserably raised animals or support CAFOs, so I have made it my business to support local farmers. The meat is so much tastier. Sure, it's a little more expensive, but I'd rather eat a beautifully raised piece of meat once a week than the CAFO offerings every day. To find out more about naturally raised meat and to find a local farm, visit *www.eatwild.com*. I found the nearest farm to me, called them, and set up a monthly mail-order arrangement. That way, I always have something fabulous in my freezer. Alternatively, you can go to *www.diamondorganics.com* and they will send you the most wonderful grass-fed meat or wild fish.

Even if you can't get to a farmer's market, just get into the habit of reading a few labels in your supermarket. You will be amazed at some of the far-flung places that many of your regular items come from.

The best local thing to do is to try to find a farm selling meat that is humanely reared and grass-fed. You can just go online and search about a bit. It is so important to start eating meat that isn't injected with hormones and antibiotics. Meat is a complicated area because it may be labeled "raised without the use of hormones or antibiotics," but that could still mean that the animal has lived in a cage the size of your microwave for its entire life. You just have to ask yourself what is important to you.

We are so used to eating chicken that has been produced in a way that you don't even want to think about. Suffice to say, it would make you sick and sad, never mind that the meat is tasteless and spongy compared with eating chickens that have been able to peck around as they please.

Purchasing eggs can be very confusing because of the labeling: "free-range" doesn't necessary mean the chickens have been allowed to roam around freely. To put "free-range" on a label legally means that the animal or chicken has been given access to the outside for as little as five minutes a day. That could mean that a door to an enormous factory farm is simply opened for five minutes a day so that the animals could go out if they wanted to! Give up your vision of a beautiful green pasture with free-roaming birds and beasts, because it rarely happens. Most significant is the fact that according to the U.S. Department of Agriculture (USDA) standards, the producer does not have to feed these "free-range" animals hormone- or antibiotic-free food. The only label you can trust is "organic," which means that the chickens are uncaged and fed an organic all-vegetarian diet free of antibiotics and pesticides. It is the only label that is subject to any government regulations.

O—Organic Foods

I admit it—until a couple of years ago, I still thought organic food was a bit of a rip-off. Even if it wasn't, how was I expected to be able to afford to feed a family with food that costs a fortune? Since becoming Gorgeously Green, I have not only realized the importance of eating food that isn't going to harm me, but I have found a way to make it affordable.

Organic food is important because it is better for your health and it is healthier for our planet. Organic means the food is produced without the aid of artificial fertilizers and pesticides. Some may question whether these chemicals are really harmful to human health. It's vital to realize that the chemical residues that remain on conventional foods accumulate in our fatty tissues over time and can influence our immune and endocrine systems as well as affect our neurological health. For a food to be labeled organic, it must also steer clear of sewage sludge, bioengineering, and ionizing radiation.

There are other benefits inherent in organic food: the organic regulations commonly prohibit hydrogenated fat (can cause heart disease, cancer, and diabetes), aspartame (thought to be a neurotoxin), phosphoric acid in sodas (can cause osteoporosis), antibiotics (can cause reduced immunity, hormone disruption, gender confusion, obesity, and cancer), pesticides (can be carcinogenic), genetically modified organisms (can cause intestinal disorders), or any of the seven thousand artificial colorings, flavorings, preservatives, and processing aids (can cause cancer, liver disease, gut problems) that are allowed in conventional food. So it kind of makes sense to go organic!

In order to avoid being ripped off, it's really important to understand the labeling scenario. Never buy something just because you see the word *Organic* on the packaging.

Here's the skinny on labeling:

1. **One hundred percent organic** *means that the food contains only organically produced ingredients.*
2. **Organic** *means that 95 percent of the ingredients must be organi-*

cally grown, and the remaining 5 percent must come from nonorganic ingredients that have been approved by the National Organic Standards Board.

3. **Made with organic ingredients** means that a product must be made with no less than 70 percent organic ingredients.

The green and white USDA organic stamp has been designed to inspire your confidence. This label can be used only on "100 percent organic" or "organic" products.

Also know that if a food is labeled organic, it has not been made with genetically modified organisms (GMOs) and has not been irradiated. Irradiation is very controversial: meat, fruits, and vegetables are basically nuked with radioactive materials that kill bacteria and prolong their shelf life. This widely used procedure has been deemed safe by the Food and Drug Administration; however, critics postulate that there are no scientific studies to assure us that it's safe, and we *do* know that molecules in food are broken down, creating free radicals that deplete the vitamin/enzyme content.

❀ Avoid packages that say "pure" or "natural." It means nothing and is a way that some companies try to get through a loophole and make their foods seem healthy.

❀ Avoid claims of "made with real fruit" or "made with whole grains." That basically means that the food has a minute amount of real fruit or whole grain in it.

❀ Avoid products that have been "enriched" with anything. It just means that the natural makeup of the food has been messed with!

Top Twelve Nonorganic Fruits and Veggies to Avoid

1. Strawberries
2. Bell peppers (green and red)
3. Spinach
4. Cherries
5. Peaches
6. Cantaloupe (Mexico)
7. Celery
8. Apples
9. Apricots
10. Green beans
11. Grapes (Chilean)
12. Cucumbers

The reason to avoid these fruits and veggies unless they are organic is that some fruits and veggies consistently contain higher levels of pesticide residue than others, even after washing. The Environmental Working Group did a huge analysis and found these twelve to be the absolute worst.

Twelve Cleanest Fruits and Veggies (contain the least amount of pesticide residue in tests)

1. Avocados	7. Grapes (non-Chilean)
2. Corn	8. Bananas
3. Onions	9. Plums
4. Sweet potatoes	10. Green onions
5. Cauliflower	11. Watermelon
6. Brussels sprouts	12. Broccoli

Since many of the women I know still balk at the idea of organic prices, I thought I would conduct my own experiment to see exactly how much more I was spending on organic versus conventionally grown food. I went to three different stores and did a huge imaginary shop. I got everything I would need for one week, including the basics. I wrote down all the prices, and at the end of the day, I calculated that the "organic shop" was only 15 percent more than the "conventional shop." I also realized that the extra 15 percent was incurred from buying grass-fed organic meat and that some of the other organic items were actually less expensive than the nonorganic ones. So if I'm willing to cut down on meat, I can easily afford to go completely organic—phew!

In Barbara Kingsolver's fantastic new book, *Animal, Vegetable, Miracle,* she makes an interesting point about how little we Americans are willing to spend on food:

> *Grocery money is an odd sticking point of U.S. citizens, who on average spend a lower proportion of our income on food than people in any other country, or any heretofore in history. In our daily fare, even in school lunches, we broadly justify consumption of tallow-fried animal pulp on the grounds that it's cheaper than whole*

grains, fresh vegetables, hormone-free dairy, and such. Whether on school boards or in families, budget keepers may be aware of the health tradeoff but still feel compelled to economize on food—in a manner that would be utterly unacceptable if the health risk involved an unsafe family vehicle or a plume of benzene running through a school's basement.

I also love what David Steinman says in his extremely informative book *Safe Trip to Eden:* "If you worry about some of the added costs of purchasing organic foods but you give to charity, think of organic food as giving to the most effective environmental charity today, more powerful even than the American Cancer Society."

The absolute rule is to go for what is in season, as it will always be less expensive and better quality. With the average price of organic produce being only about 15 percent higher than regular produce, you also need to take into account that organic produce contains on average 26 percent more dry matter (less water), therefore actually making it cheaper to buy organic. If you experiment, you will notice that nonorganic produce shrinks more when cooked because it loses all its excess water.

If you are too busy to go in search of organic produce or you just want to indulge yourself, you can get your organic fruits and veggies delivered. Go to a great company called **Fresh Direct** *www.freshdirect.com*, or for everything organic, including ice cream, go to *www.diamondorganics. com*—I love, love this company!

I used to use a company in southern California called **Pax Organica** (*www.paxorganica.com*). They delivered me a box of the most juicy and succulent produce every week. It was an absolute blessing, since I had just given birth and couldn't face trekking around any kind of market. I loved coming home and finding that box by my front door— always full of surprises. The company will give you only the cream of that week's crop and can't predict what that will be. You will also get to try things that you wouldn't normally buy.

W—Whole Foods

A whole food is as close to its natural state as possible. Its production involves little or no processing—nothing added, nothing taken away. Whole foods taste better and are healthier because they retain all of their natural nutrients, enzymes, and probiotics, which processing often removes. Food is processed for a variety of reasons: to give it a longer shelf life, to make it look better, to make it taste sweeter/saltier, to bulk it out, or to turn it into a diet food. Whole foods are assimilated and absorbed by the body more efficiently than processed foods. They also provide you with the most natural source for all your vitamins and minerals.

Whole foods include raw fruits and veggies; nuts, seeds, and sprouts; unpolished grains; unprocessed meat and fish; and nonhomogenized milk. Don't confuse whole foods with "organic food," as we are dealing with two separate issues: processed food can be organic and whole foods can be nonorganic.

Wandering up and down the aisles of my local grocery store yesterday, all I could see was a blur of lurid, plastic packaging, selling me nothing other than processed food; I was hard pushed to find *any* item that could qualify as a whole food! No wonder this nation is becoming sicker and sicker; however, we are going to see things change over the next few years as American citizens take charge of their health and demand the food that nature intended for us to eat.

Keeping It Simple

We are bombarded with information about the perils of eating hydrogenated fats and trans fats, not to mention monosaturated and polysaturated fats. Which ones really are harmful to our health and which ones will make us live longer?

Most importantly, what is the most eco-friendly oil to use? There is no particular oil that is more earth-friendly than another; however, many environmentalists argue that if you buy only one organic item for your kitchen, make sure it is oil. The reason is because heavy metals and chemicals such as pesticides tend to stick to the fats.

To keep it supersimple, you just need to know which fats to avoid and which to use.

❊   Avoid foods with labels that read "partly hydrogenated fats/oil" or "trans fats." Mercifully, all foods that contain trans fats (bad for your heart) must now have this information clearly on their labels. Many of the huge fast-food chains have been forced to change to healthier cooking oil, which is hard for them, because it's these unpleasant oils that give the fries their characteristically yummy flavor.

❖   Avoid frying olive oil at high temperatures.

❖   Avoid margarines unless they are organic and do not contain any of the harmful fats as already described.

❖   Use extra-virgin cold-pressed olive oil for dressings. You can use it for cooking, but do not fry with it when a recipe requires high temperatures, as it doesn't have a particularly high smoking point. It will burn once it reaches a certain temperature, and certain chemical reactions will take place that are not good for your health. If you use olive oil raw, it is the most delicious and healthful oil imaginable.

❖   Use grapeseed oil. It is fantastic for frying, baking, and grilling, as it has a high smoking point, meaning it will not burn or smoke even if you get it really hot. It is a light and nutty oil, which is not only delicious on salads but is also very good for you.

❖   Use coconut oil. There is a lot of controversy about this oil because at one time it was considered to be bad for the heart; however, recent research has found unbelievable health benefits. It contains lauric acid, which can destroy viruses; it is great for brain development and the nervous system; and it can protect against cancer and heart disease. Coconut oil is even thought to aid in weight loss because the body doesn't store it as fat; rather, the liver converts it straight into energy. I have been cooking with it for years, and I am a great fan. Try frying pancakes or french toast in unrefined coconut oil and you will never look back. To find really good-quality coconut oil, go to *www.gardenoflife.com*.

❖   Use butter. Anything fried in butter is simply delicious, and I strongly recommend it for taste. I always add a few drops of olive oil (okay for high temperature if it's just a few drops), as it will prevent the butter from burning. If you don't use it every day, it's worth splurging on the really good stuff. Make sure it's organic, as you will taste the difference.

Oil Care

It's very important to store your olive oil in a cool, dark place, as it can go rancid with too much heat and light. In the summer, I put mine in the fridge. Beware that "extra-virgin" olive oil doesn't mean much in the United States. We are not a member of the International Olive Oil Council. Most of the oil you buy from large stores will be mass produced and partially refined. Try to find oils that are cloudy, cold-pressed, and unfiltered. Cloudy oil means the oil has retained all of its nutrients. Good-quality oil lasts for a few years, but most of the oils we buy at large stores will last for only about a year.

Oil Neurosis

Some women are paranoid that they will put on weight by eating too much olive oil. Well, just for the record, many women I know eat avocados almost daily, copious amounts of olive oil on everything, daily fish oil supplements, and more, and they have never struggled with a weight issue. We need the good fats for our health and our beautiful skin, so get the olive oil out and start dipping!

High-Fructose Corn Syrup

High-fructose corn syrup is huge now—it's in everything from bread to sushi. Many claim that this corn syrup is a major cause of obesity in the United States, and I don't think they are wrong. The crafty thing about it is how well it is hidden. I bought some brown rice sushi the other day from a reputable health food shop. It was delicious—even my daughter gobbled it up—and no wonder, on closer inspection, I saw that the spicy sauce and even the rice had this sweet syrup in it.

High-fructose corn syrup is cheaper than sugar, so companies shove it in almost all processed food to make it taste better. The next time you go to the grocery store, label-read for it and you will be surprised. Avoid it whenever you can, because not only are you eating a chemically processed sweetener, but you are also ingesting something that is very likely genetically engineered. That combo doesn't sit well with the Gorgeously Green girl.

Other ingredients that are typically processed from genetically engineered corn are xanthan gum, mannitol, sorbitol, fructose, citric and lactic acids, glucose, maltodextrin, and MSG, among many others.

Sugars

"Refined" sugar has been given a bad rap in recent years. Does it deserve it? Yes, and this is why: It is actually an unnatural substance produced by an industrial process. It comes from sugar cane or sugar beets, which are refined down to sucrose and at the same time are stripped of all vitamins, minerals, proteins, and any other nutrients you could think of. Brown sugar is not so far down in the refinement process—the molasses from the cane or beet is refined into brown sugar and then finally into white crystals that are an alien chemical to the human body. Sugar can rot teeth; can cause diabetes, hyperglycemia, and hypoglycemia; and can contribute to heart disease, depression, hypertension, and cancer. It also unbalances the endocrine system. To add insult to injury, non-organic sugar production wreaks havoc on the environment, so always go organic when buying sugar, and eat in moderation!

Artificial sweeteners are questionable safety-wise, so I avoid them. The following are better for your body and the planet:

- Stevia—use sparingly, as it's really sweet.
- Organic honey
- Manuka honey—it's expensive but has health benefits beyond regular honey.
- Agave syrup—it's yummy sweet syrup, which has a low glycemic index, so diabetics can use it.
- Barley malt syrup—very healthy and not too sweet, it's great for baking.

Salt and Pepper

I am a salt freak. I justify my excessive intake by knowing that I am using "healthy" salt. Regular iodized salt is not the best choice because it has no minerals. If you buy sea salt, however, it not only tastes better, but it will also get minerals into your system. Since I got turned onto sea salt, there's no going back. They say you use less because the taste is more pronounced—another good justification for heavy sprinkling. Try dipping a stick or celery or a radish into a bowl of flaky sea salt—it's heaven.

As for pepper, every girl needs to own a good pepper mill. There are so many different kinds of peppercorns on the market that it's fun to try new ones. Freshly ground pepper is a must for many recipes.

It's Smelling Fishy

I love sushi, but which roll can I now eat in good conscience? We all know our oceans have been overfished to the point of extinction for many species. Some scientists even say that in forty years eating fish will be a luxury reserved for the superrich.

For those of you who are fish lovers, the best thing you can do for the moment is to order the most sustainable fish that you can. You can find a sustainable seafood guide at *www.eartheasy.com*. For quick reference, check out my list. These choices have taken into account the status of the wild population, the fishing method, the by-catch, and the general impact on the environment.

BEST CHOICES

anchovies
bluefish
calamari
catfish (farmed)
clams
crab: blue, Dungeness, and
    king
crawfish
Pacific halibut
Atlantic mackerel
mussels
Pacific octopus
farmed oysters
Pacific black cod
trap-caught, Pacific prawns
wild Alaskan salmon
sardines
scallops (bay-farmed)
Pacific squid
farmed striped bass
farmed tilapia
Pacific albacore tuna
sea urchin (uni)

EAT ONLY
OCCASIONALLY

lingcod
lobster (Atlantic)
mahimahi
octopus (Atlantic)
prawns (U.S. farmed or wild)
scallops (sea, bay, wild)
shrimp (domestic, trawl-
    caught)
snow crab
sole
squid (Atlantic)
swordfish (Pacific)
tuna: yellowfin or skipjack

AVOID

Atlantic cod
Alaska king crab
caviar
grouper
haddock
Atlantic halibut
monkfish
orange roughy
imported or tiger prawns
farmed Scottish salmon
Chilean seabass
red snapper
skate
swordfish
bluefin tuna
turbot
yellowtail flounder

Mercury Rising

It's also very important to understand the dangers to your health in eating fish high in mercury. If you are pregnant, you should avoid the following: shark, swordfish, king mackerel, tilefish, tuna steak, canned tuna, sea bass, Gulf Coast oysters, marlin, halibut, pike walleye, white croaker, largemouth bass.

You can also visit **Got Mercury** (*www.gotmercury.org*) and use their mercury calculator. Simply type in the weight amount of fish that you plan to eat, and your own weight; it will calculate your mercury risk. It's actually pretty scary to realize that a six-ounce can of tuna contains way too much mercury for someone of my weight. It's really annoying that the one source of protein that my daughter *loves* is tuna!

Farmed Versus Wild Fish

By the way, another name for farm-raised fish, which is just a marketing ploy, is ocean-raised fish. Either way, the fish are raised in pens where they don't get much swimming room and are prone to disease (and thus given antibiotics). They can also escape and infect wild fish. Moreover, they are high in mercury.

We are told to eat a lot of salmon because it contains omega-3, which has a multitude of health benefits; however, farm-raised salmon are fed soy, cornmeal, and canola oil, which completely changes the concentration of omega-3. As salmon are carnivorous, they are often fed fish feed pellets, which may contain mercury and dioxins. Wild is also preferable for tuna, halibut, and snapper, as they, too, are carnivores. Farm-raised salmon is often fed dye to give it that lovely pink color that wild salmon possesses. It also doesn't taste as good because of its diet. It's important to know that most of the omega-3 oils are found in the skin of the fish, so if you remove it, you are removing the good stuff. My recommendation is to get most of your omega-3 from good-quality supplements (see step 2). When wild salmon is in season, the price will come down a bit, so serve it for a very special dinner or an occasional treat.

Some farmed fish, like tilapia, char, and catfish, are better bets because they are vegetarians and live in brackish water (mixture of fresh and salt water).

Forget "Convenience" Food

The crazy thing about "convenience" food is that it is not very convenient at all. Given that the definition of *convenient* is "not troublesome," I would argue that it is not convenient packaging-wise—all that plastic and cardboard to dispose of—and it's not convenient for our health. Take, for example, a bag of salad. We think that bowl of mixed baby greens is so healthy, but it is not. In order to keep the leaves fresh in those sealed bags, the leaves have to be gased with some horribly toxic chemicals. Buying unpackaged and preferably organic lettuce does require a little more elbow grease in that you do have to run some water over the leaves and get out your salad spinner, but oh the difference! The leaves actually crunch, taste of lettuce, and are full of vitamins and minerals—a small time price to pay for something utterly delicious.

The joy and the sensuality in food has been lost in the pursuit of convenience. Food should be sexy. Have you ever watched chefs like Gordon Ramsey and Nigella Lawson? (Brits are always the sexiest!) They talk about food preparation with lust—touching, smelling, tasting, they titillate our senses and get our salivary glands working overtime.

In the supermarket fast-food world, food has become sanitary and dead. It may be inexpensive, but it's lacking in quality and soul. I tend to go brain-dead in a large grocery store. I can't get it together with all those garish labels and plastic wrap. It's not a fun place to be. Conversely, I love to mooch around the farmer's market, sampling crumbly goat cheese from a local farm or thick, fruity olive oil drizzled on a puff of bread. I even enjoy buying veggies, as the choice is limited to what is in season. Another blight of modern-day food is that there are too much choices. It's overwhelming and confusing. Do I buy snow peas from South Africa, green beans from Chili, zucchini from Mexico, or broccoli from Canada—eek, too much—can someone make some decisions for me please! At least at the farmer's market, the season tells me what to buy.

Some of my favorite movies are about food as a metaphor for love. *Like Water for Chocolate* and *Babette's Feast* are must-sees for the girl who enjoys eating. I firmly believe that a meal cooked with love in my heart is a hundred times more delicious than something I slap on the table because I have to. Admittedly, when I'm tired or strung out after a chaotic day, it's hard to find the love in my heart for anything, least of all a pot of brown rice, but dig deep I must or I end up with a glutinous pile of mush. Risotto is a good love food because it can't be rushed. You actually have to stand at the stove for twenty minutes as you gently stir. It can be very therapeutic and can be practiced in place of meditation. See how Zen you can become!

Eco-Kitchen Tips

1. Pour water that you have used to cook pasta or veggies into a bucket. When it's cool, use it to water your yard.
2. Keep all your old egg cartons and bring them back to a local egg supplier.
3. It's hard to avoid using resealable plastic bags altogether, so get into the habit of washing them out. Turn them inside out and stuff your hands inside, then wash as though you were washing your hands. Hang the bag over a bottle or a wooden spoon in your dish rack to dry.
4. Fill a bowl in your sink with cold water when washing veggies rather than letting all that precious water disappear down the drain.

Must-Have Utentils and Gadgets

There is some controversy about nonstick coatings on pans breaking down at high temperatures and giving off dodgy fumes, associated with a man-made chemical called perfluorooctanic (PFOA), which has become very persistent in the environment. It is not, however, clear or proven that these chemical are dangerous to humans. Not being a big risk-taker in the man-made chemical department, and as most of my old nonstick pans are pretty scratched, I put them in storage in my overstuffed garage (I can't bear to get rid of them as they were wedding presents), I have begun a collection of good quality stainless steel and cast-iron pots and pans.

I love cast-iron as it heats food evenly, goes from stovetop to oven, is inexpensive, and lasts several lifetimes. It is also acts nicely as a nonstick pan if you "season" it, which simply means coating it with vegetable oil, placing on a low heat for five minutes, and then wiping off excess oil. I was thrilled to find a large cast-iron skillet at a yard sale last year. I paid a dollar for it and I use it practically every day!

Also check out a new brand called **Green Pan** (*www.green-pan. com*). They use a patented technology called Thermolon, which is eco-friendly and polytetrafluorothylene (PTFE-free), another controversial man-made chemical.

Make sure that your spatulas are stainless steel as well. Sharp knives are a necessity for the Gorgeously Green girl. You cannot cook without seriously sharp knives, so it's worth investing in a good knife sharpener—try eBay or Craig's list. You will feel like a superchef once your knives are razor sharp, and it makes food preparation so much easier.

There are three things that the Gorgeously Green girl can easily make herself: yogurt, bread, and carbonated drinks. You will save money and help your health and the environment if you invest in the following items.

Yogurt Maker

I love yogurt and have started making my own for two very good reasons. First, I couldn't get over how much packaging I was wasting with all those little plastic pots. I never dared to buy the larger ones for fear that I'd end up throwing half of the yogurt out. With my homemade yogurt, I just make as much as I need. Second, I couldn't believe that most yogurts I bought, even though organic, were filled with sugar and gum and ingredients that I didn't want or need. Homemade yogurt is super-healthy, and if you are lactose intolerant, you can make lactose-free yogurt very easily. I add fresh fruit and organic honey when needed.

I suggest going to **Lucy's Kitchen Shop** (*www.lucyskitchenshop.com*) and ordering its yogurt maker with a couple of starter kits. It comes with a plastic bowl. Since I don't recommend heating plastic, order the additional glass bowl, which you can use instead. Sitting down on a leisurely Sunday morning with a bowl of homemade yogurt and granola is more than a Gorgeously Green girl could ever ask for!

Bread Maker

I have saved a lot of money with my bread maker. I love that I can control what goes into it. It's so much fun to experiment with adding unusual grains such as millet, spelt, and rye. My family's favorite is my cinnamon, raisin, and walnut bread—still warm and slathered with organic butter. Amazon (*www.amazon.com*) stocks a huge variety of reliable and inexpensive models.

Soda Stream

This is a must for the green girl if anyone in your family drinks sodas or carbonated water. We used to go through boxes of sparkling water every month, and I cringed at the amount of waste, even if it was going into the recycling bin. Then our **Soda Club** (*www.soda-clubusa.com*) arrived and we've become very smug. It's inexpensive, requires no electricity or batteries, and will last you for many years. It is operated by compressed air in a carbonator. When it runs out, you send the empty carbonator back, and they will clean and refill it for you. To make sparkling water, fill up one of the bottles they send you with filtered water, screw it into the machine, and press a button that makes a rather rude buzzing sound—that's it! This company will also send you a variety of syrups to make flavored soda; however, I prefer to add the carbonated water to naturally sweet, organic fruit juices.

Inspection Task

This task is hugely satisfying. You are going to get in the kitchen, roll up your sleeves, and begin sorting out your cupboards and/or your pantry. When I first did this, I was amazed at how many jars were lurking in the back that were either past their sell-by date or had no chance of ever being used.

Put everything on the kitchen table and have a good look at each item. If an item is still good but you aren't likely to use it in the next three months, put it in the "donate" bag. I filled two large bags with cans of lentils, pinto beans, and water chestnuts, then dropped them off at my local church. It's like clearing your closets—put back only what you know you love and will use a lot. While you are at it, look closely at the labels. Don't throw anything away because it's not organic; just be aware of what you have and plan to search out the organic version on your next shopping spree.

I also became fascinated with the labels on my cereal and cracker boxes—so many of them claimed to be organic, but on closer inspection, they had only a few organic ingredients. Also don't forget to look out for the insidious ingredient called high-fructose corn syrup.

Shopping List for the Basics

Now we're going to talk about how to stock your cupboards and your fridge with all the basics so that you can be well on your way to creating a Gorgeously Green kitchen. If you fill your kitchen with everything I have listed, you will be set. Even on a crazy day, you will be able to knock up something healthy, delicious, and eco-friendly.

Fridge Must-Haves

1. Organic milk, soy milk, or rice milk
2. Organic butter
3. Pitted kalamata olives
4. Sun-dried tomatoes
5. Good-quality goat cheese or feta cheese
6. Course-grain Dijon mustard
7. Ketchup
8. Dozen free-range organic eggs
9. Mayonnaise
10. Sandwich pickles
11. Ground coffee
12. Chocolate bar
13. White wine
14. Large slice of the best-quality Parmesan cheese you can afford

Pantry Must-Haves

1. Cider vinegar
2. Best balsamic vinegar you can afford (cheap balsamic is flavored with caramel)
3. Extra-virgin cold-pressed olive oil
4. Grapeseed oil
5. Toasted sesame oil
6. Extra-virgin cold-pressed coconut oil
7. Worcestershire sauce
8. Soy sauce
9. Tamari (similar to soy but tastier)
10. Peppercorns and good wooden pepper mill
11. Sea salt (large flaked if you can get it—it's more delicious and you don't use so much)
12. Herbs: dried bay leaves, chili flakes, mixed Italian herbs
13. Spices: cumin, nutmeg, cinnamon, turmeric

14. Capers
15. Peanut butter
16. Cans: coconut milk, diced
    tomatoes, tomato paste,
    garbanzo beans
17. Whole-wheat pasta
18. Soba noodles
19. Brown rice and basmati rice
20. Red and green lentils
21. Dried fruits: apricots, raisins
22. Seeds: pumpkin and sunflower
23. Free-range chicken stock
24. Vegetable stock
25. Rice or almond milk
26. Nuts

Check your kitchen cupboards and fridge. You may already have many of the list items. Make a shopping list for your next trip to the store. And when making the recipes that follow, remember to use as many organic ingridients as possible.

We need to get past the notion that it's too time-consuming to create a meal from scratch. It really isn't, unless of course you are competing with a microwave TV dinner. I can knock up a wonderful chicken soup in less than ten minutes—it lasts for three days and can feed an enormous family. All my organic pasta dishes take under twenty minutes to make, as do most of my weekday meals.

Gorgeously Green Breakfast

I adore breakfast. It really sets me up for the day. If I eat nutritious whole foods, I often don't feel hungry until lunchtime. Even if I'm in a horrible rush or I don't feel like eating, I never leave the house without something in my tummy. It was drummed into me at an early age, as most mothers, including myself, find it hugely satisfying to watch their child devour a huge healthy breakfast before school. My mother used to lay on quite a spread. Since everyone wants something different in my family, I make sure I have the fridge and the freezer stocked with Gorgeously Green breakfast goodies.

If one of us is in a terrible rush, a smoothie is the way to go—it fills you up and can get all those good nutrients inside you in one great gulp. I often make my daughter a smoothie so that I can sneak in flaxseeds or greens without her batting an eyelid.

Gorgeously Green Smoothie

Hemp is one of the most complete foods you can eat: it is rich in omega-3 and omega-6 essential fatty acids (called *essential* because it's essential we get these nutrients, as our bodies don't naturally produce them). You can purchase ground-up hemp seeds and powdered greens separately, but I suggest **Hemp n' Greens** (*www.rawganique.com*) for this recipe. The blended mixture is organic and fair trade. If you want a little more protein in your smoothie, try **Living Harvest's Vanilla Spice Hemp Protein** (*www.livingharvest. com*).

8 ounces of chilled rice or almond milk
handful of berries or half a banana
1 tablespoon Hemp n' Greens

Serves 1

Place all the ingredients in the blender and see it turn a wonderful shade of green. You will be addicted. It's great for kids, and you can get creative with names for it. I had to really use my imagination, as there was no way my daughter was going to drink something of that color, unless of course it was called "Dragon Juice." I add a dash of honey or agave syrup to sweeten.

Gorgeously Green Granola

I love homemade granola. You can find organic granola in stores, but it will never ever taste like this. It's a bit of an effort to get all the ingredients, but plan to make a bunch, as you can store it in an airtight container.

3 cups rolled oats

¼ cup sunflower seeds

¼ cup pumpkin seeds

¼ cup hemp or flaxseeds

½ cup almonds or pecans

½ cup coconut flakes

1 tablespoon cinnamon

1 teaspoon nutmeg

2 tablespoons grapeseed oil

2 tablespoons apple juice

½ cup maple syrup

¼ cup honey

½ cup dried cranberries

Serves 8–10

Preheat the oven to 350 degrees F. Lightly grease a baking sheet. Combine all of the dry ingredients in a bowl, except the cranberries. Combine all of the wet ingredients in a small measuring cup and add to the dry ingredients. Mix well and spread evenly over the baking sheet. Bake for about 30 minutes, until the granola looks brown and crunchy. Add cranberries and yum. I eat this granola with rice or almond milk.

Scrumptious Veggie Tofu Scramble

1 tablespoon grapeseed oil

½ cup chopped onions

½ cup diced tomatoes or red bell pepper

½ cup diced zucchini

1 cup fresh spinach

1 cup vegetable stock

16 ounces extra-firm tofu, drained

sea salt and freshly ground pepper

¼ cup chopped cilantro

Serves 4

Heat the grapeseed oil in a sauté pan, add the onions, and sauté until translucent. Add the tomatoes, zucchini, and spinach and sauté over medium heat for about 5 minutes until soft. If the mixture becomes dry, add some vegetable stock. Crumble up the tofu and add, continuing to cook until the tofu is heated through. Add the salt and pepper to taste and sprinkle the cilantro on top. Serve with a warmed organic tortilla or some sliced avocado.

Banana, Raisin, and Flaxseed Muffins

These are the healthiest muffins imaginable. I make a bunch of them and either freeze them or put them in an airtight container (good for a week). If I don't eat them on the day of baking, I just warm them up slightly before serving. I love them as they are, but my husband and daughter favor butter and fruit juice–sweetened jelly. Don't be put off by the amount of ingredients in this recipe, as once you have them, the muffins are supereasy to make.

¾ cup all-purpose flour

¾ cup whole-wheat flour

¾ cup ground flaxseeds

1 teaspoon baking soda

½ teaspoon cinnamon

¼ teaspoon nutmeg

2 tablespoons peanut oil

2 eggs

½ cup unsweetened applesauce

3 tablespoons honey

2 mashed ripe bananas

1 cup soy milk

½ cup raisins

Makes 12 muffins

Preheat the oven onto 375 degrees F. Grease a muffin tin with a little butter or peanut oil. Combine all of the dry ingredients together in a bowl. In another bowl, mix the peanut oil, eggs, applesauce, honey, soy milk, raisins, and banana, then add to the dry ingredients and combine well. Scoop the mixture into muffin cups and bake for 20 minutes or until a toothpick comes out dry. Cool on a wire rack.

Gorgeously Green Lunch

One of the three S's works for most of us girls. So I will show you the healthiest and greenest soups, salads, and sandwiches I have found.

In the winter, there's nothing like a thick and hearty soup to warm you up. The following four are very easy to make and are filled with essential nutrients to keep your energy high and your skin glowing. Another great thing about soup is it is very inexpensive to make, even if you're buying organic ingredients.

If you're going to make soup, it will be well worth your while to buy one of those hand blenders. It's so much easier than having to slop the whole thing into a blender. I can't be hassled by the washing up. With the wand, you can just screw off the stick and rinse under the tap.

Carrot and Parsnip Soup

This is so velvety on account of the parsnips. Serve with warm, crusty bread.

2 tablespoons grapeseed oil
2 celery stalks, finely chopped
1 leek, finely chopped
sea salt and freshly ground pepper
dash of Bragg Liquid Aminos
8 large carrots, chopped
4 parsnips, chopped
chicken or vegetable stock

Serves 4

Heat the grapeseed oil in a stainless steel stockpot over medium heat. Add the celery and leek, and sauté until soft. Add salt, pepper, and the liquid aminos. Add the carrots and parsnips and cook for 2 minutes. Add the stock and simmer with a lid on for 30 minutes. Let the soup cool for about 10 minutes and then purée with the blender until creamy smooth. Serve in warm bowls with a sprinkling of chopped fresh parsley if desired.

Lentil Soup

This sounds boring, but it is totally delicious. Lentils are high in protein and provide enormous amounts of energy, so if you are running ragged, have a large bowl of this soup and you'll be good to go.

4 tablespoons olive oil

1 large onion, thinly sliced

4 garlic cloves, thinly sliced

1 teaspoon cumin

2 cups brown, green, or yellow lentils

3 cups cold filtered water

1 cup roughly chopped spinach

sea salt and freshly ground pepper

Serves 2–4

Heat the olive oil in a stockpot over medium heat. Add the onion with a pinch of salt, and sauté for about 10 minutes while stirring now and again until golden. Add the garlic and cumin, and heat for another minute, then add the lentils and water. Bring to a boil, then simmer covered for 20 minutes. Remove from the heat and purée until smooth. Return to the pot and add the spinach. Add salt and pepper to taste. Cook for another couple of minutes. Serve with warm whole-wheat pita bread and some yummy black olives.

Miso Soup

I am a huge fan of Japanese food, particularly miso soup. It is considered to have many health benefits, including suppression of various cancers, lowering of cholesterol, anti-aging properties, and for the Gorgeously Green girl, it is thought to maintain a beautiful complexion.

The beauty of miso soup is that it is very easy to prepare. I have included udon noodles in the following recipe to make it more of a meal. You will be able to buy all of these ingredients at any well-stocked grocery store—just head for the Asian aisle.

2 tablespoons brown miso paste

2 tablespoons rice vinegar

2 tablespoons soy sauce

1 tablespoon chopped ginger

4 ounces shiitake or enoki mushrooms, chopped

udon noodles cooked according to packet and rinsed in cold water

1 cup bok choy, cut into 1-inch pieces

2 tablespoons toasted sesame seeds

Serves 2

Mix the miso paste, rice vinegar, and soy sauce in a saucepan, and then stir in 2 cups of boiling water. Squeeze the chopped ginger with a garlic press into the soup. Add the mushrooms to the pan, and put it on the stove, on a low heat until slightly softened. Stir in the noodles and bok choy, allowing the bok choy to wilt. Divide between two bowls and scatter the sesame seeds over the top.

Gorgeously Green Crunchy Wrap

I make this a lot for myself when I'm on my own. It is simple, delicious, and superhealthy. I always find that my wraps fall apart while I'm devouring them, and I like to be on my own when the whole thing becomes delightfully messy.

1 whole-wheat tortilla

3 tablespoons hummus (see next recipe)

1 avocado

4 black olives, chopped

extra-virgin olive oil

sea salt and freshly ground pepper

1/4 cucumber, thinly sliced

several crunchy lettuce leaves

1 carrot, grated

Serves 1

I like to warm the tortilla a little so that it is soft. Lay it out flat and spread with the hummus. Mash the avocado and spread on top. Add the black olives, a drizzle of olive oil, salt, and pepper. Add the cucumber, lettuce, and carrot. Roll up the wrap as tightly as you can.

Leah's Humus

Whenever my girlfriend Leah makes her delicious humus served with warm pita bread, I am in danger of devouring the entire bowl! It is ridiculously easy to make and much more tasty than the store-bought kind. You also save on plastic, which we love.

15-ounce can of garbanzo beans

3 tablespoons tahini

juice of 2 lemons

grated zest of 1 lemon

2 cloves of garlic, crushed

1/4 teaspoon cayenne pepper

1/4 teaspoon sea salt

1/2 cup of olive oil

1/2 teaspoon paprika

Serves 4 (or 1 if you're greedy like me)

Simply place the garbanzo beans, tahini, lemon juice and zest, garlic, cayenne pepper, and salt in the food processor and blend for 30 seconds. Keep the food processor running as you slowly add the olive oil, until you get the desired consistency. (I like my humus quite runny, so sometimes add a little more oil if needed.)

Spoon the mixture into a pretty bowl. Add drizzle of olive oil and a sprinkling of paprika to make it look beautiful. Serve with warm whole-wheat pita bread.

Tabbouleh

This is a traditional Moroccan recipe that couldn't be easier. The common mistake is that not enough parsley is used—so go heavy with the green, as it contains vitamins and minerals to make you even more gorgeous.

3/4 cup bulgur wheat

2 large ripe tomatoes, roughly chopped

4 scallions, trimmed and chopped

1/2 cup mint, roughly chopped

2 cups flat-leaf parsley, roughly chopped

Dressing:

1 garlic clove, crushed

1/4 teaspoon cinnamon

sea salt and freshly ground pepper

2 tablespoons lemon juice

3 tablespoons olive oil

Serves 2

Put bulgur wheat in a bowl of cold water for about 3 minutes and then through a sieve. Add the tomatoes, scallions, mint, and parsley and combine well. To make the dressing, add the garlic, cinnamon, salt, and pepper to the lemon juice and stir. Then slowly add the olive oil. Combine the dressing with the bulgur mixture and enjoy with some good black olives and warm whole-wheat pita bread if you are hungry.

Gorgeously Green Quick and Easy Suppers

Best-Ever Bell Peppers

My mom taught me to cook this years ago, and I have done it so many times for a quick lunch or supper. If you like Mediterranean food, this will be up your alley.

4 small tomatoes

2 large red bell peppers

8 pitted black olives

4 anchovies

1 bunch basil

8 tablespoons extra-virgin olive oil (divided)

sea salt and freshly ground pepper

Serves 2

Preheat the oven to 400 degrees F. Skin the tomatoes by putting them in a small bowl of just-boiled water. Leave for about a minute, then drain the water. Pick them up carefully to avoid burning yourself and slip off the skins. (Note that if you're using tomatoes in a salad, skinning them is a nice touch.) Cut the tomatoes into quarters.

Cut each pepper in half lengthwise; even cut through the stem, as it looks pretty to keep it on. Discard the pulp and seeds from the center of each half and place them open-side up in a baking dish. In each half pepper, put 2 tomato quarters, 2 black olives, 1 anchovy and 2 or 3 basil leaves. Into each half add 2 tablespoons of olive oil and salt and pepper. Bake for 40 minutes or until the edges of the peppers begin to blacken. Let them cool to room temperature, and serve with crusty bread to mop up the delicious juices.

Gorgeously Green Beans

The Gorgeously Green girl doesn't need to eat meat every night. I have become a huge fan of simple vegetarian dishes that are so delicious that even my long-suffering husband approves. This is insanely simple and mouthwateringly good.

1 pound green beans, ends removed
1 tablespoon olive oil
sea salt and freshly ground pepper
½ cup crumbled goat or feta cheese
½ cup pine nuts
¼ cup sun-dried tomatoes, chopped

Serves 2

Preheat the oven to 400 degrees F. Put the green beans in a bowl and add the olive oil, salt, and pepper. Toss with your fingers. Place in the oven for 30 minutes or until the beans look shriveled. Remove and let them cool to room temperature. Arrange on plates and crumble the cheese on top. Toast the pine nuts in a hot skillet (no oil) on high heat for about 3 minutes, constantly stirring, and add to the beans. Top with sun-dried tomatoes and serve with warm garlic bread (next recipe).

Garlic Bread

1 baguette

4 garlic cloves, crushed

5 tablespoons olive oil

Serves 4–6

Cut diagonal slats all the way down the baguette. Mix the garlic into the oil in a bowl. With a teaspoon, pour and spread a little of the mixture into each slat and over the top of the bread. Wrap in aluminum foil and bake in the same oven as the beans (previous recipe) for 10 minutes.

Warm Golden Beet Salad

Visit your local farmer's market in the winter months to find golden, red, and orange beets. I always used to be a bit baffled by these odd-looking vegetables. What on earth should you do with them? They certainly have no resemblance to the dark red, soft, sliced stuff on salad bars, but I've recently found out that they are supereasy to prepare. This recipe is a slam-dunk.

2 large golden beets

½ cup pine nuts

romaine salad leaves

½ cup chopped dried apricots

½ cup goat cheese

1 ripe pear, sliced

olive oil

½ lemon

Serves 4

Preheat the oven to 400 degrees F. Cut off the beet tops and wash them. Coat them with vegetable oil and put them in the oven for an hour or until the skins are really black. Spread pine nuts on a baking sheet and put in the oven for 4–5 minutes, turning once. Be careful as they can burn easily. Meanwhile, assemble the lettuce leaves on pretty plates, fanning them out. Let the beets cool and peel off the skins. It's messy, but they will slide off easily. When they are totally cool, cut them lengthwise into half-inch slices and set about four or five slices on each bed of lettuce. Sprinkle with the apricots, goat cheese, and pine nuts. Decorate the plates with the pear. Drizzle with good olive oil and a squeeze of fresh lemon juice.

Portobello Mushroom Pappardelle

Pasta is so ubiquitous now that it has to be really good for me to make the effort. I love this recipe because it's simple and meaty. It will satisfy a ravenous appetite.

8-ounce packet of pappardelle pasta
2 ounces butter
1 tablespoon olive oil
3 large portobello mushrooms, sliced thickly
½ cup freshly chopped parsley
Parmesan cheese
sea salt and freshly ground pepper

Serves 4

Cook the pasta according to the package directions. Meanwhile, melt the butter and oil in a skillet over medium heat. Add the mushrooms and sauté for 5 or 6 minutes, turning over once or twice with a pair of tongs. Drain the pasta when it is al dente and put in bowls. Place the mushrooms on top and drizzle with the buttery sauce from the skillet. Sprinkle with chopped parsley and grated Parmesan. Season with salt and pepper.

Roasted Vegetable Couscous

Carrots, parsnips, yam, zucchini, bell peppers, or squash—whatever is in season can be peeled and chopped into bite-size pieces.

veggies (see above)
olive oil
sea salt and freshly ground pepper
1 garlic bulb
1 cup couscous

Serves 2

Preheat the oven to 400 degrees F. Place the veggies on a large baking sheet and generously coat with olive oil, salt, and pepper. Break up the garlic bulb and add separate cloves—don't peel. Get your hands involved, making sure every bite is coated. Bake for 20 minutes. Put the couscous in a bowl and add 2 cups of boiling water. Cover with a plate for 5 minutes and then fluff up. Arrange a few spoons on each plate. Top with the veggies.

Gorgeously Green Summer Dinner Party

And now here's how to make a wonderful dinner that will blow your friends away! So many of my girlfriends tell me they can't really cook and certainly wouldn't attempt a dinner party, which in my mind is crazy because it is so simple. For those of you that fall into the latter category, promise me you'll give this a go.

Crisp and Cool Cucumber Soup

My English friend Fiona makes this and always gets groans of pleasure from her guests. I'm actually quite jealous of her cooking prowess!

2 seedless cucumbers, chopped

4 avocados, chopped

juice of 2 limes

4 tablespoons sour cream

4 scallions, chopped

32 ounces chicken stock

sea salt and freshly ground pepper

¼ cup freshly chopped cilantro

grated zest of 1 lime

Serves 4–6

Put the cucumbers, avocados, lime juice, sour cream, and scallions into the blender and whiz until smooth. Slowly add the chicken stock and give it one more whiz. Season with salt and pepper as needed. Chill before serving and then garnish with cilantro and lime zest. Serve with warm crusty bread.

One-Dish Roasted Mediterranean Chicken

This is surprisingly easy and yet very impressive when you serve it up. Don't worry if you can't get organic red potatoes or Roma tomatoes—just get what you can.

8 garlic cloves

2 teaspoons lemon juice

3 tablespoons olive oil

sea salt and freshly ground pepper

2 chicken breasts, with skin and bone left on

8 Roma tomatoes, halved lengthwise

2 pounds red potatoes, quartered

½ cup pitted kalamata olives

1 tablespoon freshly chopped rosemary

2 cups fresh arugula

Serves 4

Preheat the oven to 425 degrees F. Lightly grease a large baking dish with olive oil. Mince 4 garlic gloves and mash to a paste. Add the lemon juice, 2 tablespoons of olive oil, salt, and pepper. Cut the chicken breasts in half and place skin-side-up in the baking dish. Brush generously with half of the garlic mixture.

Toss the tomatoes, remaining garlic cloves, and potatoes in the rest of the olive oil and coat well. Arrange them around the chicken and sprinkle with the olives and rosemary. Put in the oven for 15 minutes and then take out to brush with the remaining garlic mixture. Roast for another 15 minutes and serve on a bed of crunchy green arugula.

Summer Pudding

In England, a pudding is a spongy, delicious, fattening thing! In the winter, I like chocolate or syrup sponges with heavy cream. This is a beautiful, light, summery version—a British classic that will elicit gasps of delight from your guests. It's also very green because you are using up leftover bread.

3/4 cup water

13/4 pounds soft summer fruit: raspberries, blackberries, strawberries, and blueberries

3/4 cup unrefined sugar

7–8 medium slices white bread or brioche, crusts trimmed

Serves 4–6 (generous portions)

Put the water, fruit, and sugar in a saucepan and simmer over medium heat until the sugar has melted. Lightly grease a glass or ceramic bowl.

Cut bread slices lengthwise and line the sides and bottom of the bowl. Fill in any gaps with small pieces of bread so no juice escapes when you add fruit. Fill the bowl with the fruit mixture and cover with more slices of bread. Put a plate on top of the bread and weigh down with something heavy like a can. Chill overnight. When you are ready to serve, turn out onto a pretty plate, dust with confectioners' sugar, and serve with full-fat yogurt or heavy cream.

Gorgeously Green Winter Dinner Party

Twice-Baked Soufflé

This recipe is seriously impressive. Whenever I serve it, my guests are talking about it for weeks afterward. Everyone thinks that you have to be a gourmet cook to pass off a good soufflé; however, this is a good way around the worry of the whole thing caving in. It's foolproof and quite wonderful. I strongly suggest you make it a day in advance so that you can enjoy pampering yourself before the dinner, knowing that you have something ingenious up your sleeve.

1 cup whole milk

1 bay leaf

1/2 teaspoon nutmeg

6 whole black peppercorns

2 tablespoons butter

1/2 cup all-purpose flour

sea salt and freshly ground pepper

6 ounces Gruyère cheese, grated

2 large eggs, separated

3/4 cup heavy cream

2 tablespoons Parmesan, grated

Serves 6

You will also need 6 ramekins (small individual ceramic dishes), a baking tin (about 6 inches deep), and a baking dish. Preheat the oven to 350 degrees F. Heat the milk, bay leaf, nutmeg, and peppercorns in a saucepan until the mixture simmers, then pour through a sieve into a small bowl and chuck away the spices.

Rinse the pan and melt the butter in it. Add the flour and stir until smooth and glossy. Cook for 3 minutes, then gradually stir in the milk, whisking all the time until the sauce is thick. Add the salt and pepper and cook for 2 minutes more on very low heat. Remove from the heat, let cool for 5 minutes, then beat in the egg yolks, one at a time. Stir in the grated cheese.

Make sure the egg whites are in a really clean bowl. Beat them until they are in peaks. Using a large metal spoon, fold them into the sauce mixture. Divide among the six ramekins.

Set the ramekins in the baking tin and fill the tin with 1/2 inch of boiling water. Place in the center of the oven and bake for 20 minutes. When the ramekins are cool, turn each soufflé out into the palm of your hand, then place right-way-up on a shallow baking dish. You can cover them with parchment paper and store in the fridge for up to 24 hours. (Don't worry if they collapse a little, as they will rise when you cook them again.)

Exactly 40 minutes before you plan to serve them, preheat the oven to 350 degrees F. Sprinkle the soufflés with Parmesan cheese. Cook in the center of the oven for 30 minutes. Just before bringing them out, drizzle each with a large spoon of heavy cream. A sprig of watercress or a small pile of arugula will make this dish picture perfect.

Stuffed Squash

My husband loves this recipe, as it's very satisfying. Once set on dishes, you'll want to get your digital camera out, as they look so beautiful. I buy my acorn squash at a farmer's market, where they are plentiful for all the winter months.

4 small acorn squash, halved lengthwise and seeded

sea salt and freshly ground pepper

2 cups brown rice

3 tablespoons grapeseed oil

1 large onion, finely chopped

5 celery stalks, chopped

4 carrots, chopped

1 teaspoon dried oregano

1/2 teaspoon dried basil

3 tablespoons tamari or soy sauce

1 cup raisins

1 cup toasted pine nuts

1/2 cup crumbled feta cheese

Serves 8

Preheat the oven to 400 degrees F. Place the squash halves, cut-side-up, in a large baking pan and add about 2 inches of water to the pan. Brush a little olive oil over the squash, then season with salt and pepper and bake for 45 minutes.

Rinse the rice and put in a heavy saucepan with 3 cups of water and a little salt. Bring to a boil, cover, and simmer on low heat for 45–50 minutes. Meanwhile, in a large skillet, heat the grapeseed oil and add the onion, celery, and carrots. Gently sauté until soft. Add the oregano, basil, and tamari or soy sauce, then stir in the raisins. When the rice is cooked, add to the vegetables and mix well.

Pile the mixture into each squash half and sprinkle with the pine nuts and feta cheese. Serve with a side of steamed greens or a simple salad.

Wicked Little Chocolate Pots

These were a big treat when I was little. My mother is an amazing cook, and she would serve this dessert in little white porcelain pots with lids on them so that you couldn't vie for the biggest. "You get what you get and you don't get upset," she'd say!

6 ounces best-quality dark chocolate, broken into small squares

¼ cup strong black coffee

1 teaspoon butter

3 eggs, separated

½ teaspoon vanilla

2 teaspoons brandy (optional)

Makes 6–7 little pots

In a saucepan, warm the chocolate and coffee over low heat until the chocolate melts and becomes creamy. Beat in the butter with a whisk. Allow to cool for 5 minutes. Then beat in the egg yolks one at a time. Add the vanilla and brandy. Whisk the egg whites in a clean bowl until they are stiff, then stir briskly into the chocolate mixture. Pour into small pots or pretty glasses and chill overnight.

Gorgeously Green Treats

Macaroons

My husband can be persuaded to do almost anything with the promise of a couple of my homemade macaroons. He has no idea how easy they are to make!

12 ounces shredded coconut

½ cup rice syrup

½ cup maple syrup

2 tablespoons soy milk

Serves 2 greedy girls!

Preheat the oven to 325 degrees F. Mix all of the ingredients in a bowl, then divide the mixture into little triangular piles on a greased baking sheet. Bake for 15 to 20 minutes. The macaroons should be nicely browned on top and gooey in the center.

Kids

Supersmart Smoothie

Numerous studies have concluded that omega-3 oils are really helpful for the brain development in kids. One of the best ways to ingest these precious oils is by eating hemp seed. My daughter would rather eat dirt, so it has to be carefully hidden away in a smoothie. If you can't get ground hemp seeds at your local health food store, you can try the following Web sites: *www. globalhempstore.com* and *www.momsoriginal.com*.

½ cup plain yogurt

1 banana

1 tablespoon ground hemp seeds

1 cup pineapple or orange juice

1 teaspoon honey to sweeten (optional)

Serves 1

Put yogurt, banana, and hemp seeds in a blender and blend until smooth. Slowly add the fruit juice and blend for another 30 seconds. Taste to see if you need to sweeten with honey.

Chocolate Chip, Walnut, and Banana Cookies

Okay, these are incredibly delicious and a firm favorite of every child who graces my kitchen; they are also a snap to make. I take comfort in the fact that they contain a lot of healthy whole foods. I rarely buy cookies anymore, because the really good organic ones are expensive, and the grocery store kind aren't an option because of the unhealthy fats in most of them.

This recipe will make about three dozen small cookies, so you can keep them in a sealed container for a week or go feed a class of hungry kids.

1 cup all-purpose flour

1 teaspoon baking soda

1 teaspoon baking powder

¼ teaspoon salt

¼ cup coconut oil

2 tablespoons butter

1 cup brown sugar

1 large egg

1 large egg white

½ cup agave syrup

1 tablespoon soy milk

2 teaspoons vanilla

2 cups rolled oats

1 cup semisweet chocolate chips

1 cup walnut pieces

1 ripe banana, mashed

Makes 36 cookies

Preheat the over to 375 degrees F. Combine the flour, baking soda, baking powder, and salt in a bowl. Put the coconut oil, butter, brown sugar, egg, egg white, agave syrup, soy milk, and vanilla into a food processor and blend until smooth. Pour this mixture into the dry ingredients and mix well. Stir in the oats, chocolate chips, walnuts, and banana. With a tablespoon, drop the dough onto a greased baking sheet, making sure the cookies are spaced 2½ inches apart. Bake for 7–10 minutes. Cookies should be slightly soft when pressed with your finger. Take care not to overbake them.

Slow Cookers

Slow cookers have always annoyed me. I'm not sure why—maybe it was my mom's insistence that I should get one. Ever since I left home at age eighteen, she's been banging on about it. So naturally I steered clear of them until a few months ago. Now I love my bubbling pot, and yes, my least favorite three words are "I told you!" Slow cookers are the way to go for the Gorgeously Green girl, as they use the least amount of energy out of every cooking device you can think of, and they save time and money. I love that I can throw in a bunch of veggies, some stock, and a dash of wine in the morning and then forget about it. I come back at night and a bubbling, cozy stew is waiting. *Simple Vegan Slow Cooking* by Michelle Rivera has lots of great stockpot recipes.

Gado Gado Stew

½ cup peanut butter

¼ cup rice vinegar

1 cup of green beans, trimmed

1 red or yellow bell pepper, sliced

8 ounces water chestnuts

4 or 5 large mushrooms, sliced

1 tablespoon freshly grated ginger

8 ounces tofu

½ cup chopped peanuts

2 tablespoons soy sauce

2 teaspoons toasted sesame oil

2 cups vegetable broth

1 cup broccoli florets

5 ounces rice noodles or soba noodles

Serves 4-6

Mix the peanut butter and rice vinegar together in a bowl. Put all of the other ingredients in the slow cooker except the broccoli and rice noodles. Add the peanut butter mixture and cook on high for 3 hours or low for 7 hours. Thirty minutes before serving, making sure the temperature is high, add the broccoli florets and rice noodles.

Every Girl Needs Her Goodies

Far from denying myself the goodies, I just think about the ones that are going to make me feel good and then stock up. Although dietitians and nutritionists suggest munching on carrot or celery sticks, it doesn't really do it for me. Here are some one-bite goody ideas:

- A couple of squares of rich dark chocolate
- A large square of Greek halvah (made with almonds, tahini, and honey)
- A rice cake slathered with fruit-juice-only jelly or almond butter
- Half a papaya with a squeeze of lime juice
- A handful of cashew nuts or smoked almonds
- A handful of garlicky soy nuts

All of these items are nutritious whole foods that will give you energy and put a smile on your face.

Drinks

Tea

Being a Brit, I'm a great tea drinker; however, I have now gone totally green. I drink green tea at least twice a day because I love the flavor, and the health benefits are incredible. It is said to be helpful for cancer, arthritis, high cholesterol, cardiovascular disease, infection, and impaired immune function, because it contains polyphenols, which are powerful antioxidants. It is often grown organically, so you won't be harming the earth. Green tea can also help dieters to burn more calories—hello! As if that's not enough, it helps prevent tooth decay—so go green, girls.

Here are some recommendations if you want to purchase really good-quality tea:

- ❀ I'm obsessed with the **Tea Garden** (*www.teagarden.com*), and luckily for me, unluckily for my bank balance, there are two stores within cycling distance from me in Los Angeles. They have literally hundreds of different kinds of green and black teas, and they'll spend hours telling you all about the different brewing times and benefits. The owner is the eccentric and fabulous Dr. Tea. He has his own radio show, often appears on TV, and has recently published a book that I can't wait to read called *The Ultimate Tea Diet.* The Web site is informative, as you can learn a lot about the different teas, especially the ones that promote weight loss.
- ❀ **Rishi Tea Company** (*www.rishi-tea.com*) shows you photographs of all the different leaves and blends. If you are new to tea drinking, you can enjoy trying different brews until you find your favorite. I am addicted to genmaicha (*jen-my-cha*). It is mixed with toasted rice and has a rich, nutty flavor.
- ❀ **Numi** (*www.numitea.com*) is a wonderful organic tea company with fantastic eco-friendly practices. I adore its Flowering Tea—you pop your little bud into a glass cup or teapot and watch the "rare Leaves of Art" blossom.
- ❀ **Tazo Tea** (*www.tazo.com*) has a cute little canister for loose-leaf teas with a lid that doubles as a tea infuser. I also like to buy tea in tins, as they are obviously recyclable and keep the tea really fresh. When you purchase your teas, pay specific attention to the brewing instructions. Each tea differs in how long you need to steep it.
- ❀ **Garden of Life** (*www.gardenoflife.com*) has a great tea concentrate that I love. It comes already brewed in convenient individual liquid packets.

Make Your Own

It is so easy and delicious to make your own herbal tea. After completing step 6, you will, if you already don't, have an herb garden, so you are all set. Just grab a bunch of mint leaves, put them in a warmed teapot, and add boiling water. Serve with organic honey. Kids will love it. You can also add some orange or lemon rind to give it a fruity flavor.

Cocoa

Sipping a cup of creamy, hot cocoa on a winter night is almost as good as it gets. Goes without saying that the cocoa must be organic and fair trade. For a special treat, try one of the following:

❀ **Green & Blacks Maya Gold**   (*www.green&blacks.com*)
❀ **Xocolatl**   (*www.dagobachocolate.com*)

Coffee Substitute

If you're trying to cut down your coffee intake, try **Teeccino** (*www. teeccino.com*)—another favorite of mine. It's an herbal coffee made of grains, fruits, and nuts. It has all the same enjoyment as coffee but is caffeine-free, and you don't get the acidity that is in coffee (and not good for you). Yummy flavors like vanilla nut and amaretto make this brew a treat, especially if you are craving something sweet.

Soda

We never have soda in our house. It is totally gross—even if it's diet soda, it contains benzene, a chemical that has been linked to many horrible health conditions. Moreover, it can be fattening and rots your teeth.

Because I don't want to deny my daughter the zing of a cool, sparkling lemonade, I make my own: I buy organic lemonade or cranberry juice and add sparkling water. For a fancier version, make this **Gorgeously Green Deluxe Soda**: Fill a third of each glass with organic lemonade (not the sparkling kind). Grab a few sprigs of lavender and a few leaves of basil and mint. Crush the herbs between your palms and add to the lemonade. Add crushed ice and fill the rest of the glass with sparkling mineral water.

Coconut Water

Coconut water is an amazing alternative to those foul-colored sports and energy drinks. It replaces lost electrolytes, so if you're gasping of thirst, it's the way to go. If you have been sick, it's a great way to get rehydrated. It has a bunch more potassium than most sports drinks and is great for digestion. Check out:

❀ *www.zico.com*
❀ *www.onenaturalexperience.com*

Drinks for Kids

I give my child water over juice almost all the time because she has a very sweet tooth and doesn't need the extra sugar. I never give her the little plastic bottles because they can leach chemicals into the water, and they require energy to produce and recycle. I love the metal **Sigg** bottles for kids (*www.reusablebags.com*). They come in divine designs, are indestructible, and ensure zero percent leaching.

Gorgeously Green Kitchen Tips

❀ When you are boiling the water for a cup of tea, boil only the amount you will be using, as it uses considerably less energy to heat a small mug's worth as opposed to a full kettle. You could invest in an **Eco-kettle** (*www.eco-kettle.com*), which is cordless and saves a great deal of energy.

❀ Boiling water in a tea kettle is quicker and more energy efficient than bringing water to boil in a pan, so when cooking veggies, boil the water in your kettle before transferring to a pan.

❀ A microwave is the most eco-friendly way to cook, as it uses the least amount of energy.

❀ Invest in a slow cooker, as it is the most energy efficient of the lot.

❀ Wooden cutting boards are better than plastic because they don't pollute during the manufacturing process, and the wood has natural antibacterial properties.

❀ In the winter, leave the oven door open after turning it off, as it will help heat the kitchen.

Recipes—For even more scrumptious and sustainable recipes, go to *www.gorgeouslygreen.com* and type in the password that you see below. Password: **Yummy**.

Task

Go to your local grocery store and make your way to the produce section. Pick up the fruits and veggies you would normally buy, but instead of putting them in your cart, read the label to see if it is grown locally (within one hundred miles). If it is not, put it back and pick an alternative. See if you end up with fewer produce items than normal when you get to the checkout.

Savasana

Not a good idea to practice this pose with a full belly. Great idea to do it before you eat—that way, you will eat more slowly and enjoy your food a whole lot more. Lie down as usual. Take a few yogic breaths as you relax your body. Focus on the miracle that your physical body is—the perfect precision with which everything works, from your digestion, to your heart pumping blood. Focus on what feels good in your body. Allow your belly to be soft and let go.

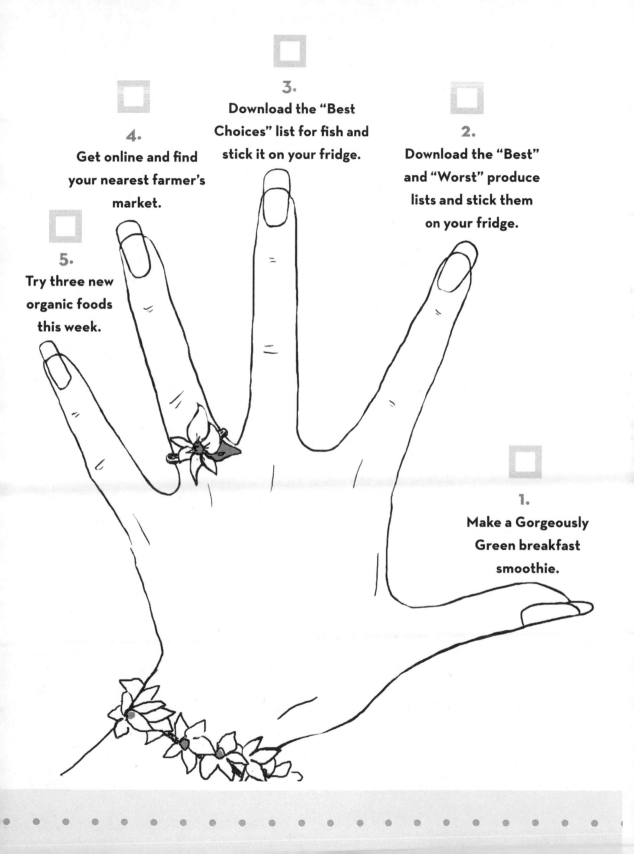

3.
Download the "Best Choices" list for fish and stick it on your fridge.

4.
Get online and find your nearest farmer's market.

5.
Try three new organic foods this week.

2.
Download the "Best" and "Worst" produce lists and stick them on your fridge.

1.
Make a Gorgeously Green breakfast smoothie.

Chapter Seven

STEP 7: Out and About
Having Fun

I know, we all know—our cars are the worst environmental culprits of the lot. They spew out their ghastly emissions into our already polluted air and will take global warming to the next level as more and more people drive. It's amazing that we didn't even think there was a problem a few years ago. We thought big cars were cool, and here in California, we used to laugh at small European-style cars. Not anymore—it's the owners of the teeny "Smart" car (which looks like one of my daughter's Polly Pocket toys) who are laughing at us in our silly four-by-fours. It clearly doesn't make sense to drive a whacking gas-guzzler anymore—it harms our pocketbook and our planet.

IT'S TRUE: Cars are responsible for more than 60 percent of air pollution, which causes global warming, acid rain, and smog.

We also know that we are dependent on oil and that it is going to run out in the not-too-distant future, and then what are we going to do? It's such an awful prospect to get our head around that we tend to ignore it, hoping it won't happen in our lifetime or our children's. It's unfathomable to think of a life without oil—nothing would work! It's not just cars but *everything* that we take for granted in our day-to-day life, from heat and light to food. The gloom-and-doom merchants would have us believe that the lights are going to go out and that a hot shower will be a distant memory in only a few years' time. I think we've got a bit longer and that alternative technologies are going to go some way to helping the situation. I do, however, know that I need to take responsibility right now and inspire every woman I know to do the same. I'm discovering that it feels great to be accountable and to really care. Every time I flick off a light switch, I'm helping; every time I walk instead of drive, I'm helping, and I get to tone my tush for free.

Driving a car is the most obvious "dependent-on-oil" nightmare. It's a twofold issue that we need to consider:

1. *The gas that we pump into our cars is only going to get more expensive and isn't going to last forever. There really is a finite amount of oil buried in the earth. We've managed to drill down and get most of it out in just three hundred years, and there isn't that much left.*
2. *The amount of gas we use is directly related to our tailpipe emissions. It's a total bummer—just when we have gotten used to our cozy, comfortable, and cost-effective cars, we're being told that they are the most lethal monsters ever to have been invented.*

Change the Way You Look at Your Car

I try to look at my car as a luxury now. It is very expensive to run and very costly to the environment, so I try not to take it for granted. My car is very personal; she even has a name, Hilary! Much as I love her, she's got to be left at home whenever possible. The other day, I decided to walk the three miles rather than drive to pick up my daughter from school, and then we took the bus back. Given the fact that nearly everyone drives in L.A., this was a courageous step to take. The other moms in the carpool line, sitting in their comfortable Volvo station wagons, looked at me with derision as I stood at the bus stop with Lola, trying to make sense of the timetable. We had to wait an hour in a sudden downpour for the number 210 to come sputtering along. Lola was hungry, cold, and not amused; and did mom bring along snacks and a sweater—I don't think so! We'll be more prepared next time, although Lola categorically says, "There won't be a *next* time."

There is no perfect alternative to using your car, other than walking or cycling. Did you know that walking one mile in twenty minutes uses as much energy as doing aerobics for sixteen minutes? So maybe you want to donate your leotard to Goodwill and put on your walking boots.

If you live in a city that is not an urban sprawl like Los Angeles or has a good mass-transit system, you are very lucky. When I used to live in London, public transport was a way of life and you hardly needed a car.

We all have such different lifestyles, so let's consider some of the alternatives to guzzling the gas:

❀ **Car-pooling**   is an excellent idea, and I am forcing myself to do more of it. I have to admit, I do like being by myself in my car, blaring the radio or singing at the top of my voice, but it's a small sacrifice to make for the planet.

Call a friend or someone who lives nearby and suggest going to the store together. I actually love shopping with a girlfriend. I like to see what she puts in her cart, and we can share tips, recipes, and gossip.

If you are going out to a restaurant or movie with friends who live nearby, suggest carpooling. You'll need only one designated driver.

Post a note at work or on the gym/yoga studio bulletin board saying you are looking for people in your area to carpool with—many of these situations have ended up in romance! (Obviously, check that the office or gym knows the person well who you are going to ride with.)

❀ **Car sharing** (*www.carsharing.net*) is different from carpooling. It's a relatively recent thing. More and more car-sharing companies are springing up all over the United States. It will work well for you only if you live an urban, low-mileage lifestyle. You simply take out a membership with your local car-sharing company, and for a nominal monthly fee, you get to use their cute hybrid car for as little as a two-hour window. The advantage is that you will save on parking, insurance, car payments, repairs, and fuel bills. The disadvantage is that you have to go pick up the car when you need it. The difference between car sharing and car rental is that you don't have to sign forms, get insurance, and pay through the roof. Everything is included and taken care of.

❀ **Cutting back** on certain trips is possible—my husband keeps telling me, thank you very much! I understand it's all about organization—something that doesn't come naturally to me but definitely something I need to get the hang of in order to be green. If I make an extensive and well-organized—ugh, I hate that word—shopping list at the beginning of the week, then I am less likely to have to rush out and buy the items that I forgot or didn't think I would need.

I have also started to plan errands around the route I am taking that day rather than the other way around. If it's not on my school pick-up route, I'll go to the bank or post office when I'm next in that area of town. You may be lucky enough to have everything nearby or even within walking distance, but Los Angeles is horrendously spread out—witness, the drugstore I like is eight miles from my favorite deli.

I have also got into the habit of always calling up stores to see if they have what I need ahead of time, as last December I learned my lesson when I went off in search of recycled holiday cards. After an entire morning's trek around L.A., I went home exhausted and irritated and had to suffer my horribly smug husband singing, "I told you so."

TIP: Make a list with the phone numbers of all the main stores in your area where you frequently shop—hardware, grocery store, and so on. Stick it to your fridge door next to your superorganized shopping list to remind you to make the short call before taking the long trip.

❀ **Bicycling** is a must! I've got my eye on a powder pink bicycle, but my husband is very nervous about cycling in Los Angeles. You do take your life into your hands in this busy city where cycle lanes are virtually unheard of, but I'd like to be ahead of the curve. I use to bicycle everywhere when I lived in London—my thighs, butt, and bank balance were in very good shape as a result. If you live anywhere that is cycling-friendly, ditch your car whenever you can. Consider buying an electric bicycle (*www.electrabike.com*) and brag about your ride having zero emissions.

❀ **Backpacking** is the new cool thing to be seen doing around town. Adults with backpacks used to conjure up images of spotty adolescents with student travel cards or crusty weirdos. Not anymore. Invest in a really cool and colorful backpack, and get it as large as possible. You are going to walk or cycle to the grocery store and not worry about how to cart the bags home, because you have your new trendy back accessory. The other day, I needed my daily aerobic exercise, so I decided to kill two birds by walking a few miles to the store. I slung my gorgeous new ruck-sack over my shoulder and set off. The return journey was challenging, to say the least, because the sun decided to suddenly increase the temperature by almost twenty degrees. Add a twenty-pound backpack to the equation and you have a very sweaty girl. However, it's great for the legs, butt, pocketbook, and environment, so give it a go.

The Skinny on Alternative Fuels

Aside from walking, a lot of people are pushing alternative fuels as a way to cut down on our energy consumption. I'm not convinced that they are the way to go, but we'll take a look at the options.

We've finally cottoned on that there is a *finite* supply of oil, and most of what's left isn't in our country. It has to be said, however, that there is no perfect solution to this monumental problem. The best daily contribution that any of us can make is to cut down on our personal fuel consumption.

It's also important to realize that in creating biofuels or ethanol, we could create even more serious global catastrophes: instead of the arguments being over oil, they will be over food, water, and habitable land. A good example of a bad situation is Brazil: the country's largest crop is sugarcane, yet half of it is being switched to ethanol for biofuel. This fuel is not only for domestic use but also for export. Brazil's landscape is being devastated to make way for more plantations. Forests are being slashed down at an unprecedented rate, which causes serious greenhouse gases. So you see, the golden ethanol that we see in the news comes with a massive price tag and may not be sustainable in the long run. Most significant is the fact that it won't be possible for us to grow enough crops to feed our demand—ever!

IT'S TRUE: If high-yield biocrops were grown on all the farmland on earth, the resulting fuel would account for only 20 percent of our current demand.

❀ **Ethanol** is made out of primarily corn and sugarcane. It is typically mixed with regular gas and is usually used as an additive. Almost

50 percent of us use some form of ethanol in our cars without even knowing it. It pollutes less than gasoline; however, there are problems that make it less than ideal.

It takes a lot of food crops to produce a relatively small amount of ethanol, and car mileage is lower on this alternative fuel. More importantly, it generates a ton of carbon dioxide, which contributes to global warming; and ethanol produces more smog than regular gas. Finally, U.S. corn is treated with larger quantities of toxic pesticides and fertilizers than any other crop, so a drastic increase in its production would be disastrous for our water supply because of the runoff.

❀ **Cellulosic ethanol** is similar to regular ethanol. This variation is made from wood chips and agricultural waste products. It can also be made out of switchgrass. The great news about this one is that it doesn't eat up the food crops needed to feed this hungry world. The technology and infrastructure for production is still a little way off, but the future looks promising.

❀ **Hybrid technology** is becoming popular. Most of us know about the trendy hybrid car. Many celebrities drive the Toyota Prius, which gets almost forty miles to the gallon and has really low tailpipe emissions.

Hybrid cars use gas and electricity. They have electric batteries, which power electric motors. A combustion engine (this is the most technical I will ever get) generates electricity to recharge the battery. When you drive slowly, the car will just use electricity, and when you put your foot on the pedal, it'll click into gas mode and you'll see a little picture on your monitor of dots pouring out of a gas can. You will save a bit on your gas bill with hybrids, although not as much as the manufacturers would have you believe.

There is a lot of controversy, however, because many say the whole life of a hybrid car from dust to dust uses more energy and produces more pollution that that of a regular car. Why? Because the car's elaborate battery system causes a massive environmental impact due to the mining needed to produce the batteries and the caustic substances that power them. These substances are really poisonous and cause untold damage when released into the environment.

If the battery and car is disposed of responsibly at the end of the car's life, it may be a good choice—but do weigh the pros and cons. Since hybrids are expensive, if you are considering a new car, you may be better off buying the most fuel-efficient nonhybrid you can find.

❀ **Biodiesel** is made mainly from soybeans, which is a huge U.S. crop. It can also be made from old restaurant grease and fat. I'm not sure I love the thought of all that stinky burger grease running Hilary, but it's fantastic that it is being put to good use.

If you already own a diesel car, you can switch to biodiesel. I strongly advise you to make the change right this minute, because regular diesel spews out horrendous smog-forming emissions—much more so than regular gas. Go to *www.biodiesel.org* and find the nearest biodiesel supplier. If you switch, you will be so Gorgeously Green that you will hardly be able to stand it. No more harmful emissions and no more dependence on foreign oil—what could be better?

Putting biodiesel in a regular gas-powered vehicle is a big mistake. The fuel must fit the engine for which it is made. The vehicle must have a diesel engine that runs on diesel number 2.

Biodiesel is probably one of the best alternative choices to date, especially when you consider that the fast-food industry produces over three billion gallons of fryer oil a year and that amount is only going to increase.

❀ **Electric cars** are definitely not the way to go if you are going on a journey of a hundred miles or more. The battery will run out, and in the unlikely event that you find somewhere to plug it in, you may be sitting for a good hour or two waiting for it to charge!

The good news is that electric cars reduce many of the really bad tailpipe emissions, especially the ones that cause ozone depletion and acid rain. Electricity, however, is electricity, and the power plants from whence it comes are big polluters. So it's not the perfect solution, but certainly better than a gas-guzzler in the city.

❀ **Hydrogen** is made from natural gas but can also be produced from water. Many people think that hydrogen cars are going to be a future hit. The big problem right now is that it takes a lot of energy to produce hydrogen, so it sort of defeats the purpose. Also, hydrogen produces carbon monoxide like any other tailpipe emission and is very expensive to produce.

❀ **Blue-green algae** is an exciting new discovery for cars. We are going to be hearing a lot more about it over the next few years. Algae needs water, sunlight, and carbon dioxide to grow. The oil that it produces can be harvested and converted to biodiesel, and the carbohydrate content can be fermented into ethanol. Because algae "eats" carbon dioxide, it can also clean up dirty fumes and emissions from power plants.

So now you can impress all your friends with your technical knowledge of alternative fuels. Some people love to get on a soapbox and pontificate about the perfection of whatever alternative fuel they happen to be using—they can make us feel useless and pathetic, not to mention guilty the next time we're gassing up, but just know that the perfect solution hasn't yet been found.

If you're not ready to get into the whole alternative fuel scene, there are a number of things you can do right now that will make your driving experience greener. Remember, becoming Gorgeously Green is all about making simple changes that work for you right now.

Thirteen Tips for Making Your Old Banger Eco-Friendly

1. *Get your tire pressure checked weekly—yes, weekly.*
2. *Look around for the best gas prices. They can really vary, even between gas stations that are opposite each other.*
3. *Don't use a higher-octane gas than you need. Only 10 percent of cars require high octane, which is not only more expensive but releases more hazardous pollutants into the air.*
4. *Use your computer to shop instead of taking another trip.*
5. *Avoid crazy road-rage-style driving. It's easier said than done, but gas mileage rapidly decreases when you are over 60 mph.*
6. *If you're hot, open the windows! Pretty obvious, but most of us automatically reach for the A/C button without realizing that this uses more gas.*
7. *Try not to strap a sofa, bathtub, or human being to the top of your car on a regular basis, as the extra weight and wind resistance will drain your gas.*
8. *Remember that sitting with the engine on while you're girly-gossiping means you are getting zero miles to the gallon. To add insult to injury, you're polluting.*

9. *Get your car serviced on a regular basis. Dirty air filters and underinflated tires can increase the cost of gas considerably.*

10. *Don't ever top off your gas when it's clicked off, as the spillover is really bad for your precious little self and the environment.*

11. *Fill your tank at night, as there'll be less evaporation. It will also reduce emissions during the peak daylight hours when ozone formation is most likely to occur.*

12. *Park in the shade. The heat of the sun causes toxins to evaporate from the fuel tank of your car.*

13. *Don't use conventional antifreeze—it's very toxic. Try to get some made from propylene glycol, which is less toxic, or use recycled antifreeze.*

TIP: When you get your car serviced, call around a few service stations in your area to see if any of them use re-refined motor oil; also check that they recycle oil. If you do it yourself, drain oil into a sealed container and take it to your nearest service station that recycles oil. Never pour oil down a drain.

Car Vanity

If you want you car to look shiny and cute, you may be wondering about the car wash. Is it green? Obviously, the most eco-friendly thing you could do would be to wash you car as little as possible. Let it get really dirty until you can't stand it anymore, but if you want the hand-wax thing 24/7, it is greener to go to the car wash. There are very strict laws in the United States that make commercial car washes drain their wastewater in the sewer so that it gets treated properly. Many of them also reuse and recycle the rinsing water. The worst thing you can do is wash your car out on your driveway. All the detergent chemicals and dirty, oily water will run straight into the storm drains; from there, it'll make it's way into creeks, streams, and rivers. As a typical car wash uses up to forty-five gallons of water, check out Green Earth Waterless Carwash (*www.greenearthcarwash.com*). This company was started by a couple whose daughter suffered from chronic allergies. Since most car wash detergents are filled with toxic chemicals, they developed their products to be VOC-, fragrance-, dye-, and paraben-free.

To Fly or Not to Fly—That Is the Question

First off, don't you hate flying nowadays? It is a highly unpleasant experience unless you are able to fly first class, which isn't the norm for most of us. From the moment I set foot inside an airport, my anxiety level rises—the endless lines of disgruntled faces and velour sweats is enough to put anyone off. The appalling security measures that are only going to get worse and then sitting for hours in smelly, cramped conditions—ugh. I always come off a plane looking ten years older and feeling like I need a long weekend at a spa. To add to the horror of flying is the fact that it is an environmental nightmare. It's much worse than driving, because the toxic chemicals that are spewed out are much closer to the ozone layer—they go straight in, whereas on the ground, many of them evaporate on their way up.

IT'S TRUE: Travel and tourism are the world's biggest industries. By the year 2010, one billion people will travel to another country for a vacation, causing unprecedented amounts of greenhouse gases.

So how can we become Gorgeously Green travelers? The good news is that you can make a number of changes that will make a huge difference. Here are three things you can do to help ease fuel consumption on the plane:

1. *Pee before you get on, as each flush uses a great deal of jet fuel.*
2. *Refrain from taking any luggage on the plane at all. Get used to traveling with a toothbrush and a couple of T-shirts; it's the only eco-friendly thing to do.*
3. *Make sure you pick an airline that doesn't offer blankets, cushions, food, or drinks, as all these things weigh down the plane and thus burn more fuel.*

Only joking! I have to say that there are some airlines in China that are seriously suggesting the above measures, as they are so worried about pollution. Although these extreme measures aren't realistic for the average flier, you can try to pack lighter. It'll save your back and the biosphere!

You can also choose to invest in an eco-friendly airline. A few airlines have started to offer customers the opportunity to take part in a program where they can offset carbon emissions that were spewed out during their flight. It's actually a great idea for the Gorgeously Green girl. For a negligible amount of money, we can become accountable for an extremely polluting yet very necessary form of transport. Delta was the first U.S. airline to offer passengers who buy tickets from their Web site the opportunity to offset their emissions by paying $5.50. This money is donated to the Conservation Fund for planting trees—for a little over the price of a chai latte, it feels great to do the right thing (more on carbon offsetting from page 253 on).

IT'S TRUE: A single flush at 30,000 feet uses a quarter of a gallon of fuel.

According to a physicist at Boeing, a single takeoff of a 747 is akin to "setting the local gas station on fire and flying it over your neighborhood." Dan Imhoff, author of *Paper or Plastic*, says that a two-minute takeoff by a 747 is equal to 2.4 million lawn mowers running for twenty minutes. Air travel is going to triple in the next twenty to thirty years. Can you imagine our ghastly, crowded airports getting any worse!

IT'S TRUE: In 2008, air travel is responsible for 2 percent of total global carbon emissions. By 2050, it will be responsible for 10 to 17 percent of emissions, because more people will be flying.

Like a Bird

An eco-plane has recently been designed and may be up and running in the next ten years if we are lucky. The fuselage and wings meld into each other in an aerodynamic design that looks like a seagull in flight. It's much lighter than a normal airplane and is noiseless. So we have that to look forward to when we're grandmothers!

Green Tripping

So how does the Gorgeously Green girl vacation? The greenest vacation would obviously be somewhere close to home. Rent a cottage or a cabin, grab some bicycles, and you're good to go. With airfares continuing to rise, I think a lot more of us are going to forgo those aqua tropical waters in favor of something a bit more local. The cleanest way to travel is by train, so if you can take one anywhere for your summer break, do it. I adore riding on a train. I like to kick back and catch up on magazines or plug into my iPod and get jostled to sleep by Joni Mitchell.

Count yourself lucky if you have a good rail system in your city, because here in Los Angeles, we don't. Talking about trains, I've always fantasized about going on the Orient Express.

Go Green on the Road

1. Try a road trip this year instead of flying somewhere. It will save your money, your stress levels, and your eco-conscience.

2. Stay in a "**Green Seal**" certified hotel. This is an independent agency that certifies hotels that only do all the cool stuff regarding conserving energy.

3. Pick one of thousands of fabulous hotels from this Web site, (*www.greenhotels.com*) that will take care of your every eco-need. Many of these hotels are deluxe and not the rustic, sweat-lodge scenario that eco-travel typically suggests.

4. **Kimpton Hotels** (*www.kimptonhotels.com*) are in major cities all over North America, and their mission is "to support a sustainable world." These are deluxe hotels that won't compromise you on any level.

5. Impress your friends by taking a risk. Do something really altruistic and wonderful, like going on a conservation vacation (*www.keytocostarica.com*) where you will help to support rural communities in Costa Rica.

6. If you are hell-bent on getting on a plane, go on a Spiritual

Quest (*www.himalayanhightreks.com*) to the Buddhist region of Bhutan, Mongolia, Nepal, or Tibet.

7. If you are low on cash this year, check out the following Web sites for really cool volunteer vacations:

For half a day's work, you can get your accommodations and meals at a wonderful organic farm (*www.wwoofusa.com*).

If you want to learn about women's struggles in Afghanistan or fair trade in Tanzania, these folks will arrange an unforgettable trip (*www.globalexchange.org*).

For just $130, you can go on an exciting volunteer hiking trip where you help the planet and your butt at the same time (*www.americanhiking.org*)!

This is one of my favorites. You can go on a fabulously exotic vacation and stay in an affordable hotel that is eco-friendly (*www.responsibletravel.org*).

8. Check out the **International Ecotourism Society** (*www.ecotourism.org*) as they hold auctions for the most incredible eco-trips imaginable.

9. Do a home exchange with someone in a different country. This could turn out to be a wonderful adventure and is much more affordable than a regular vacation. One of the most well-known Web sites is *www.homeexchange.com* (the Web site that was featured in the movie *The Holiday*).

· ·

Seal of Approval

There are a number of certifications that have been set up so that the traveler can be assured that the hotel/tour operator's claims are trusty.

❀ **Green Globe** participants (*www.greenglobe21.com*) have to prove that they are operating at a very high environmental standard.

❁ **Sustainable Tourism Eco-Certification Program** *(www.sustain-abletravelinternational.com)* means the tourism providers get together and agree to make the best environmental effort they can.

❁ **Ecotels** *(www.concepthospitality.com/ecotel)* are hotels that are awarded from one to five "Ecotel Globes."

❁ **Blue Flag Beaches** *(www.blueflag.org)* are assessed on their water quality, environmental education/management, and safety. They must have their blue flags renewed every year.

❁ **Green Key** participants *(www.green-key.org)* have to complete an application that details exactly what they are doing to help the environment.

You may also be surprised at how many regular resorts are turning to eco-friendly practices. If you have your heart set on a particular country or area, call a few hotels and ask them what they are doing about helping the environment—that information might influence your choice. My husband and I recently wanted to find a family resort in Hawaii. I made a few calls, did a bit of research, and found a fabulous resort with many eco-friendly aspects to it, including the fact that every little wooden cabin was made out of coconut fronds: *www.konavillage.com*.

Cruising

With a bit of thought and planning, you can always come up with a more eco-friendly choice. A good example is cruise ships: Large liners can pump up to 25,000 gallons of untreated sewage into the ocean daily. Some of the smaller lines offer more environmentally friendly alternatives:

❁ *www.cruisenorthexpeditions.com*
❁ *www.expeditions.com*

If you're thinking of taking a tip with one of the major cruise lines, do your research because a few of them have been sued for environmental damage, such as the dumping of toxic chemicals and raw sewage.

Hotel Perks

I love staying in hotels period. I love the fluffy white towels—as many as I want—and the bathrobe that I can fling to the floor to be cleaned every day if I choose. I have a clean sheet fetish. My husband was a little surprised the first time he heard me groan with pleasure when I slid into a freshly made-up bed. He thought something fruity was going on and wouldn't believe that it was simply the cool, fresh linen that was pleasuring me. My husband is thrilled that in becoming Gorgeously Green, I have had to find another avenue for my bedtime pleasure! Daily clean sheets, towels, and robes are not earth-friendly. I don't have them at home, so I can't, in good conscience, have them in hotels either. Most hotels have signs asking you to refrain from tossing your towels into the laundry every day. I guess they want to save money, too, so it's win/win for them if you comply.

Eco-Indulgence

Who doesn't love a spa? But beware: there are good spas and really bad spas! Again, watch for that ubiquitous buzzword, *spa*, which brings to mind infinity pools and holistic massage, but it's not always the case. In England, a spa is a hangout that incorporates water—lots of it, and preferably of the healing variety. Here in Los Angeles, I have come across numerous day spas that offer nothing more than a couple of shabby treatment rooms and a bad-tempered receptionist; the only water being in the heavily chlorinated shower that you are shoved into after an unpleasant mud wrap. Many of the treatments offered in such establishments sound good but can be completely bogus. Moreover, the Gorgeously Green girl needs to be on high alert for any "healing" treatments that could involve what we now understand to be toxic chemicals. If I have a facial, I need to know the products that are going on my skin. There is no way that I am going to pay over a hundred bucks for fancy creams that do little more than mess with my endocrine system. I tend to pass on the body scrubs, as I can take along a pot of my own home-made polish and spend my money on a really good massage.

The great news is that many women are demanding a truly holistic experience with products that are even superior to the ones they use at home. These same women want everything to be organic and even environmentally friendly—and so the eco-spa has evolved.

The online Spa Resource Directory, **Spa Finder** (*www.spafinder. com*) offers us a great definition: "Eco spas are set in natural or protected areas and incorporate organic gardening, water conservation and ecological building design. They encourage sensitivity to the natural environment and wildlife, and they may also promote the well-being of local people and culture by preserving indigenous healing traditions and ingredients." The International Spa Association says that any spa can declare itself to be an "eco-oasis," and there are no official regulations to police its practices. So you need to be supersavvy and do your research. Ask these questions:

1. *What skin care products do you use? (If you've never heard of the product, enter it into the Skin Deep database (see page 28).*
2. *Do you use indigenous products and practices from the area in which you are located? (A good sign if they do.)*
3. *Is all your food organic and/or local? (Great sign if it is.)*
4. *What are your environmental practices: do you recycle, compost, use solar power, etc.?*

The Gorgeously Green Road Trip

I'm taking my family on a green road trip this year. I haven't decided exactly where yet, but living here in southern California, I've got a lot of choices. My husband doesn't like surprises, but I've told him to trust me on this one. The last one I planned had him negotiating his way around rocks and thick foliage while contending with an extraordinarily aggressive mule—I love an adventure!

I plan to book us into a "Green Seal Certified" hotel for two or three nights. We will load up the car with all our goodies: organic snacks, juices, chocolate, and fruit packed in a no-waste picnic hamper.

No-Waste Picnic Hamper

Cloth napkins, reusable plastic or glass containers, real (as opposed to plastic) cutlery, and reusable cups and mugs. There is nothing worse that using paper plates and plastic cutlery for a picnic, especially if any cutting is involved, and it's totally unromantic.

If you are using a cooler, instead of buying ice packs, use old plastic bottles, fill half full with water, and put in the freezer—*voilà!*

We'll make frequent stops at coffee shops en route and fill up our reusable coffee mugs and water bottles. We are going to be really old-fashioned and play car games like "animal twenty questions" and I spy." I don't love the idea of an in-car DVD system. I have such great memories of road trips as a kid: my brother and I would snuggle in with pillows and toys, and the hours would be spent chatting, fighting, and driving my mother crazy. That being said, we all connected with each other, which wouldn't have been the case had we been watching movies for six hours.

Vacation at Home

Many greenies have started vacationing at home, and it's not a bad idea. My neighbors decided to try it this year and they had a riot. They drew up a family rule sheet before the week began: no phones, no computers or Blackberries, and obviously no work of any description, including home projects. They said it was blissful—they planned all kinds of local excursions to museums and funny little pockets of town they had never had time to visit. They took naps, watched movies, went for long nature walks, and most importantly, avoided the hassle and expense of regular travel.

Travel with Good Purpose

No matter where you are going or how you are getting there, you can take these Gorgeously Green steps:

1. Never, ever litter. Obvious for most, but amazing how some people still don't get it.
2. Use your cute little digital camera instead of taking "natural" souvenirs like rocks and shells. My daughter always used to

collect shells. I thought a few wouldn't make a difference, but then I realized that if everyone thought like me, there would be nothing pretty to look at on the beach.

3. Again, obvious—but keep to the trail. Our ever-expanding population is trampling all over what few scenic places we have left.

4. Study the culture of where you are going so that you can respect the people. They may believe that taking photos robs them of their souls. Always ask before entering a shrine or sacred place.

5. Never have your picture taken with a wild animal. Many of them were probably removed from their mothers when young and will have had claws and teeth removed or may even be drugged.

6. Don't support dancing bears. They are removed from the wild when young, and training involves standing on a hot metal plate while music is played, forcing the bear to "dance" to avoid the pain.

7. For your souvenirs, avoid items from endangered species such as ivory, tortoise shell, feathers, and animal skins. If you are buying items such as frames that are made of wood, ask what kind of wood it is and find out if it's harvested responsibly.

8. Try to shop and eat locally, as it will boost that area's economy.

9. There can be risks when taking part in swimming with the dolphins. These gorgeous, intelligent animals can be injured by your jewelry or develop infections from your suntan lotion.

Eco-Travel—Go online to *www.gorgeouslygreen.com* for the latest green in earth-friendly travel and type in the password that you see below. Password: Dreamy.

Entertainment and Entertaining

What does the Gorgeously Green girl do to entertain herself? I cannot believe the ridiculously small amount of time we devote to having fun. Most people I know, myself included, are to some extent workaholics. We just don't know when to stop. For me, the Internet has a lot to do with it. I am definitely addicted to checking my e-mail; it makes me feel connected—so connected, in fact, that I get in a panic when I can't check in to see who wants, needs, or loves me today, and that's just the start of it. Shopping online or surfing for health-related information can be a dangerously addictive pastime. "What *are* you doing on that computer?" my husband will ask. "Just checking e-mails," I'll reply. "But you've been on it for hours," he'll complain. "Important business," I'll reply as I hastily attempt to remove all traces of retail therapy. Thank goodness for all the laborious forms you have to fill in with personal details to register—that at least in some ways deters me from making outrageously impulsive decisions.

So sadly I have to admit that I spend much of what little leisure time I have sitting in front of an inanimate techno gadget. I'm also alarmed to see that many of my e-mails have been sent from girlfriends at either eleven thirty at night or five thirty in the morning. Talk about drudgery.

Where's all the girly fun gone? Bellyaching laughter over cocktails, great food, and conversation; reading a brilliant novel while chomping on gourmet chocolate. When my mom was my age, computers were strictly a man's office thing, cell phones were unheard of, as was call waiting and answering machines. How on earth did she manage? I was horrified to see that in the intermission of my daughter's school play last week, I glanced across the aisle and noticed that every single mom was checking her e-mails on her Blackberry. Not one word was passed among these women. Something's not right about all this. I still refuse to use a Blackberry, and I've promised my husband that the Gorgeously Green me is going to be on computer curfew from 6 p.m. onward.

Entertainment *Can* Be a Deeper Shade of Green

Most things we do for entertainment can be made a good deal greener by taking a few simple steps:

❁ **Movies and concerts:** I always take my own water in my reusable water bottle for obvious reasons, and water is horribly expensive at the theater. I also bring some really good fair-trade organic chocolate.

❁ **Amusement parks:** Take your own picnic, as you will avoid standing in long lines to buy expensive, tasteless food. You will also be helping the environment by refusing to buy low-quality burgers and pizzas that are served in enough paper and plastic to send chills down the trunk of a tree.

If you buy something at the souvenir store, lead your treat-seeking missile to something that will last, like an alarm clock or a snow globe. If you buy the cheaper candy items, they'll not only rot teeth but also be packaged in nonrecyclable plastic, which will sit in an overstuffed landfill for years.

❁ **Circuses:** The Gorgeously Green girl doesn't want to take her kids to a circus where the performers are being cruel to the animals. Fortunately, there are now fantastic circuses that don't even use animals. Go to *www.friendsofanimals.org/animalfreecircus.html.*

❁ **Zoos/Aquariums/SeaWorld:** I'm not a great zoo girl. I don't love seeing animals in captivity, and I don't think it's educational for my daughter to see unhappy animals in dingy, cramped pens. She's much better off seeing them in their natural habitat on some of the wonderful nature TV programs available. That said, if you do decide to go, take a thermos of cold water in the summer or hot cocoa in the winter. You can also pack small containers of organic carrots, celery, raisins, and crackers so that you can avoid all the packaged junk food. I'm not a total party-pooper, I promise. Ice cream and the occasional cotton candy is a must.

SeaWorld is not green, because it doesn't have any kind of positive impact on the environment. I hate that a huge whale lives in a large swimming pool, and I detest the way that these creatures are treated. Richard O'Barry used to be a dolphin trainer (he actually trained the famous Flipper of the 1960s hit show), and he has revealed how the dolphins are captured for amusement parks and aquariums—they are chased down until they are exhausted, then the mainly female babies are taken away from their mothers. They are trained by punishment so that we can enjoy them doing tricks while we sip on buckets of soda. Flipper actually died in Richard O'Barry's arms, so O'Barry has dedicated his life to stopping this terrible kind of entertainment. Go to *www.thedolphinproject.org* to find out more and see what you can do. I take my daughter to IMAX movies to watch whales and dolphins so that she can see them in their natural environment.

I'm a huge supporter of an organization called Born Free. It is an international wildlife charity that seeks to alleviate the suffering of animals and to protect endangered species. Will Travers, the CEO, was inspired by his parents, who starred in the film classic *Born Free*. He has devoted his life to ending the incarceration of wild animals for "fun" and to keeping wildlife in the wild. I met with him last week and he said, "Our world is still green, it's still gorgeous. Let's keep it that way—it's the only one we and the animals have!" Visit the organization's Web site (*www.bornfreeusa.org*) and find out about some of the atrocities that are happening every day of the year and what Born Free is trying to do to prevent them.

❀ **Beaches:** This just has to be a reusable container and cloth napkin experience. Don't even think about plastic resealable bags and wipes—

tons of fossil fuel to make and stuff to clog up the landfills. I have found a brilliant alternative to regular sandwich bags: it is a reusable sandwich wrap and placemat in one. When you are done, you can put it in the dishwasher and let it air-dry. Go to *www.wrapnmat.com* and buy a bunch of them.

You can buy the most wonderful biodegradable bags, disposable cutlery, plates, and cups from *www.excellentpackaging.com*. I love their "Spudware"—cutlery made from potatoes and corn. Also find a bunch of great eco packaging at *www.simplybiodegradable.com*.

Buy an old-fashioned wicker picnic basket with real stainless steel cutlery. You can always take along a small cooler for the beers. I just purchased one from *www.tenthousandvillages.com*, where everything is created by local artists from around the world; I could actually read about the man who created my basket, and everything is very reasonable priced.

Grab some natural sunblock that doesn't contain the toxic chemicals mentioned in step 2. Some say that skin cancer is on the rise, because even slathered in high-protection sun cream, we shouldn't be baking ourselves like roast chickens—the sunscreen gives us a false sense of security. You're much better off using a low-protection factor and staying out for just fifteen minutes. You will develop the vitamin D you need to feel great and a have a gorgeously healthy glow.

❀ **Sporting events:** To a certain extent, "when in Rome . . ." when we go to events like football or basketball games. My husband would refuse to sit by me if I took a picnic salad to the Lakers. Every now and again, I'll just order junk food and thoroughly enjoy it, knowing that it's a twice-a-year experience that tastes fantastic but never makes me feel that good afterward. I do take my own water, though.

❀ **Kids' entertainment:** I try to make sure that when I entertain my daughter and her friends, we stay away from "consuming" as much as possible. I have stopped taking my daughter to megamarts and malls where she can be tempted by all the doll and teddy bear corporations that insinuate that mommy is insensitive and cruel if she doesn't shell out. I have gotten over the fear that she will miss out if she just stays at home and plays in the backyard. Funnily enough, she and her friends are so much happier. The other day, my daughter and her best friend started groaning and moaning that they were bored. I suggested helping me with some chores and they were off before I could blink. Ten minutes later, I saw them out of the kitchen window. They had found a couple of old yoga mats and had turned them into "princess cloaks." They had a whole thing going on that lasted for two hours—thank goodness I didn't take them to the mall to spend money on a load of junk.

I keep old bags full of fabric, buttons, twine, egg cartons, and more. In the winter months, I have a permanent arts-and-crafts table in my kitchen. It keeps the kids busy for hours, doesn't cost a penny, and all they are using is recycled bits and pieces.

Kids' Arts and Crafts

The Gorgeously Green mom really needs to consider eco-friendly art supplies. Many crayons, paints, and clays contain toxic chemicals.

- ❧ I have found fabulous modeling clay that is made out of beeswax and is available from **Eco Art Work** (*www.ecoartwork.com*).
- ❧ Prang Soybean Crayons are nontoxic and are made from soybean oil and are biodegradable. You can purchase them at **Prang Power** (*www.prangpower.com*).
- ❧ A great Web site for all kinds of art supplies at the right price is **Budget Art Kids** (*www.budgetartkids.com*).

Try to be really conscious of the amount of paper your kids waste. It sounds obvious, but make them aware that they need to cover *both* sides of the paper before pulling out a new sheet. This could prompt a great discussion about why we need to save the trees.

I never buy art kits for kids because they involve way too much packaging—all the individual little plastic bags. It's less expensive and more fun to take your children to a craft store and let them pick out the individual things they really want. Better still, just get out your recycling bin and encourage them to get creative. Lola and her gang have made incredible "villages" out of egg cartons, toothpaste caps, yogurt cups, and plastic bags. I love *www.progressivekids.com* for kids—everything from really cool language flash cards to creative writing kits for teens.

Kids' Birthday Parties

I am horrified at the amount of waste that is generated at the average children's birthday party. I see it week after week as I trail after Lola from party to party: enormous black trash bags filled with barely used paper napkins and plates, wrapping paper, juice boxes, plastic cups and glasses, and so on. I see very little of this waste being recycled, so into the landfill it goes.

I decided that I couldn't celebrate a life in good conscience by using up all these precious resources just because they are convenient, so the last few parties have been an eco-adventure for our family. I encourage Lola to pick a theme that is in some way connected to nature. This year she had a Native American party, which was easy because we did it outside and used leaves, flowers, and rocks; she made her own newfangled tepee, and she and her friends created a play. Many of us remember the good old days when birthday parties involved a few simple games like pin the tail on the donkey and a wheelbarrow race, followed by a slice of birthday cake, perhaps a run through the lawn sprinkler, and good-bye! The bar has been raised too high for my liking over the past few years. The birthday party scene here in Hollywood is bizarre and sometimes quite obscene. Lola has come away with "Oscar"-style gift baskets filled with more toys than she gets at Christmas!

Here are ideas for the Gorgeously Green mom:

1. Use a real cloth tablecloth and napkins.

2. Buy plates and cups that are made from postconsumer waste and can be reused or composted. I love the bright colors that **Recycline** *carries (www.recycline.com). Its products can be used over and over and are made from recycled yogurt cups.*

3. If you don't want to do the washing up, buy cutlery made out of corn or potatoes—they can be composted. You'll find this stuff at www.nau-ur.com.

4. Make your own cake or cupcakes. It will save you some money and will be a lot of fun to create. You can easily buy organic cake mixes now at most large grocery stores. I love **Dr. Oetker** *(www.oetker.com).*

5. Give earth-friendly favors: A small trowel, fork, and a packet of seeds tied up with a bit of raffia always goes down well. An organic cotton napkin wrapped around a bamboo spoon and fork (www.bambu.com) is great. Just make sure that whatever you give can be reused and won't just be chucked in the trash.

*6. I know, juice boxes and mini water bottles are incredibly convenient for crowds of kids, but resist, because typically one or two sips are taken and then they are discarded. Buy a water dispenser from **Igloo** (www.igloo-store.com) and use recyclable paper cups. Alternatively, make a bowl of organic fruit juice punch.*

7. Try to judge the right amount of food to serve wisely. Typically, a lot of food is thrown away after a kids' party.

IT'S TRUE: If every household in America replaced a forty-count pack of conventional paper plates with just one pack made from 100 percent recycled paper, 487,000 trees would be saved (Ideal Bite).

A Gorgeously Green Dinner Party

I adore entertaining and I love that it's so easy to make the few simple changes that turn dinner into an eco-friendly deal.

1. Never use paper napkins, cups, or plastic cutlery, as the environment doesn't like it. Anyway, do you like eating off a paper plate? I don't think so!

2. Serve organic wine and beer if you can—they say it lessons the effects of a hangover.

3. Only burn 100 percent beeswax or soy candles that do not contain lead. I love the beautiful honey color of beeswax, and I've gone off the strong smell of artificially scented candles.

4. Make a fresh room spray by purchasing a small spray bottle and filling it with water. Add a few drops of lavender and geranium essential oils. Give your curtains a few quick sprays before everyone arrives.

5. For a really special occasion, order an organic bouquet from www.organicbouquets.com. If you can grow your own flowers to pick, even better. In the winter, I cut loads of greenery from all sorts of different trees and bushes and put it in an old vintage tin.

6. For a more elaborate affair, I make tiny name cards out of recycled paper.

7. Refrain from serving beef, as it is the least sustainable food available. If you serve fish, make sure that it's not from the endangered list.

8. I try to do a lot of vegetarian dinners, because lots of my friends and my husband have an idea about this kind of "health" food and the idea isn't good. I make it superdelicious (see step 6), and they don't even think about the fact that they haven't touched a piece of meat.

9. If you are looking for some new plates, glasses, or vases to spruce up your table, go to **Viva Terra** *(www.vivaterra.com)*. It carries the most beautiful recycled glass, wine carafes, and unusual vases.

A Gorgeously Green Wedding

Weddings are huge consumer events. An average wedding in the United States costs $25,000. To save money and lighten your imprint on the planet, plan a gorgeously green wedding using the following tips:

1. An outdoor spot is a lovely idea. The bride and groom will feel connected to nature.

2. Try to have the ceremony and the reception at the same location. You don't want to increase your carbon imprint by having your guests travel by car from place to place.

3. Buy an organic, cotton, or hemp silk wedding dress. Alternatively, you can purchase a beautiful vintage dress from a thrift or vintage store. Either way, make sure the dress is reusable.

4. Buy 100 percent recycled invitations that are processed without chlorine. Another lovely idea is to buy paper with seeds embedded in it so that your guests can plant their invites after the wedding *(www.twistedlimbpaper.com)*.

5. *Use a reply postcard without an envelope.*
6. *Create a Web site for directions, events, and hotel arrangements rather than printing out more paper.*
7. *Use a location that is willing to use organic food or bring your own organic caterer.*
8. *Have an organic wedding cake. It's likely there's a pastry chef in your area who will make a vegan, organic, even gluten-free cake for you—shop around.*
9. *Try to use an organic florist (www.organicbouquet.com).*
10. *Use potted plants for table centerpieces and give them as gifts to people who have worked hard on your wedding.*
11. *Throw wildflower seeds instead of rice or confetti.*
12. *At the end of the service, collect the programs to recycle.*
13. *For a favor, give each guest an 11-watt CFL lightbulb with a little note saying that if they replace their regular 50-watt bulb with this, they will save 685 pounds of carbon dioxide.*
14. *Another good favor idea is to make your own organic jelly and put it in pretty glass jars with a label saying "from the wedding of . . ." I did that for my wedding and everyone talked about the lemon jelly for months after the event!*
15. *Make sure your makeup and hair artist will use only nontoxic products for your big day.*

Holidays and Gifts

It makes me crazy to see the amount of holiday waste—the paper that is thrown away is unconscionable. It is so easy to make your holiday or birthday green, and here's how:

1. *Send only e-cards. It's not just the paper that you'll save but also the fossil fuel to deliver your epistles. My mother digs her heels in on this one. She wants a tangible card that she can actually put on her mantle—a computer printout just doesn't do it. I see her point, so I send cards to her and a few family members who live far away. The rest get the electronic version.*
2. *Avoid wrapping paper that is not recycled. If you can't get any,*

wrap presents in old newspaper or magazines. It'll leave a bit of print on your fingers—but dirty hands, clean conscience. This year, I persuaded my extended family to wrap their gazillion holiday gifts in newspaper. It was so satisfying when it came to cleanup time, stuffing all the ripped-up wrapping into the recycle bins—no new trees cut.

3. You can find a green version of any gift you want to give and you won't need to go near the megamarts. Order from the comfort of your living room from the following Web sites:

- ❀ **Vivaterra** (*www.vivaterra.com*) has the most beautiful ideas for gifts—everything from organic robes to recycled glassware to jewelry.
- ❀ **Eco Express** (*www.ecoexpress.com*) creates gift baskets to suit every occasion.
- ❀ **Trees for a Change** (*www.treesforachange.com*) will plant a tree in the United States as a gift and will make a cute personalized card for the recipient.

Make Your Own

Making your own gifts is the hippest thing you can do. The recipients of these homemade offerings will be absolutely delighted that you have taken the time and the care. Last year, I knitted a scarf for every woman I loved, which was a gargantuan task given that the last time I had attempted to knit was twenty-five years ago. I had a blast. I picked the most outrageously complicated yarns, as they were so beautiful, and I created a signature tassel or pompom on each piece. I even had woven labels made so that my girlfriends would know that their gift was handcrafted by me! The joy was in the making. As I produced each scarf, I spent hours thinking about the person for whom I was knitting: What colors did she wear? Would she prefer an evening show-off scarf or a winter wonderland number? If you are a knitter or a wannabe knitter, make sure you go for eco-yarns. Here are three great companies:

- ❀ *www.spinnery.com*
- ❀ *www.handweavers.com*
- ❀ *www.theyarngrove.com*

The year before, I made face oils for the girls. They had all been commenting on how good my skin looked, and I was convinced it was either my new haircut or my new essential oil preparation. I bought dozens of small brown glass bottles and filled them with my miracle oil (see step 2). The fun was making the labels, which I personalized for each of my friends. I put them in little recycled cardboard boxes filled with straw and rose petals. It is deeply satisfying to know that your gifts are not harming the environment.

Fail-Safe Homemade Gifts

A great birthday gift for kids or adults is a little planting kit: a really good trowel and fork, gardening gloves, and seeds according to the theme you want to do. It could be for an herb garden, a vegetable garden, flowers to cut in the summer for your dinner parties, and so on. Just think about the time of year and the climate you are living in. If you are not up on gardening, go to your local nursery or get online. It's easy to figure out what works seasonally (see step 8).

❀ I am always thrilled to get a **tree**. It is the most gorgeous and sometimes extravagant gift, depending on the age of the tree. When I was little, my dad bought me a pear tree, and it is still in the garden where I grew up, yielding fat, juicy pears every summer. Find out what your girlfriend's favorite fruit is and buy accordingly. If she doesn't have enough space to plant a tree, you can get dwarf versions in planters, which can easily sit on a small deck.

❀ **Pomanders** and other sweet-smelling goodies to spruce up the lingerie drawer are wonderful. For a holiday gift, get an orange and a large tub of cloves. Simply stick the cloves very close together all over the orange (you don't want one bit of orange showing). You can attach a pretty ribbon to the top so that it can be hung in a wardrobe to give off a rich, spicy aroma. Always grow lavender in the summer so that in the fall you can harvest the flowers to gather a large bunch and bind with twine or string. Hang upside down in a sunny window to dry.

❀ **Jellies** are really easy to make, and people are superimpressed. Just grab a bunch of whatever is in season in the summer: peaches, strawberries, blackberries, and so on. See the recipe in step 6. Create you own fabulous labels stating that the jelly is 100 percent organic.

Such a Waste

Always consider the waste that you may be creating when you buy and wrap a gift. If the gift is plastic, it probably isn't going to last long, and then it will not decompose, particularly kids' stuff, because a lot of plastic may be involved. So think carefully when buying presents for children. Expensive techno gadgets will need to be replaced in less than a year when the new one comes out. Consider the packaging that things come in even before you wrap them: Styrofoam, plastic, paper, and cellophane—it's outrageous how we have become almost immune to this waste. It's irresponsible if we don't even attempt to recycle.

A great idea for a kid's gift is to go to **Born Free USA** and adopt an animal (*www.bornfreeusa.org*). Lola wanted some ghastly plastic toy that all her friends at school were getting excited about. I suggested that instead we could adopt an animal of her choice from Born Free. We looked at the Web site and she picked out a baby chimp. It'll cost you what you'd pay for a large plastic toy; however, your child will receive a package containing an adoption certificate, framed photographs, information on his or her particular animal, and more. Lola was so delighted that she could barely contain herself. She placed the photograph of "Fluffball" in a place of pride, and every day she imagines him happily playing. She says if her contribution was enough to get the medicine he needs, . . . and on and on—a million times more entertaining than a plastic toy, so now all her friends are into the adoption thing big time!

IT'S TRUE: Every person in the United States produces more than twice his or her weight in waste every day.

It's amazing to realize that half of what ends up in the landfill is paper, most of which is packaging, newspapers, and magazines. The really scary thing is that we are literally running out of ideas of where to put it all. Landfills have been closed all over the place because they are chock-full, waste mountains are accumulating in underdeveloped countries, and many other nations try to ship their garbage anywhere they can. We can't turn a blind eye anymore.

It's strange that we have grown up in a culture where we don't have to think about consequences. I tell my daughter to put her trash in the can, but that's only half the story. I also need to teach her that we've got to find some way to reduce the amount we throw away, too. Kids are incredible when they understand the whole picture. They come up with really creative solutions that we may be too busy to think about. My daughter marvels at packaging now. At the age of six, she realizes that it's better to buy certain things in bulk rather than to buy loads of tiny packages (much as she misses them because the tiny thing is cuter).

I have to admit that I sometimes love packaging. In a perverse sort of way, I enjoy pulling clothes and the like out of layers of tissue and paper—I like the feel and the smell. So it's taken a bit of getting used to, to change my habits. I have had to realize that a few sheets of tissue paper are not going to prevent my new jeans from creasing or getting dirty, and that they're just there for the fancy effect.

Wow—that's enough for this step.

Task

Plan a green event: If you are planning to throw a birthday or holiday party, a wedding, a baby shower, or a family gathering, start thinking green—what can you do that will *really* make a difference? If you haven't got an event coming up, why not plan a potluck picnic or a cookout for the people you love? Tell them you are doing the eco thing and get them to bring organic wine and food in reusable containers. Gather all the tips you've learned from this chapter and inspire your friends and family.

Savasana

There's a lot to think about for this step. Remember you don't need to do it all at once. Use this week's savasana to mull over some of the things we have covered. What is the most important issue for you? It may be your car or your paper waste; it may be that you just want to forget the whole thing and go buy a new pair of shoes. I have to admit that shoe visions do occur sometimes when I am deep in meditation. Either way, lie down on the floor with your customary supports, relax, and observe your breath. When you are superrelaxed, breathe in joy and breathe out compassion.

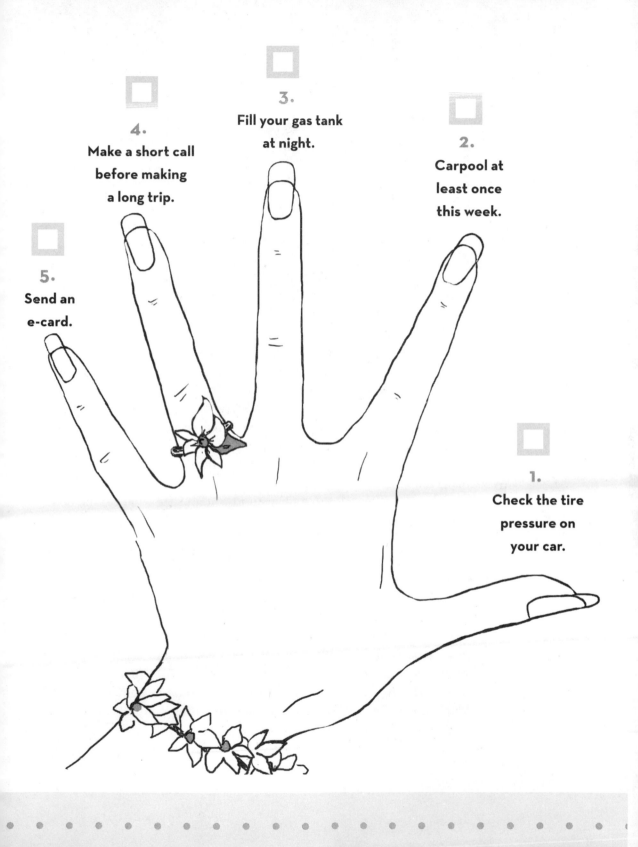

5.
Send an
e-card.

4.
Make a short call
before making
a long trip.

3.
Fill your gas tank
at night.

2.
Carpool at
least once
this week.

1.
Check the tire
pressure on
your car.

Chapter Eight

STEP 8: Go Supergreen

Congratulations for making it to the last and final step of the Gorgeously Green program. You now have a pretty good idea of how to green every aspect of your life. Hopefully, you will have picked one change to make for each step—that's seven changes. However insignificant your tiny contribution may seem, it has a cumulative effect, which in itself will create great change.

If you have walked up the seven steps, you are pretty near the top of the green mountain. It's now time not only to look back on the progress you have made but also to look around you and see what can be done out there in the world.

Going the Extra Green Mile

Assuming that you have made your home as green as you can over the past few weeks, think about your work, office, school—all the places in which you or your children hang out during the day. There's no point in making your home toxin-free if you are sitting in chemical hell at your office. Granted, this becomes a lot more difficult, because you may be dealing with people who don't want to know about your new-found green thing. Trust me, I've had to suffer a great deal of eye-rolling and sharp intakes of breath.

"What chemicals do they use to clean the classrooms?" I asked my daughter's long-suffering headmaster. "I haven't a clue," he answered as he became very involved in tidying up his pens and fiddling with paper clips. I got the impression that he didn't really want me to get involved with the cleaning crew. I was a mom—and probably an irritating one—and it wasn't really my business. I persisted. Slowly but surely, I got them to switch to eco-friendly nontoxic cleaners.

Although you might initially be treated with indifference or even derision, I can assure you that in the final analysis you will be respected and thanked. No one is going to dislike you for making the air in his or her immediate surroundings cleaner and safer.

It's so easy to be defeated by the apathy of many who cling to the belief that there is nothing really wrong. The annoying thing about pollution and global warming is that most people can't see it, hear it, or smell it—*yet!* It's not tangible unless you get taken to landfills or helicopter over devastated rain forests. Here in the United States, we can live in comfortable denial for quite sometime, until it's too late.

The big shift for me was having a child. It suddenly became about her and not me anymore. I care—we all care—about the future of our children. I would feel horribly irresponsible if I just said, "Well, never mind, as long as I get my creature comforts, as long as I can go on shopping, I don't really care—you'll figure it out. Technology will come up with something." Technology may not. I hasten to add that "technology" is partly responsible for the mess we are now in. I am the first to enjoy everything at the touch of a button and a comfortably convenient life, but I'm willing to compromise a little to create a better future.

Be an Absolute Pest

The most important thing we can all do is to become pests. We have all the power because we are consumers. We have a voice. Hurrah—you can shout as loudly as you want because the large companies and corporations are going to have to listen to you or you'll go somewhere else. It's that simple. A great example is the recent explosion of organic food. Until a few years ago, it was confined to a pitifully small area of the produce section and looked totally off-putting: a few scraggy old lettuces and shriveled apples sitting alongside their perfect gleaming rivals. I'm not surprised that shoppers turned their noses up, even ridiculed the deluded hippie mom who would actually fork out an extra few bucks for these measly offerings. The savvy modern shopper, however, is with the program. Upon learning about the health hazards of conventional production, shoppers have demanded more organic food, and the grocery stores have had to oblige.

The great news is that because of technology, it's easy to become a pest. You don't have to sit down and write laborious letters or make annoying phone calls. Simply switch on your computer and search for the company you are targeting. Send the company a quick three-line e-mail telling them why you want them to change or you'll take your business elsewhere. Consider these places:

❀ Your local home delivery Chinese/Thai restaurant: Tell them that you want them to switch their packaging to paper and cardboard that can be recycled. You could even suggest they look into some of the new biodegradable options that are now becoming available. Guide the place to a good source for biodegradable goods, such as *www.sunterra.us.com* and *www.biodegradablestore.com*.

❀ Your favorite cosmetic company that still uses parabens: You could write a letter to the head office saying that you would love to continue using its products, but being the Gorgeously Green girl that you now are, you need to know that your cosmetics are safe. Is the company going to reformulate its products?

❀ Your favorite clothes store that you suspect may indulge in non–fair-trade practices: Ask the store about clothing production.

❀ Your favorite restaurant that serves fish on the endangered species list: Tell the restaurant that you would be so much happier if it would serve only sustainable fish. Take the place the list if necessary.

❀ Your favorite restaurant that doesn't offer organic veggies: Tell the restaurant that it needs to get with the program and start offering organic.

❀ Your local grocery store: Ask to stock up on all the organic and non-GMO products that you'd like.

Go easy on your friends and neighbors who you see polluting the environment. I am such a wimp when it comes to confrontation, yet I feel even worse if I walk away without saying anything.

A case in point is lawn fertilizer. One of my next-door neighbors is eco-obsessed and uses manure that stinks to fertilize his yard. Although it is gross, I applaud him for not allowing dangerous chemicals to waft over into my yard while my daughter is skipping, jumping, and swimming. The other next-door neighbor is out there every season with a huge spray gun of toxic chemicals. He has a bright green lawn—but at what price? He wasn't thrilled when I approached him with all the British charm I could muster and asked him to consider changing to a nontoxic alternative. "They don't work," he replied, "Actually they do," I said, pointing at my lawn, which wasn't perhaps as neon as his but was holding up pretty well. "I just love feeling good about using stuff that's not harmful," I explained, and I didn't push it any further. I delivered him some fair-trade chocolate as a peace offering. Two weeks later, I saw him with a giant bag of organic fertilizer.

I would go insane if I tried to confront everybody I see during the day who is unwittingly harming our planet, so I don't even try; however, if you can convince just one person this month to switch to a product or behavior that will help save his or her health and the planet, it would go a long way.

When pointing out something to friends, they almost always say, "I had no idea that was bad!" So you are doing your girlfriends a huge favor by throwing out a few home truths that can only make them happier and healthier in the long run.

Here are two checklists that you can download as a PDF file at *www.gorgeouslygreen.com.* Take them into your school or office and make your whole world Gorgeously Green.

CHECKLIST FOR YOUR OFFICE

1. *Do you use compact fluorescent lightbulbs?*
2. *Do you recycle all your paper?*
3. *Do you print and copy on both sides of paper?*
4. *Do you use 100 percent recycled stationery?*
5. *Do you use recycled toner cartridges?*
6. *Do the office cleaners use nontoxic products?*
7. *Do you reuse shipping boxes?*
8. *Are there plenty of indoor green plants in every room?*
9. *Do you use regular air fresheners in the restrooms?*
10. *Would you consider purchasing organic fair-trade coffee?*
11. *Do you encourage carpooling?*
12. *Do you use paper/Styrofoam cups?*
13. *How do you dispose of printer cartridges and batteries?*
14. *How do you dispose of all computers and telephones?*
15. *Do you recycle?*
16. *Do you turn off all electrical appliances at the end of the day, including computers, printers, and copiers?*
17. *Do you provide plastic water bottles to employees?*
18. *Would you consider putting in a water filtration system?*
19. *Do you invest in any carbon offsets for business travel?*
20. *Do you video conference in order to save on travel?*

CHECKLIST FOR YOUR SCHOOL

1. *Are all the heating and A/C vents regularly cleaned?*
2. *Does the school recycle all its paper?*
3. *Does the school cleanup crew use nontoxic cleaners?*
4. *Do the sinks have antibacterial soaps for use?*
5. *Is there adequate ventilation in each classroom?*
6. *Does the school offer organic food/snacks?*
7. *Does the school have an edible garden?*
8. *Does the school encourage no-waste lunches?*
9. *Does the school encourage carpooling?*
10. *Do the teachers and students turn off all appliances when leaving the room?*

You can make an amazing difference at your child's school by implementing a no-idling rule in the carpool lane. I'm surprised that more schools don't do it already, as it's not difficult to turn your engine off. It's a total myth that turning your car on and off uses more gas. At my daughter's school, some cars used to sit idling for up to half an hour—crazy when you know that 10 percent of our fuel is used up when the car is just sitting still. Talk to the principal. Tell him or her that you will make a flyer or send an e-mail to every parent in the school, informing them of the new earth-friendly rule.

Edible Yard

Many of you have heard of Alice Waters, owner of the world famous Chez Panisse restaurant in northern California and founder of the "Edible Yard" movement for schools. She has always been passionate about using fresh, local food whenever possible and wants to encourage children to become leaders in the movement. Many asphalt schoolyards have been ripped up and replaced with abundant gardens, where the children can learn about their food and connect to nature. She inspired me to get into my school and do the same. It makes no difference where you live—you can start this movement anywhere.

My daughter's school is in the inner city and has relatively little greenery or spare space. I cased the entire area, back alleys and all, looking for somewhere that *anything* could be grown. I finally came across a small rectangular area in the back of the art building. It seemed to be a dumping place for broken bleachers and basketball nets, but it had potential. I asked for permission, got the science and art teachers involved, and set to work. We had a handyman build four large raised beds and brought in a bunch of enormous terracotta planters.

Before long, we had beans growing up wire fences, strawberries tumbling out of pots, and tomatoes growing toward the sky! Each class made a mosaic stepping stone for the garden. Every child wanted to be a part of it. We were able to teach our children about organic gardening, which is invaluable, especially for the kids who didn't have a yard at home. Your school may already have an edible yard, but if it doesn't, there's great opportunity for you to be the change.

Hanging with Like-Minded People

It's a great idea to find a few friends who feel the same way as you do about the planet. You will feed ideas to one another and keep the torch burning. If you are single and want to find an eco-mate, go to one of the following Web sites:

- ❀ www.veganpassions.com
- ❀ www.greensingles.com
- ❀ www.ewsingles.com

I love browsing through the success stories on the Green Singles site (notice how I spend my time). Some of them even provide photographs of quite presentable-looking men. One woman tells of how her honey proposed in their bean patch. Don't be turned off—these Web sites are not always a hotbed of mental health; many strike it lucky!

Keep a Journal

Buy a beautiful recycled pad and keep a Gorgeously Green journal. Each day, write about the changes you are making or want to make. I find that putting pen to paper brings all sorts of ideas up from my subconscious. I love to take a sort of inventory of the day: How eco-friendly was I today? How can I improve on things? What were my mistakes? What were my successes? It helps me to stay connected to my deepest values on a daily basis. I also put recipes in my journal as I collect them. I particularly like taking my journal when traveling, as it's quite fascinating to note down what other cultures are doing about the environment.

Our Future

Our children are our future. Whether it's your own kids or your nieces, nephews, or godchildren, they need to know that they will be the stewards of this planet at a vitally important time in history.

If nothing else, I want my daughter to truly understand the impact that she has on the environment. I want her to treat the planet with as much care and respect as she treats other people. I want her to be a Gorgeously Green girl!

My daughter is like a sponge right now. At six years of age, she soaks up everything she sees and hears. Mercifully, I've caught the green bug just in time. She always asks me if something needs to go in the recycling bin or the "other" one. She understands all the basics about not wasting water or electricity, and she despises Hummer cars. She loves makeup and malls as much as the next little girl, but I make sure that the nail polish is nontoxic and the mall is a superspecial treat where we will be strictly window-shopping.

Go to *www.earth911.org*. It is a brilliant educational Web site for kids that includes games, exercises, cartoons, and really cool competitions—the theme being helping to heal the planet. It is suitable for every age; you just click on the grade level your child is in.

For second graders and up, my favorite site is *www.kidsregen.org*. It's great fun, informative, and covers everything that might interest your child, from easy recipes to organic gardening.

For younger children, I love *www.kidsplanet.org*. It's a cute, animated Web site. If children click on "Web of Life," a spider will teach them about the interconnectedness of all things. I just read it to my daughter while she sat on my lap, managing the mouse. She was so excited by the whole thing.

Mini-Activist

We can teach our kids that they have a voice, too. I would have loved to be told that when I was young—that my opinions counted, so I should voice them. Maybe I was too precocious for anyone to dare lead me in that direction.

Our kids can become activists at a really early age, thanks to the glorious Internet. They are going to be on their computers whether we like it or not, so let's get them to focus on some really life-changing, exciting work. Children love to feel that they have a purpose and that they can make a difference. The beauty of many of the campaigns and petitions on the Web is that you don't have to be a certain age to sign them. So point your little ones to some earth-friendly Web sites. Stick them on their "favorites" link and encourage them to get active.

Your kids can get to know the "Green Squad" on *www.nrdc.org/greensquad*. This site will show them how to green their schools. There are assignments and different levels to aspire to, like "detective" or "super-investigator." Also go to the official National Resources Defense Council (NRDC) Web site and click on "Take Action." The NRDC makes it really interesting and easy for kids to find what sparks them, and then how they can do something about it. Leonardo De Caprio is very involved with this organization. In its Santa Monica, California, resource center, there is a large area that he created where anyone can sit down at one of the five computers, and within seconds, take an action that will make a difference.

The other day, my daughter had a friend over, and for fun I got them to create heart-shaped cards out of old paper and then write "stop cutting the trees down in Liberia"—it was a campaign that I had read about on the Friends of the Earth Web site. They had such a laugh—drawing pictures on their hearts of cut-down trees with people crying, their imaginations started working overtime. I explained that I would send their artwork to a particular senator and that I was sure he would take note and that their actions would make a difference. They haven't stopped talking about the poor people who can't breathe due to lack of oxygen in Liberia—six is a good age to get them started!

Totally Gorgeously Green

Now that you are green inside and out, it's time to put your money where your mouth is. Ugh—we are bombarded with requests for our hard-earned money every day. I just switch off when I am asked to contribute. My community, my school, and my daughter—everyone's got a hand out. I think long and hard before I'm willing to part with my dollars. However, because I do want a planet for my great-grandchildren to enjoy, I give some money to organizations that are really making a difference.

It doesn't have to be a wad of cash either. For just $15, you can go to one of the following Web sites and feel good about being green:

❀ *www.futureforests.com*
❀ *www.climatecare.org*
❀ *www.planttrees.org*

I love an organization called **The Ten Dollar Club** (*www.tendollar-club.com*). It is a group of caring individuals who have pooled their resources of just $10 a month. They realize that many people can't afford to make a massive difference on their own, but if a bunch of people get together and pool just ten bucks, huge changes can be made. It costs $10 for me to buy just two ice-blended drinks or chai lattes. I can easily go without a couple of these a month, because it'll make little difference to me but a huge difference to the people who receive my contribution. I also know that 100 percent of the members' contributions go the field projects in developing countries—not a cent is held back for overheads. So make your latte at home and help to relieve some serious suffering abroad. The Web site tells you about all the projects that they are currently working on.

Greenie Points

Here's how to score some serious Gorgeously Green credibility: become a Green activist now, before you close this book. *You can get people to listen to you at the click of a button*—how great is that! You are sitting there with great power at the end of your index finger. All you have to do is log on to *www.foe.org.* Pick out a campaign that takes your fancy, fill out your name and address, and press the "Submit" button. This Web site is Friends of the Earth, and it campaigns for every environmental concern you can think of, from stopping global warming reports from being suppressed to cleaning up marine sanctuaries. I love that it takes all of twenty seconds to be an activist and it doesn't cost a dime. You get to feel great about feeling great.

My favorite organization is the NRDC. It is the nation's most effective environmental organization. It uses law, science, and the support of more than a million members to protect the planet's wildlife and wild places and to ensure a healthy environment for every living thing. It has had major success with many huge campaigns; it even managed to halt plans to build a massive car plant on the coast of Baja, California, which is the last natural breeding place in the world for whales.

There is so much to do and see on the organization's excellent Web site, so plan to put aside time to enjoy navigating yourself around. If you want to take action, you simply click on "Take Action," which will give you a choice of three or four issues that you may be interested in. You can choose the one that matters to you most, then add your name and address (after doing this once, you only need to add your e-mail), and bingo, your signature is added to an important petition. *One signature makes a difference.*

Activism—To turn an even deeper shade of green, click on *www.gor-geouslygreen.com*, type in the password that you see below, and find even more organizations that make a difference. Password: Magnificent.

Let Your Voice Be Heard!

Your individual voice is a powerful one, and although it may not often seem to be the case, elected officials do pay attention. When members of the U.S. Congress hear from you, for instance, they usually consider that message to be shared by dozens of other people living in your district. So be the spokesperson for others who may feel powerless.

If you are seriously concerned about air and water pollution or any other environmental issue, you could take one of the following steps:

1. Make sure you know who your city's mayor is and who represents you on your city council. Drop them both a personal note

and tell them what matters to you. They really sit up and take no-
tice if you ask for a face-to-face meeting!
2. Find out who represents your neighborhood in your state legis-
lature and send a similar letter. You should be able to find out
your state representative on the Internet.
3. Check out what is happening in the U.S. Congress. Remember
that the people we send to Washington work for us. Go to www.
house.gov.writerep and simply type in your zip code to find out
your member of Congress. You could then find out when this per-
son is going to be back home in the district office and set up a
meeting.
4. What about talking to one or both of your U.S. senators? You
can find out who they are by going to www.senate.gov. I was
thrilled to see that one of my senators has an open invitation to
have breakfast with her every Wednesday and Thursday in Wash-
ington. I'm going to take her up on that when I'm next in that neck
of the woods, as I've got quite a few issues I'd like to discuss!

It will take you about ten minutes to sit down and write a thoughtful letter to send to local, state, or national decision makers. The Gorgeously Green girl can be a force to be reckoned with, so rather than getting mad about the state of the nation while sipping your nonfat latte, get writing and help to change the course of history. Handwritten letters are the most effective way to get someone to sit up and listen.

Making a Difference Every Hour of Every Day

Sounds like a tall order, but you can do it by switching to an eco-friendly credit card and/or cell phone. I have signed on for both at *www.workingassets.com*.

You sign up and support the causes you believe in just by doing what you do every day: talking on your phone. The organization donates 1 percent of your charges to nonprofit groups working for peace, human rights, and the environment. It offers competitive plans and reduced-fee phones.

The group also does a credit card where they will donate ten cents on every purchase you make to really cool nonprofit groups. Other outlets for socially responsible credit cards are **Alternatives Federal Credit Union** (*www.alternatives.org/visacard.html*) and the **Giving Card** (*www.thegivingcard.com*).

What Is Green Power?

Green power is power from the sun, wind, plants, and moving water and is obviously the most sustainable way to meet our energy needs and protect the planet. Choosing to use green power is fantastic, because electricity generation is the largest industrial polluter in our country.

Electricity generation produces acid rain and small soot particles; nitrogen oxide emissions, which form smog and stress forest ecosystems; and carbon dioxide emissions, the heat-trapping gases that cause global warming.

In order to support the cleaner technologies, you simply tell your local utility that you want to buy green power. You will pay a tiny bit more, but knowing you are making a big difference is worth it.

When power flows from the generator to your house, electrons get mixed together on the wires. You can't specify which electrons you get, but you can make sure that your money goes to support clean, sustainable generators, which has the effect of making the whole system greener.

How can you tell if utility companies are telling fibs about where your money is really going? Many states now require disclosure labels, just like labels on food packages.

Carbon Offsets—Excuse Me?

You are going to hear more and more about carbon offsetting as time goes on, so the Gorgeously Green girl should know exactly what this is or you'll be caught with you pants down!

In Europe, everyone, from huge corporations to the lowly little man on the street, is buying carbon offsets to make them feel better about the energy they are using. Cutting down on our personal energy consumption in the home is a great place to start; however, we need to do a lot more to avoid the full-on glacier melt/Manhattan-submerged underwater scenario.

The basic premise of carbon offsets is that you calculate how much carbon you use in your day-to-day life, then you compensate for that by going to a company that provides offsets, and you pay them to finance renewable energy projects. So if I calculate that I produce eight tons of carbon emissions from my heating, car, and so on, I can counterbalance that by creating eight tons of reductions. If a huge wind turbine farm is created, the less coal will have to be burned in order to create electricity, so we've got to help fund these bizarre-looking farms. That or get a wind turbine on your own roof—many in Europe are doing just that. My husband has drawn the line at solar panels.

The Web site *www.nativeenergy.com* has an online calculator. If I am about to travel to the United Kingdom, I know I will be emitting a lot of greenhouse gases into the atmosphere by choosing to fly, so I can click on "Travel Calculator" to work out how many tons of GHGs I'm spewing out, then select an offset that will reduce my GHGs by the same amount.

It is difficult to figure out which offsets are better than others. The most obvious choice would be one that plants trees—it has a nice feel-good factor built in, but it's not the best bet. It's difficult to calculate how much carbon dioxide a given forest will "breathe in," and the whole thing is often calculated by working out how much carbon dioxide a tree will take in over its lifetime, which could be a hundred years after the emissions associated with your gas-spewing activity have happened. Better to go with a more glamorous option like cow methane or cement!

Fortunately, Tufts Climate Initiative has recently conducted a useful study of carbon-emission offset programs. The following invest in the most effective projects and are the most accurate in terms of calculations:

- **Native Energy** (*www.nativeenergy.com*) invests in wind-power and methane-gas energy production facilities on U.S. family farms.
- **Atmosfair** (*www.atmosfair.com*) develops solar power in developing countries and methane entrapment in Thailand.
- **My Climate** (*www.myclimate.org*) puts your money into solar greenhouses in the Himalayas, biomass facilities in India, and farms in Madagascar.
- **Climate Friendly** (*www.climatefriendly.com*) puts the money into renewable energy in Australia and New Zealand.

I love Climate Friendly because you can click on either the car, airplane, or house icon, fill in a couple of simple details, and it will immediately tell you how many tons of carbon you are emitting into the atmosphere and how much it will cost you to offset it. It's actually a bit scary, as you get to see in black and white what your seemingly innocent lifestyle is doing to the planet. Thank goodness companies like this are stepping up to the plate and making it supersimple for those of us who want to live with a squeaky clean conscience.

I sometimes wonder how much of a difference all this renewable energy will really make. According to the Union of Concerned Scientists, if every nation increased its use of renewable energy to 20 percent of our electricity generation by 2020, it would be the same as planting nearly 130 million trees—an area the size of Colorado or Wyoming. This gives me hope that we can and will win the fight against global warming.

You can also do your own home carbon offsetting. I make little bargains with myself—for example, if I give myself the luxury, which it now is, of a lovely, hot bath, I promise myself that I will not switch on my dryer for the rest for the week.

Stonyfield Farm, the largest yogurt manufacturer in the United States, has led the way by offsetting 100 percent of carbon dioxide emissions from its facilities. It has funded a great program called Climate Counts. You can visit this Web site (*www.climatecounts.org*) and find out how all the major companies stack up against one another in the war against global warming.

Join the Stars

It is so exciting that so many Hollywood stars have become high-profile environmentalists. Many of these inspiring women are doing fantastic things in the green space. They are taking responsibility and encouraging us all to become accountable for our actions. They make us want to emulate them for more than their beauty and talent—we want to join them in their many efforts in thwarting the destruction of our planet. Some of the better-known female activists today are Julia Roberts, Julia Louis-Dreyfus, Cameron Diaz, Gwyneth Paltrow, Penelope Cruz, Diane Keaton, Meg Ryan, Goldie Hawn, and Kirsten Dunst. And think of the guys: Robert Redford, Leonardo DeCaprio, Bono, Sting, Pierce Brosnan, Orlando Bloom—not a bad bunch to join forces with.

Julia Roberts has inspired me by taking on the gargantuan task of getting school buses to switch to a less polluting fuel. She helped initiate legislation in California that will mandate the use of biodiesel in all conventional diesel school buses. I hope this will lead other states to follow suit, and moms all over the nation will be thanking her. Julia is passionate about reducing air pollution, as she is only too aware of the alarming rise in cases of juvenile respiratory disease. She is the quintessential Gorgeously Green girl, who walks the walk in every area of her life.

Laurie David has created great change in the green scene by bringing the whole issue of global warming into the mainstream media. She is a tireless activist who should be applauded.

Daryl Hannah has been at it for years. She lives off the grid in the Rocky Mountains and is currently attempting to establish a biodiesel standard with Willie Nelson.

It feels great to join hands with these inspiring women and commit to making a difference.

Task

What would you like to change? What do you feel passionate about? Close your eyes, deepen your breath, and take a few minutes to think about it. This step is about volunteering your time. Pick something, anything that you care about, and get online to find out how you can get involved. It doesn't have to be a massive time commitment, so don't worry about signing your life away. I was really upset because I didn't want to take Lola to my nearest beach—it was too dirty—so I joined Heal The Bay, and volunteered my family to come to help clean up every few months. If you're not sure about which organization to choose, I suggest browsing *www.environmentnow.org*. It'll give you some great ideas.

Here is the last "Pick One" hand of the program, so choose wisely and enjoy!

And Finally . . .

Consider passing this book on to every female you know and telling her that it feels great to live in good conscience.

You deserve a massive hug for completing this life-changing eight-step program. Congratulations. Give yourself a huge hug for making a

GORGEOUSLY GREEN LIFESTYLE CHECKLIST
(YES/NO ANSWERS)

Your Beauty

☐ 1. Do you know what the ingredients are in your cosmetics?

☐ 2. Do you ever read the labels on your lotions and creams?

☐ 3. Do you know what is in your nail polish?

☐ 4. Do you use drug-store hair dye?

☐ 5. Do you buy your products from a department store?

☐ 6. Do you believe labels that say "natural" or "organic"?

Your Home

☐ 1. Do you know what energy-efficient appliances are?

☐ 2. Do you buy energy-efficient appliances?

☐ 3. Do you know what compact fluorescent lightbulbs (CFLs) are?

☐ 4. Do you buy CFLs?

☐ 5. Do you purchase paper items made from recycled or postconsumer material?

☐ 6. Have you ever cleaned your refrigerator coils?

☐ 7. Do you shut things off when not using them?

☐ 8. Do you unplug appliances and chargers when not using them?

☐ 9. Is your thermostat set at 68 degrees Fahrenheit or lower?

☐ 10. Is your air conditioner set at 78 degrees Fahrenheit or higher?

☐ 11. Is your water heater wrapped?

☐ 12. Do you use space heaters?

☐ 13. Do you purchase green energy?

☐ 14. Do you use your washer/dryer almost every day?

☐ 15. Do you ever air-dry your clothes?

☐ 16. Do you take your clothes to a regular dry-cleaner?

☐ 17. Do you have low-flow toilets and showers?

☐ 18. Do you use recycled trash bags?

☐ 19. Are you aware of how many bags of trash you generate weekly?

☐ 20. Do you use toxic cleaners in your home?

☐ 21. Do you chuck used batteries in the trash?

☐ 22. Do you know what volatile organic compounds (VOCs) are?

☐ 23. Are VOCs present in your home?

- [ ] 24. Have you ever visited a hazardous waste facility?
- [ ] 25. Do you have green houseplants in your home?
- [ ] 26. Do all members of your family try to conserve water?

Your Yard

- [ ] 1. Do you have a garden?
- [ ] 2. Do you grow herbs?
- [ ] 3. Do you know about native plants?
- [ ] 4. Do you grow native plants?
- [ ] 5. Do you use lawn fertilizer?
- [ ] 6. Do you use garden pesticides?
- [ ] 7. Is your garden organic?
- [ ] 8. Do you irrigate your lawn every day?
- [ ] 9. Do you hose your driveway to clean it off?

Your Ride

- [ ] 1. Do you drive an energy-efficient car?
- [ ] 2. If not, are you considering purchasing one?
- [ ] 3. Do you ever carpool?
- [ ] 4. Do you use a reusable mug?
- [ ] 5. Do you drive to the store every day?
- [ ] 6. Do you own a bicycle?
- [ ] 7. When you change your oil, do you recycle it?
- [ ] 8. Do you check your tire pressure once a week?
- [ ] 8a. Do you wash your car at home?

Your Shopping

- [ ] 1. Do you buy organic cotton clothes or bed linens?
- [ ] 2. Do you buy clothes not made with sweatshop labor?
- [ ] 3. Do you try to eat locally grown food?
- [ ] 4. Do you eat organic food?
- [ ] 5. Do you try to buy things with less packaging?
- [ ] 6. Do you shop at farmer's markets?
- [ ] 7. Do you buy from small local stores?
- [ ] 8. Do you avoid factory-farmed meats?
- [ ] 9. Do you buy organic produce?
- [ ] 9a. Do you Buy Fair-Trade Items?
- [ ] 10. Do you purchase genetically modified organisms (GMO)-free food?
- [ ] 11. Do you purchase antibiotic- and hormone-free dairy?

Your Desires

- [ ] 1. Do you wish to become healthier?
- [ ] 2. Do you want to become more vibrant?
- [ ] 3. Do you want to live according to your deepest values?
- [ ] 4. Do you want to feel exhilarated?
- [ ] 5. Are you ready to become Gorgeously Green?

difference. We are all connected to this earth and are made from the same atoms and molecules. Everything is interrelated. Every thought you have has an effect, just as every action has an impact. You are that powerful. So take your newfound power out there, and as Gandhi is so often quoted as saying, "Be the change you want to see in the world."

Checklist Revisited

Remember the checklist from step 1? Here it is again. In just eight weeks, you may not see huge changes, but I'm sure you've made a few. This is only your first time through the course, so use a pencil in case you want to revisit it. I have a built-in forgetting mechanism in my brain, so I need to do the course every few months to refresh the old gray matter.

No More Separation

The mistake that many of us make is to assume that the environment is somewhere outside of ourselves, yet we *are* the environment. We eat, drink, and breathe it. Whatever we do to the environment, we do to ourselves. We must learn to treat our environment (ourselves) with kindness and compassion. It is interesting that green is the color of the heart chakra. In many Eastern traditions, a chakra *(shock-ra)* is a center of energy that is located in the subtle body. The green heart chakra is associated with love and humanity.

Savasana

This is the last time we will visit this pose together. You know the drill. So lie down and get comfortable. Take long, smooth breaths through your nose.

Feel the earth beneath your body, supporting your weight. Let go completely, feeling safe and supported. Know that as you nurture this earth and its inhabitants, you in turn will be nurtured and loved.

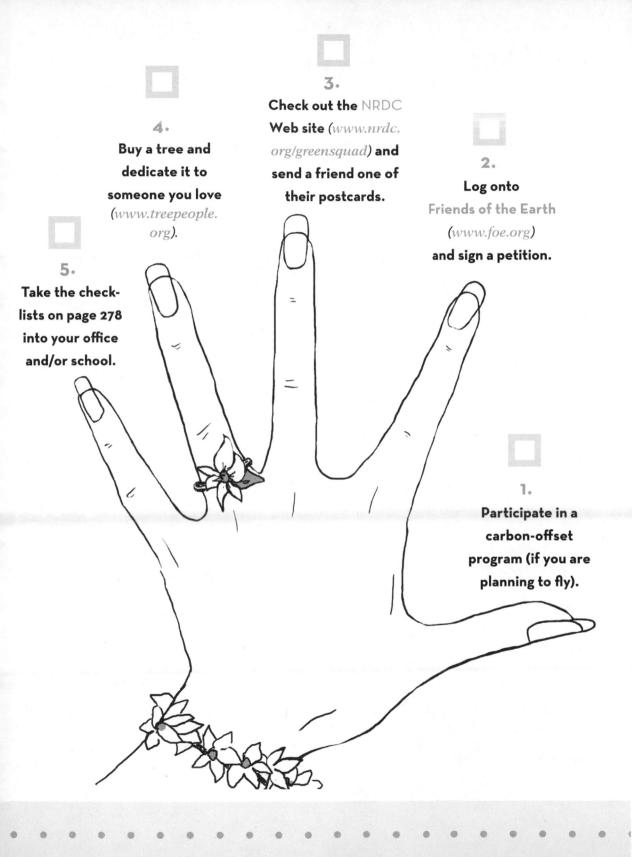

4.
Buy a tree and
dedicate it to
someone you love
*(www.treepeople.
org)*.

3.
Check out the NRDC
Web site *(www.nrdc.
org/greensquad)* **and**
send a friend one of
their postcards.

2.
Log onto
Friends of the Earth
(www.foe.org)
and sign a petition.

5.
Take the check-
lists on page 278
into your office
and/or school.

1.
Participate in a
carbon-offset
program (if you are
planning to fly).

GORGEOUSLY GREEN • MAINTENANCE PLAN

GREEN DATE—Take yourself on a weekly green date. You could go to the park, take a trip to your local nursery, or go to the beach. Find a way to connect with the natural world.

ORGANIZE your day so that you will take fewer trips. Carpool or take public transport.

RECYCLE absolutely everything.

GRAB your reusable shopping tote, coffee mug, and water bottle whenever you go out.

ENCOURAGE all your girlfriends to become Gorgeously Green.

ORGANIC whenever possible!

USE nontoxic cleaning and beauty products.

SHOP ONLINE, as it saves fossil fuel.

LOWER your energy consumption by flicking off light switches and appliances.

YOGA every day!

GENERATE a demand for earth-friendly products by voting with your dollars.

REUSE as many items as possible.

ELIMINATE as much waste as you can.

ENJOY your new sense of purpose in life.

NURTURE yourself and your planet with nothing but the best.

GORGEOUSLY GREEN
CERTIFICATION

I, _____, have completed the

earth-friendly

eight-step program.

I am officially **GORGEOUSLY GREEN**.

REMEMBER:

You have tremendous power as a woman

To create great change, so

Dig deep and discover what you believe in.

Affirm it,

Radiate it,

Fill every conversation with it.

Your life has great purpose and meaning—

Live it beautifully.

"Between stimulus and response, there is a space. In that space lies our freedom and power to choose our response. In our response lies our growth and happiness"

—STEVEN R. COVEY

A mission statement comes from the heart and reflects our deepest values. It's helpful to clarify our life purpose so that it becomes a guide or a compass, leading us into the future.

You have an enormous impact on the environment, and so this Eco-Mission Statement is a call to acknowledge that impact and take responsibility for it.

Writing a mission statement is like creating a sculpture: you have to keep on chipping away at what you don't need until you see a beautiful form emerging. The following questions will help you to build your statement. When you have a few spare minutes, sit somewhere quiet and write down your answers. Then take a plain piece of paper and write a rough draft of your statement. Read what you have written and underline the sentences that resonate with you. Pick out two or three sentences and copy them into the Eco-Mission Statement Box at the end of the study pages.

1. What are the activities of most worth in my personal life?

2. What are the personal accomplishments that I feel most proud of?

3. I admire the following traits in other women:

4. What are the traits that I want to develop and cultivate in myself?

5. What is it that I love most about this gorgeous planet?

6. What is the legacy that I want to leave behind?

7. How can I become more accountable?

8. How can I make a difference?

My personal Eco-Mission Statement:

My personal Eco-Mission Statement: I will live by the values of integrity, freedom of choice, and love for all living things and this planet. I will be accountable for every choice I make and every day I will strive to make a difference.

—Sophie Uliano

INDEX

Free ChicoBag!

Show Off Your Earth-Friendly Lifestyle

Get Your Free Gorgeously Green ChicoBag Today!

Be the first to own the uber-functional, stylish, and sustainable alternative to throwaway plastic and paper bags. Colorful, lightweight, and ultra-compact, the Gorgeously Green ChicoBag folds up into its integrated pouch for toting in your pocket, purse, or glove compartment. It's a cinch to carry and is made of strong and durable woven nylon.

Now it is yours for **FREE** (but don't tell anyone). This special deal is only for readers of Sophie Uliano's *Gorgeously Green*.

Be The First To Know!

Discover The Latest Eco-licious Tidbits

Sign Up to Get Gorgeously Green's E-mail Newsletter!

It's the insider's guide to what's hot, new, and undiscovered in the world of earth-friendly living. From the latest finds in eco-fashion and style to the grooviest green cleaning products, find it all here.

Sign up for the eNewsletter

Gorgeously Green Living
Eco-licious Tidbits on Fashion, Food and Fun

News From Sophie's World
» Recipes
» Yoga & Fitness
» Garden
» Travel
» Eco-Home
» Mom
» Beauty
» World

Featured Products
» Helen & Riegle

» Bamboo Candles

Green Kid's Birthday Party

If you are throwing a birthday party this summer, make it earth-friendly - it is easy, simple and fun.

The first concern is to reduce the amount of waste and this is how: Try not to use any paper or plastic tablecloths, cups, plates or cutlery. Instead, go to www.recycline.com and purchase a set of their brightly colored recycled cups, plates and cutlery. They are all made from recycled yogurt cups as they have a partnership with Stonyfield Farms. You can reuse them again and again and they are reusable. Well worth the investment. If you want to be a bit fancier, you may want to go to www.bambu.com and purchase bamboo plates and cutlery.

Bamboo is becoming very fashionable in the green scene as it is a renewable resouce. For younger kids, they carry a "spork" which is fabulous for birthday cake.

Instead of a tablecloth, find an old sheet and buy some non-toxic markers (available from most art stores). When the kids arrive, get them to decorate the cloth with drawings or birthday messages to your child. It's something that the birthday girl/boy can keep forever. Always use cloth napkins. They don't have to match, its a kid's party and odd ones can look more colorful and fun.

Make sure all the food you serve is organic. You can buy delicious organic cake mixes from most large grocery stores, which will save you a lot of money. It's also fun to get your child involved in designing and making their cake.

Goodie bags can be the most kid...

Sign up for your e-mail newsletter about the latest in eco-fashion, food and fun. Visit www.GorgeouslyGreen.com/eNewsletter